Bar code on back page

Charlotte Community Library
Charlotte MI 48813

NIAGARA FALLS

JOEL A. DOMBROWSKI

917.
479
D

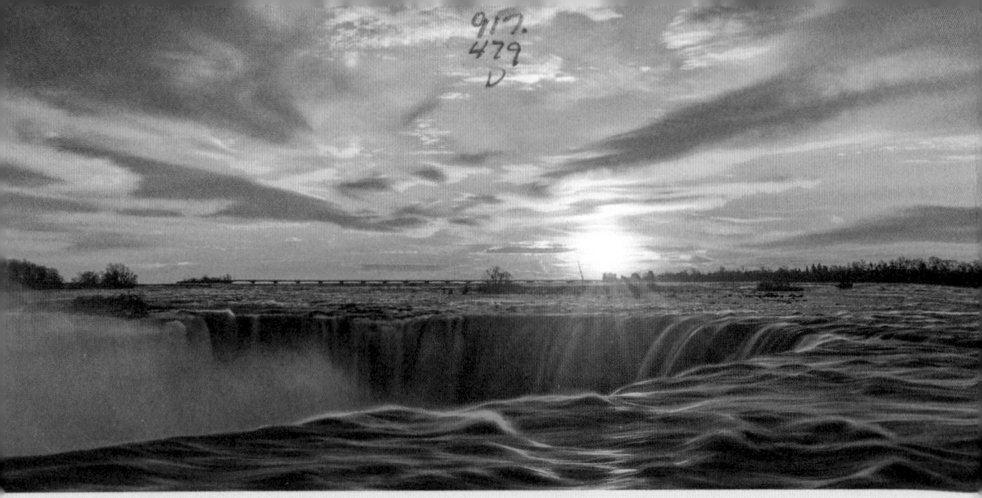

Contents

2 Sample Buffalo Wings and Brews: Home to the original hot wings (page 123) and more than 30 breweries and distilleries (page 118), this is a city that will satisfy your appetite.

3 Wander the Waterfront: Canalside is the vibrant, beating heart of Buffalo's renaissance. Stroll the waterfront, visit Naval and Military Park, and explore the city's history and heritage (page 104).

4 Revisit History at Old Fort Niagara: Costumed reenactors demonstrate how soldiers fought to protect this gateway to the New World (page 91).

1 Experience the Power of the Falls: Niagara's beauty leaves more than 10 million visitors awestruck each year. There's no shortage of photo opportunities (page 20) or ways to experience this wonder (page 17), including jetboats, cruises, and even a zipline.

7 TOP EXPERIENCES

A boat draws you into the furious tumult at the base of the falls. The bright green water roils with energy. The roar is deafening. Amid the chaos, a moment of clarity emerges. This 17-story wall of water has no equal in the world. *This* is the power of nature.

This moment draws millions of people to Niagara Falls each year. But Niagara offers more than the falls. It's a world-class destination where you can experience nature and adventure, as well as entertainment, culture, and cuisine. Stretching across both sides of the U.S.-Canadian border is a fertile wine country that produces remarkable vintages on everything from family farms to stunning, European-style estates. A 20-minute drive away is Buffalo, where a waterfront entertainment district has emerged from the ruins of the old Erie Canal. The city has embraced its blue-collar roots while preserving and redeveloping an amazing architectural legacy that includes masterpieces by renowned architects Louis Sullivan and Frank Lloyd Wright.

Yet, it all circles back to that wall of water. You have to experience the simple but visceral power of nature here for yourself.

Clockwise from top left: nighttime illumination of the Horseshoe Falls; Journey Behind the Falls observation platform; the Niagara SkyWheel; Horseshoe Falls in winter; aerial view of the Table Rock Welcome Centre; Niagara Falls.

DISCOVER

Niagara Falls

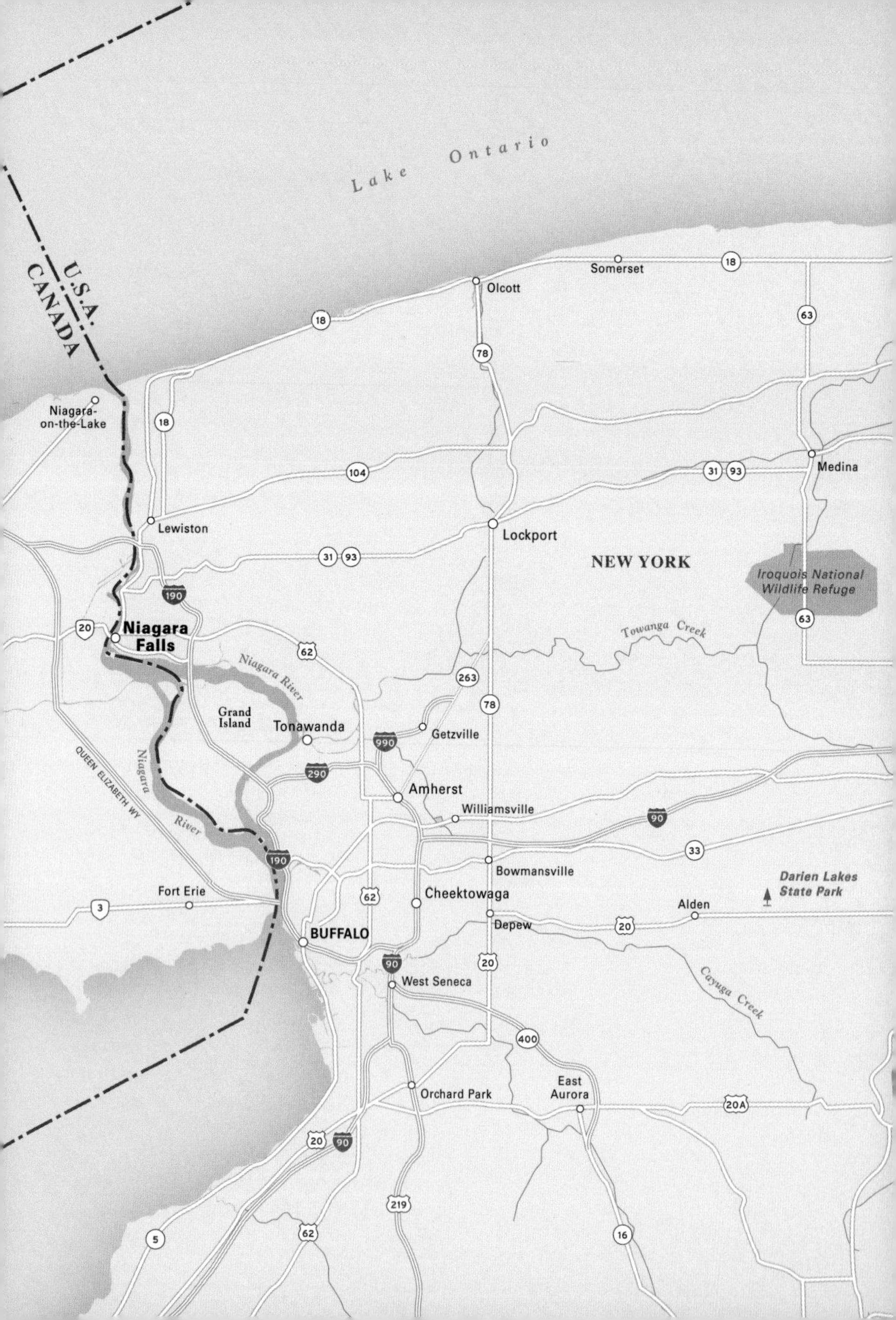

Lake Ontario
U.S.A.
CANADA
Somerset
18
Olcott
63
78
Niagara-on-the-Lake
104
31
93
Medina
Lewiston
Lockport
NEW YORK
Iroquois National Wildlife Refuge
190
20
Niagara Falls
62
Towanga Creek
Niagara River
263
Grand Island
Tonawanda
Getzville
990
QUEEN ELIZABETH WY
Niagara River
290
Amherst
Williamsville
90
33
Bowmansville
Fort Erie
3
Cheektowaga
Darien Lakes State Park
Alden
Depew
BUFFALO
West Seneca
Cayuga Creek
400
Orchard Park
East Aurora
20A
219
5
16

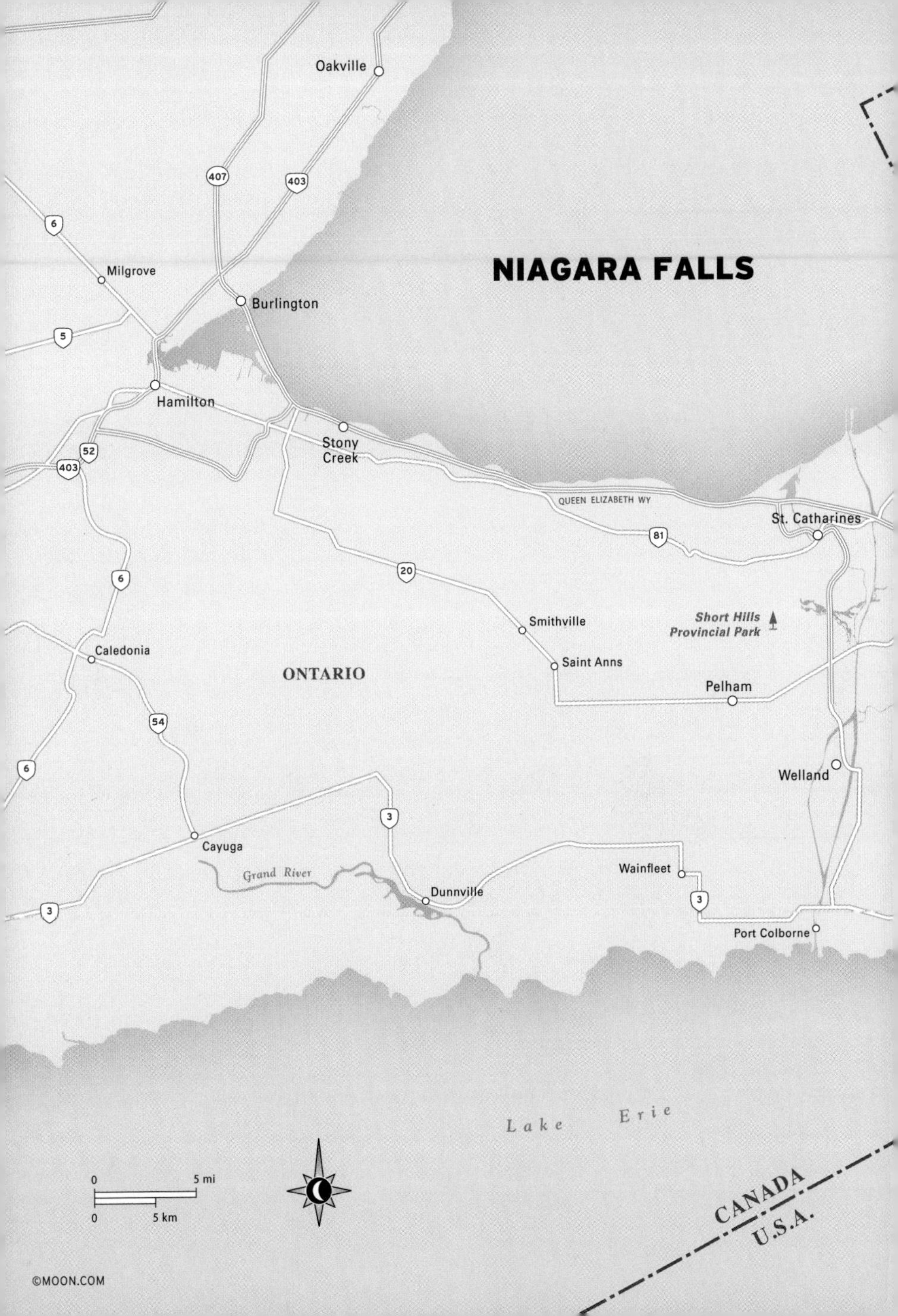

NIAGARA FALLS
Oakville
407
403
6
Milgrove
Burlington
5
Hamilton
Stony
Creek
52
403
QUEEN ELIZABETH WY
St. Catharines
81
20
6
Smithville
Short Hills
Provincial Park
Caledonia
Saint Anns
ONTARIO
Pelham
54
6
Welland
3
Cayuga
Grand River
Wainfleet
Dunnville
3
3
Port Colborne
Lake Erie
0
5 mi
0
5 km
CANADA
U.S.A.
©MOON.COM

Although every effort was made to make sure the information in this book was accurate when going to press, research was impacted by the COVID-19 pandemic. Some things may have changed during this crisis and the recovery that followed. Be sure to confirm specific details when making your travel plans.

5 Bike to World-Class Wineries: Drink in the spirit of Niagara by pedaling to its finest wineries on a guided tour (page 156).

<<<

6 Get Out on the Water: This region is perfect for kayaking, fishing, water biking, and boating (page 112).

>>>

7 See Stately Architecture: Buffalo is a living architectural museum showcasing the work of masters like Frank Lloyd Wright, H. H. Richardson, and the "father of the skyscraper" Louis Sullivan (page 101).

<<<

Planning Your Trip

Where to Go

Niagara Falls, Ontario

The beauty of this area extends beyond the three waterfalls known as Niagara Falls, but the heart of the Niagara experience is at the brink of the falls. Here, you'll find the **Table Rock Welcome Centre,** home to several major attractions that allow you to see above, below, and behind the falls. **Queen Victoria Park** provides a lush open area adjacent to the falls, with gardens and excellent vistas of Niagara. **High-rise hotels** and a **glittering casino** are found in **Fallsview,** the highly developed zone that sits atop a bluff overlooking Niagara. Downstream, the **Parkway North** area includes the scenic **whirlpool** that reveals the power of Niagara's white water.

Niagara Falls, New York

The U.S. side of Niagara offers a different perspective on the falls. Visitors spend most of their time in **Niagara Falls State Park,** which affords intimate opportunities to experience the falls. Here, you can enjoy the spectrum of Niagara's many moods, from sublime to raging. Surrounding the park is **downtown** Niagara Falls, with many hotels within walking distance of the falls. **Little Italy** offers a nostalgic and authentic taste of the city's Italian heritage. **North of the falls** are hiking trails, **Whirlpool State Park,** and the beautiful, historic town of **Lewiston.** Where the river pours into Lake Ontario is **Youngstown,** an area that has witnessed more than three centuries of conflict over the control of the Niagara River.

The American Falls is located on the U.S. side of the border inside Niagara Falls State Park.

Buffalo

Buffalo is New York State's second-largest city. At **Canalside,** the city's waterfront district, you can **kayak, sail,** and explore the nation's first superhighway—the **Erie Canal.** Buildings designed by famous architects such as Frank Lloyd Wright, H. H. Richardson, and Louis Sullivan are a stunning reminder of the city's affluent past, while the neighborhoods of **Elmwood Village** and **Allentown** are centers of the **arts and culture.** Southeast of the city, **East Aurora** is a walkable Arts and Crafts village that exudes small-town charm. To the north and northeast of the city, **North Tonawanda, Lockport,** and **Niagara County** offer **museums, wine-tasting,** and **hiking** in the countryside.

Niagara-on-the-Lake and Wine Country

Perched on the southern shoreline of Lake Ontario is a beautiful **Victorian village** called Niagara-on-the-Lake. The area expanding outward from NOTL is a fertile peninsula, home to more than 30 **wineries and vineyards.** To the west, the **Welland Canal** draws **recreational boaters** and oceangoing freighters alike, and visitors can watch massive ships traverse the canal's locks. The small towns that line the canal are charming and historic, from the garden city of **St. Catharines** to **Fort Erie,** home to **historic Old Fort Erie.**

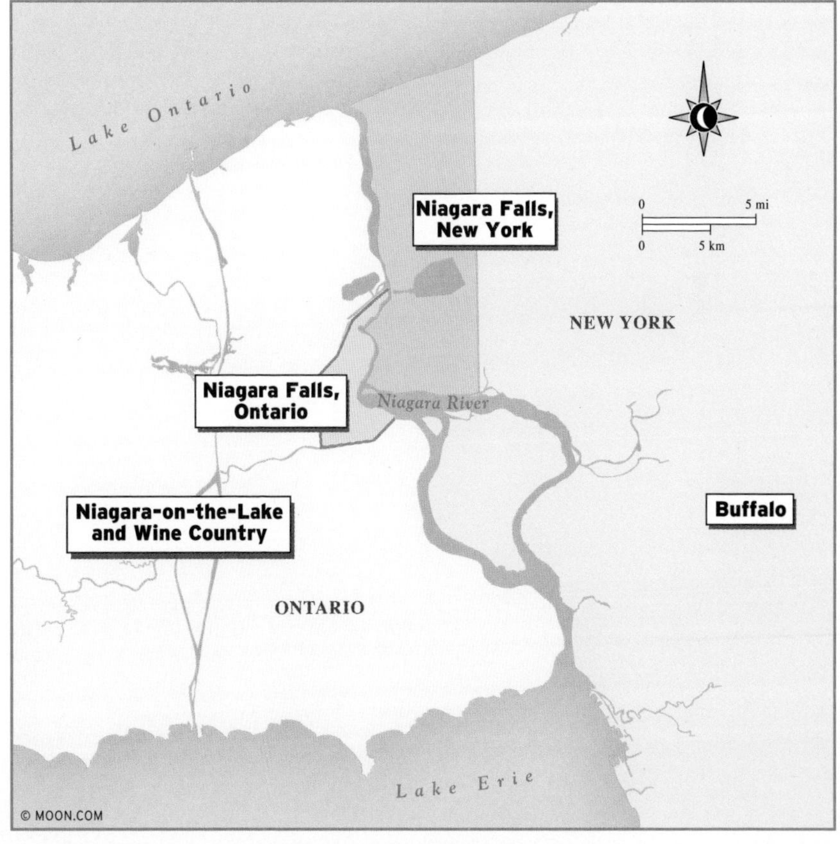

When to Go

Most people visit Niagara Falls in the **summer,** mid-June through early September. The weather is pleasant, with high temperatures averaging 81°F (27°C). During this time, you may experience **longer lines** at attractions, especially on the Canadian side of the border and on holidays such as Memorial Day, July 1 (Canada Day), July 4, and Labor Day. Avoid traveling to the falls on summer holidays, due to the crowds and lengthy waits at **border crossings.** Hotel rates peak during the summer.

Nature puts on an amazing show during **autumn,** September through October. This region explodes with color as leaves make their annual transformation from green to yellow, red, brown, and orange. The weather moderates, with the high temperature averaging 60°F (15°C) in October. Mornings and evenings can be crisp, but the days are mostly bright and sunny. Many locals favor visiting the falls at this time because the attractions are still open, but there is seldom a line. If you are a **leaf peeper,** visit this region in mid-October and hike to your heart's content while the fall colors are at their peak. Wineries have an extra romantic ambience at this time of year.

Winter is the slowest tourism season for Niagara, and with good reason. The months of December-February are snowy, with bitter wind chills and **below-freezing temperatures.** Seasonal attractions are closed and the tourist areas somewhat empty. However, the freezing weather also creates an austere landscape, and frozen mist from the falls envelops everything in a crystalline, icy coating. The best time for a brief visit is during the **Festival of Lights,** around the holidays in December. Walk around or drive your car along the Canadian side of the border and experience thousands of lights illuminating dozens of holiday displays.

In **spring,** March until the beginning of June, you'll find **off-season rates** on accommodations. As in winter, some attractions have **limited hours** or are not operating. The Maid of the Mist and Hornblower Niagara Cruises cannot safely ply the waters of the lower Niagara until the river is free of ice, so they don't typically start running until May. Spring arrives a little later here than in other parts of the Northeast due to the ice on Lake Erie. By May, the weather is more pleasant.

The Two-Day Best of Niagara Falls

For this itinerary, base yourself on the **Canadian side** of the border. The **Fallsview Casino Resort** and **Marriott Niagara Falls Fallsview Hotel & Spa** both offer excellent views and are close to all the major attractions.

Day 1

Purchase a **Niagara Falls Adventure Pass** at one of the Ontario Niagara Parks welcome centres. The clerk will ask if you'd like to reserve ticket times for **Journey Behind the Falls, Niagara's Fury,** and the **White Water Walk.** Add two hours to the current time to come up with your reservation time for Journey Behind the Falls. Reserve Niagara's Fury for one hour after that. Do not reserve a time for the White Water Walk.

Walk one block to **Hornblower Niagara Cruises** and hop on a boat for an up-close (and saturated) look at the falls. Afterward, walk south along the rim of the gorge, enjoying the excellent vista of the U.S. side of the border. In the front atrium of **Table Rock Welcome Centre,** you'll find the entrance for **Journey Behind the Falls.** Explore the falls from a tunnel dug through the gorge, emerging in time to catch **Niagara's Fury,** a 4-D movie on the 2nd floor of the Welcome Centre.

Relax and enjoy the view from the **brink of Horseshoe Falls,** located at the rear of the Welcome Centre. For lunch, treat yourself to a meal at **Elements on the Falls** for casual fine dining with an incomparable view.

Spend a leisurely afternoon exploring **Queen Victoria Park,** across from the Welcome Centre. Within walking distance are the **Dufferin Islands,** the **Floral Showhouse,** and many beautiful gardens.

the White Water Walk along the Niagara River

the nightly illumination of Niagara Falls

Hop on a green-line **WEGO bus** (included in your pass) headed north along the gorge. Get off at the **White Water Walk,** where you can spend an hour strolling close to the river's rapids. Get on another green-line bus and head farther north, stopping at the **Whirlpool Aero Car.** From the adjacent viewing area, you'll have a chance to observe the dangerous and breathtaking **Whirlpool.**

After returning to your hotel for a rest, it's time for dinner. Try the **Grand Buffet** at the Fallsview Casino Resort for exceptional value and a great view of the falls. After dinner, try your luck at the casino tables, or head to Queen Victoria Park for the nightly **illumination of the falls.** Enjoy the beauty of the lights projected on the falls and **fireworks over the falls** at 10pm each summer evening.

Day 2

Start early! Explore the **U.S. side** of Niagara with a trip aboard the **Niagara Jet Adventures** in Youngstown. Afterward, head south along the gorge and stop by the **Niagara Power Vista.** Take the brief drive from the bottom of the Power Vista to the **fishing platform** and see anglers catching huge trout and salmon. Next, continue south along the gorge to **Whirlpool State Park,** a perfect 30-minute stop for a brief walk to an excellent view of the swirling waters of the Niagara River whirlpool.

Enter **Niagara Falls State Park** and head to **Goat Island.** Here you will find many opportunities to experience the majesty of Niagara up close. Start at the **Cave of the Winds,** which takes you beneath Bridal Veil Falls. Next, head to **Luna Island,** an off-the-beaten-path spot to appreciate Bridal Veil Falls from above. On the far shore of Goat Island, **Terrapin Point** is your next stop. This is the best spot in the park for a view of the brink of Horseshoe Falls. Finally, walk along the south shore to **Three Sisters Islands,** which jut into the upper rapids of the Niagara River.

If you're looking for a quick lunch, try the **Misty Dog Grill,** or if you have time, take the 10-minute drive to **Little Italy** and go to the **Como Restaurant** for an authentic Italian

Choose Your Own Adventure

You can experience Niagara Falls in a variety of thrilling ways.

GET OUT ON THE WATER

- **Hornblower Niagara Cruises (Canada):** Catamarans ferry passengers to the base of Horseshoe Falls for a 20-minute tour. The Hornblower also provides 40-minute enhanced cruises during the nightly illumination and the summer fireworks shows (page 35).
- **Maid of the Mist (U.S.):** What begins as a gentle, 20-minute boat ride suddenly becomes a journey into the heart of the falls. For more than 150 years, the Maid of the Mist has thrilled millions of tourists and is the top attraction in Niagara (page 67).

RIDE THE RAPIDS

- **Whirlpool Jet Boats (Canada and U.S.):** These boats take you for a thrill ride through the lower rapids of the Niagara River. Jet boat rides last 45-60 minutes round trip, and are available from two Canada-based locations (page 145) and a U.S. location (page 91).
- **Niagara Jet Adventures (U.S.):** Rock-n-roll music and engaging guides create an entertaining ride through the white waters of the Niagara River (page 89).

GO BEHIND THE FALLS

- **Journey Behind the Falls (Canada):** A series of tunnels guide you to the raging sheet of water that is the underside of the Horseshoe Falls (page 33).
- **Cave of the Winds (U.S.):** This self-guided tour takes you along a series of decks leading to the foot of Bridal Veil Falls. The Cave of the Winds **Winter Experience** offers an abbreviated tour to see the falls and Niagara River in its icy, wintry glory (page 72).

Whirlpool Aero Car

GLIDE ABOVE THE FALLS

- **MistRider Zipline to the Falls (Canada):** A thrilling and quick zipline experience starts 220 feet (67 m) above the Niagara River, allowing you to glide to the base of the gorge (page 37).
- **Whirlpool Aero Car (Canada):** Departing from Colt's Point, the 10-minute ride allows passengers to float 210 feet (64 m) over the whirlpool (page 43).

lunch. Return to Canada via the Rainbow Bridge and relax before dinner.

On the Canadian side of the border, head north to St. Davids for dinner at the **Ravine Winery Restaurant.** After dinner, go to the **Skylon Tower** and watch the sunset from the observation deck, 52 stories above the falls. Take a walk down **Clifton Hill** for some kitschy entertainment. Conclude your evening with a gentle but magnificent ride on the **Niagara SkyWheel.**

Day Trips

Wine Country and Niagara-on-the-Lake

There are several ways to enjoy a tour of wine country: You can drive yourself, let someone else drive for you, or take a bike tour.

Many transportation companies like **Grape and Wine Tours** and **Grape Escape Wine Tours** offer bus or van tours of wineries, which usually include visits to 3-5 wineries and a meal. Escorted bicycle tours are another popular way to tour the area. As you cycle through the countryside, visiting wineries along the way, tour guides provide narration about the region. **Niagara Getaway Wine Tours, Grape Escape Wine Tours,** and **Niagara Wine Tours International** provide bike tours of the winery region as well as bike rentals.

MORNING

From your hotel in Niagara Falls, make the 20-minute drive to **Fort George** and be transported back to the War of 1812 with costumed docents, period music, and musket demonstrations. Plan to spend 2-4 hours here. Head to Niagara-on-the-Lake for an early lunch of authentic British pub grub at the (allegedly) haunted **Olde Angel Inn.**

AFTERNOON

After lunch, head south out of town to **Peller Estates,** a stunning French château that is large but homey. Couches surround a fireplace, making for a cozy wine-tasting experience. Continuing south along the gorge, stop at **Inniskillin Winery,** which boasts some of the region's best ice wines. Return north to visit **Stratus Vineyards** and **Jackson-Triggs Niagara Estate Winery.** Each provides an excellent introduction to the diverse wines produced in the Niagara region, including ice wine, chardonnay, pinot noir, riesling, and gewürztraminer.

vineyard in southern Ontario

The Buffalo History Museum

EVENING

Make your way back to Niagara-on-the-Lake for dinner at **Zees Grill.** Sit out on the patio if the weather is nice. Zees' wine menu features selections from Inniskillin, Peller Estates, and Jackson-Triggs. Test out your new skills in wine pairings by choosing one of these local wines to complement your meal.

After dinner, walk along Queen Street to browse some of the shops. If you love sweets, stop at the **Rocky Mountain Chocolate Factory,** where chocolate lovers will be overwhelmed by the number of tempting goodies.

Buffalo: History, Heritage, and Architecture

Frederick Law Olmsted, the designer of Central Park in New York City, called Buffalo the "best-designed city in America." When touring the streets of Buffalo, it is easy to see why.

MORNING

Start your day with a tour of the **Darwin Martin House Complex,** designed by Frank Lloyd Wright. A brief drive gets you to the **Museum District** and **Delaware Park** for a glimpse into Buffalo's golden era, after the Erie Canal flooded the city with prosperity. **The Buffalo History Museum** and the **Richardson Olmsted Campus** are within walking distance of each other and well worth a visit.

Head downtown for lunch at the **Pearl Street Grill and Brewery.** Sample some of the 16 craft beers they have on tap.

AFTERNOON

After lunch, walk two blocks north on Pearl Street to find Louis Sullivan's prototype skyscraper, the **Guaranty Building.** Directly across the street is **St. Paul's Episcopal Cathedral,** built by Richard Upjohn. The architect considered St. Paul's his best work.

Walk or drive to the waterfront **Canalside** complex. Start at the **Commercial Slip,** the unearthed and restored terminus of the Erie Canal. Here, you can explore the actual ruins of the canal, including the towpath and foundations of buildings that lined the waterway. Interpretive

Best Photo Ops

Both the Canadian and U.S. sides of Niagara Falls offer ample photo opportunities. Here's where to go to get these great shots.

NIAGARA FALLS FROM ABOVE

Photograph from:

- **Skylon Tower,** Canada (page 38)
- **Observation Tower,** U.S. (page 69)

RAINBOWS IN THE FALLS

Photograph from:

- Niagara Falls **gorge rim** *after* noon on the Canada side, and *before* noon on the U.S. side (page 78)

THE TOP OF HORSESHOE FALLS

Photograph from:

- **Table Rock Welcome Centre,** Canada (page 33)
- **Terrapin Point,** U.S. (page 73)

THE BASE OF HORSESHOE FALLS

Photograph from:

- **Journey Behind the Falls** tour, Canada (page 33)
- **Maid of the Mist** boat tour, U.S. (page 67)

  And don't forget to water-proof your camera!

Table Rock Welcome Centre

THE WHIRLPOOL

Photograph from:

- **Whirlpool Aero Car,** Canada (page 43)
- **Whirlpool State Park,** U.S. (page 87)

NIAGARA FALLS FIREWORKS

Photograph from:

- **Queen Victoria Park** north of Table Rock or Skylon Tower, Canada (page 46)
- **Luna Island,** U.S. (page 72). Arrive 30 minutes early for a good viewing spot.

signs allow you to explore at your own pace. Hop aboard the **Buffalo Double Decker Bus** for an entertaining historical tour of the waterfront, including the **grain elevators,** and hear some hidden stories of Buffalo.

The bus drops you off at the **Buffalo and Erie County Naval and Military Park,** which features three decommissioned naval vessels, including a WWII submarine, a destroyer, and a guided missile cruiser. Artifacts and displays honor all branches of the military, but the real stars are the retired veterans who act as docents.

EVENING

Dinner is just five minutes away at the **Hotel Lafayette,** a beautifully restored 1904 luxury hotel. Enjoy dining at **Lafayette Brewing Company,** just off the main lobby. Before or after dinner, stroll through the ground floor of the hotel for a reminder of Buffalo's Gilded Age.

Romantic Getaway

Niagara Falls calls itself the Honeymoon Capital of the World. This itinerary will help you appreciate the romantic mystique of the falls during a quick weekend getaway.

Base yourself on the Canadian side of the falls. Book a stay at the **Sheraton on the Falls** and make reservations at their Christienne Fallsview Spa, making certain to use the infinity hydrotherapy tub. It's worth the splurge to stay in one of the Sheraton's corner suites, which have a balcony, fireplace, and soaking tub.

Friday

Check into your hotel and use the afternoon to acquaint yourself with the falls area. Take a boat ride to the base of the falls with **Hornblower Niagara Cruises,** and then go for a different perspective with **Journey Behind the Falls.** Head 3 miles (5 km) downstream from the falls for a peek at the **Whirlpool,** Niagara's most dangerous stretch of water.

Take a **horse-drawn carriage ride** around town as dusk approaches. You can find the carriages on Niagara Parkway, close to Murray Hill. Enjoy an intimate dinner at one of Niagara's most exclusive restaurants, **AG.** Be sure to order an ice wine martini as an aperitif. Make your reservation for 7:30pm to give yourself enough time to enjoy the nightly illumination of the falls from the rim of the gorge.

After dinner, head to the **Skylon Tower.** Grab a coffee or other warm beverage at the coffee shop in the base of the tower to keep you warm once you're out on the **Observation Deck.** This is the perfect spot to watch the **fireworks display.** Your perch 520 feet (160 m) above the ground gives you the opportunity to look down on the pyrotechnics.

If you still have some energy left, go to **Clifton Hill** for a ride on the **Niagara SkyWheel,** some arcade games, or a kitschy trip through one of the numerous haunted houses.

Hornblower Niagara Cruises

fireworks display over the falls

aerial view of Goat Island

Saturday

Following breakfast, head out for a tour of the wineries in **wine country.** The best way to relax and enjoy a tour and lunch is by bus. If you and your partner are more active types, try a bicycle tour. **Grape Escape Wine Tours** offers both bus and bike tours, and will pick you up at your falls-area hotel. The bus tour covers stops at four wineries, plus a three-course meal at an excellent Niagara-on-the-Lake restaurant. The bike tour offers a picnic lunch in an orchard.

After a day of touring, it's time to relax back at the hotel. Start off with an hour-long massage for two at the hotel spa, followed by a facial treatment.

For dinner, make your way to **Elements on the Falls** after the sun goes down. Here, you'll enjoy great food and an excellent view of the nightly illumination of Niagara Falls. After dinner, head over to the **Fallsview Casino Resort,** where you can try your luck at the tables or catch a show at the casino's Avalon Ballroom Theatre.

Sunday

If you're heading back to the States today, stop at **Niagara Falls State Park** after you cross the border. The park is a wonderland of natural features and offers some different views of the falls.

Spend a few hours walking around **Goat Island,** being sure to check out **Terrapin Point** and **Luna Island.** From there, you can venture out onto the **Three Sisters Islands,** which will place you as close to the upper rapids of the Niagara River as you can safely get.

On your way out of the park, stop at the **Observation Tower Platform** for one last look at the amazing Niagara Falls.

Niagara Falls, Ontario

In the shifting fortunes of the Niagara region,

Niagara Falls, Ontario, is on the upswing as the preferred destination for tourists. Visitors are drawn to the Canadian side for the best view of the three waterfalls—Horseshoe, Bridal Veil, and American Falls—collectively known as Niagara Falls. From this side of the U.S.-Canadian border, millions of tourists are inspired by the complete panorama in all its glory.

Family-friendly attractions, 34 miles (56 km) of parkland along the Niagara River, golf courses, and accommodations offer all the amenities of a world-class destination. Though some visitors feel that the glitz and glass of the high-rise hotels obscure the natural beauty of the

Highlights

Look for ★ to find recommended sights, activities, dining, and lodging.

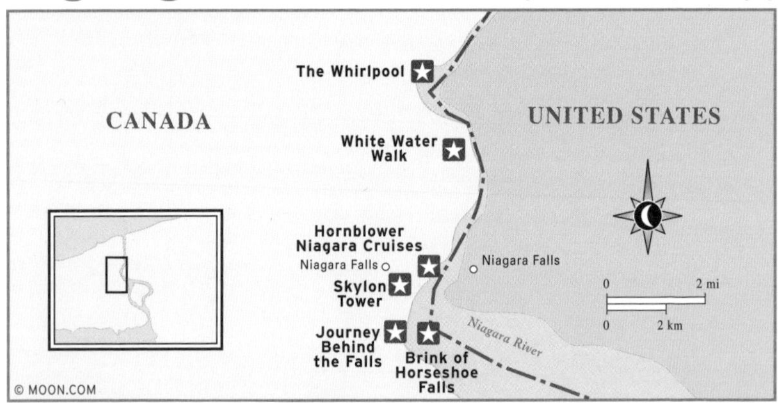

★ **Experience the brink of Horseshoe Falls:** See where nature's power and beauty combine to become Niagara Falls (page 32).

★ **Journey Behind the Falls:** Check out the world's most famous wall of water from tunnels that take you behind Horseshoe Falls (page 33).

★ **Take a voyage:** The **Hornblower Niagara Cruises** take you into the fury beneath Niagara Falls. To get any closer, you'd need to be in a barrel (page 35).

★ **Go up Skylon Tower:** Day or night, some of the best views are from the tower's observation deck, perched more than 500 feet above the falls (page 38).

★ **Walk along the Niagara River:** Follow the path known as the **White Water Walk** to experience Niagara's waters without getting wet (page 42).

★ **Discover the whirlpool:** This curious bend in the lower Niagara River is a powerful, swirling vortex that is both beautiful and deadly (page 43).

falls, most still favor the Canadian side over its American cousin across the river.

With more than 16,000 hotel rooms, Niagara Falls, Ontario, has the second-largest visitor capacity in Canada. The Fallsview Casino Resort attracts 20,000 visitors each day and is the largest gaming venue in the country.

The star of the show, though, is Niagara, the raw and refreshing apex of nature's power.

HISTORY

The early history of this region is as turbulent as the mighty Niagara River. For hundreds of years, a nation of Indians known as the Neutrals hunted and farmed this area on both sides of the river. In an effort to increase their share of the beaver pelt trade, members of the Iroquois Confederacy overpowered the Neutrals and took control of the region in the 1650s. The Iroquois, also known as the Haudenosaunee (People of the Longhouse), dominated smaller bands of native peoples, eventually controlling a region that stretched from Canada to the Carolinas.

Europeans explored the area beginning in the 1600s. The first written description of Niagara Falls was by a Jesuit priest, Father Louis Hennepin, in December 1678. By the 1700s, France and England were fighting for control of the region. English forces prevailed and, in 1759, the French military finally departed.

As the American Revolution heated up, colonists loyal to England moved to Canada. Many settled in the area that is now southern Ontario on land given to them by the British Crown. Settlers cleared the land for farming, finding the soil perfect for growing fruits and vegetables. Loyalists and their native allies proved to be an effective adversary against the Continental Army, especially in New York state and the area known as Ohio country.

The War of 1812 brought death and destruction to the Niagara frontier, with many of the bloodiest engagements occurring along the Niagara River. At the start of the war, the United States was hindered by inexperienced troops and incompetent leadership. By the end of the conflict, the United States proved that its land and naval forces were equal to those of England. Notable engagements including battles at Queenston Heights and Chippawa shaped the outcome of the conflict. At the end of hostilities, neither Canada nor the United States had lost or gained any territory.

By 1881, the Town of Niagara Falls, Ontario, was established. The Canadian side of the falls was already a popular spot for visitors but was also known as a tourist trap, where competing attractions used aggressive promotional techniques to secure customers. The Canadian government bought the land surrounding Horseshoe Falls, removed private hotels and attractions, and created Queen Victoria Park in 1885. With a goal of conservation and wise growth, the Niagara Parks Commission governs the development of the region. The commission's partnership with various government agencies and private interest groups has yielded a destination that welcomes more than 12 million visitors each year.

PLANNING YOUR TIME

Niagara Falls, Ontario, is rich in natural and developed attractions. A three-day, two-night stay allows enough time to fully appreciate all this destination has to offer.

Plan on making both daytime and nighttime visits to the pedestrian path along the gorge that connects the brink of the falls with the Hornblower Niagara Cruises complex. This 0.75-mile (1.2-km) path offers the best views of all three waterfalls that comprise Niagara. Viewing the falls at various times during your visit will reveal different aspects of this natural wonder.

Fewer tourists visit on weekdays than on weekends and holidays, when the area swells with visitors. The best strategy for

Previous: the brink of Horseshoe Falls; helicopter tour; Skylon Tower.

avoiding long lines at the Hornblower Niagara Cruises complex is to arrive early in the morning, just after 10am. The **Niagara Falls Adventure Pass Classic** (www.niagaraparks.com, $67 adults, $44 children 6-12) reserves timed tickets for Journey Behind the Falls, the Hornblower Cruise, Niagara's Fury, and the White Water Walk. If you are spending 1-2 days in Niagara and are likely to do the Hornblower Cruise and the Journey Behind the Falls attractions, the Classic Pass is a good value, saving you 27 percent off retail rates. Staying two or more days? **The Adventure Pass Plus** (www.niagaraparks.com, $90 adults, $59 children 6-12) includes everything covered in the Classic pass but adds four Parks Heritage sites, including Old Fort Erie. Either pass includes two days' unlimited use of the WEGO bus system, a wonderfully eco-friendly way to explore the region. In terms of sustainability, another benefit of any of the passes is that you may use your mobile device instead of printed tickets to gain admission to your included attractions.

Some attractions, including the Hornblower Niagara Cruises, Journey Behind the Falls, and the White Water Walk, are seasonal and are either closed or have restricted hours November-April. The **Niagara Parks** website (www.niagaraparks.com) is the best resource for information on seasonal schedules. From November through April when some attractions are closed, the Wonder Pass (www.niagaraparks.com, $25 adults, $17 children 6-12) is available.

This area is car-friendly, but the tourist transit system, **WEGO,** provides excellent, inexpensive transportation with stops at all the major hotels and attractions. If your hotel is not on the WEGO route, you can park for free at the Whirlpool Aero Car lot (3850 Niagara River Pkwy.) and pick up the bus there. Parking fees vary by season—expect to pay $20-25 during the summer to use lots close to Table Rock.

ORIENTATION

Attractions generally are clustered in three zones:

Brink of the Falls: The area from Chippawa in the south to the Rainbow Bridge, which includes Queen Victoria Park, Table Rock Welcome Centre, Hornblower Niagara Cruises, and the Dufferin Islands.

Fallsview: The developed area parallel to Victoria Park, including Clifton Hill and Lundy's Lane.

Parkway North: The area from the Rainbow Bridge north toward Queenston, which includes the whirlpool, White Water Walk, and the Butterfly Conservatory.

Sights

Unless noted otherwise, the sights listed here are presented south to north. All pricing is in Canadian currency, unless otherwise noted.

CHIPPAWA

Located just 2 miles (3.2 km) from the brink of Niagara, the quiet community of Chippawa is frequently overlooked by tourists and is known as the childhood home of film director James Cameron.

Chippawa is bisected by the Welland River, which makes for numerous beautiful waterfront views. Some of the best are from **Kingsbridge Park** (7870 Niagara Pkwy., 877/642-7275, www.niagaraparksnature.com, dawn-dusk daily), which has picnic facilities, a playground, and a wading pool. Another nearby park, the **Chippawa Battlefield Site** (Niagara Pkwy. near Ussher's Creek, www.niagaraparksheritage.com, dawn-dusk daily) memorializes the Battle of Chippawa, where more than 200 Indian, Canadian, and American soldiers died fighting during the War of 1812. The park's main feature is a

Niagara Falls, Ontario

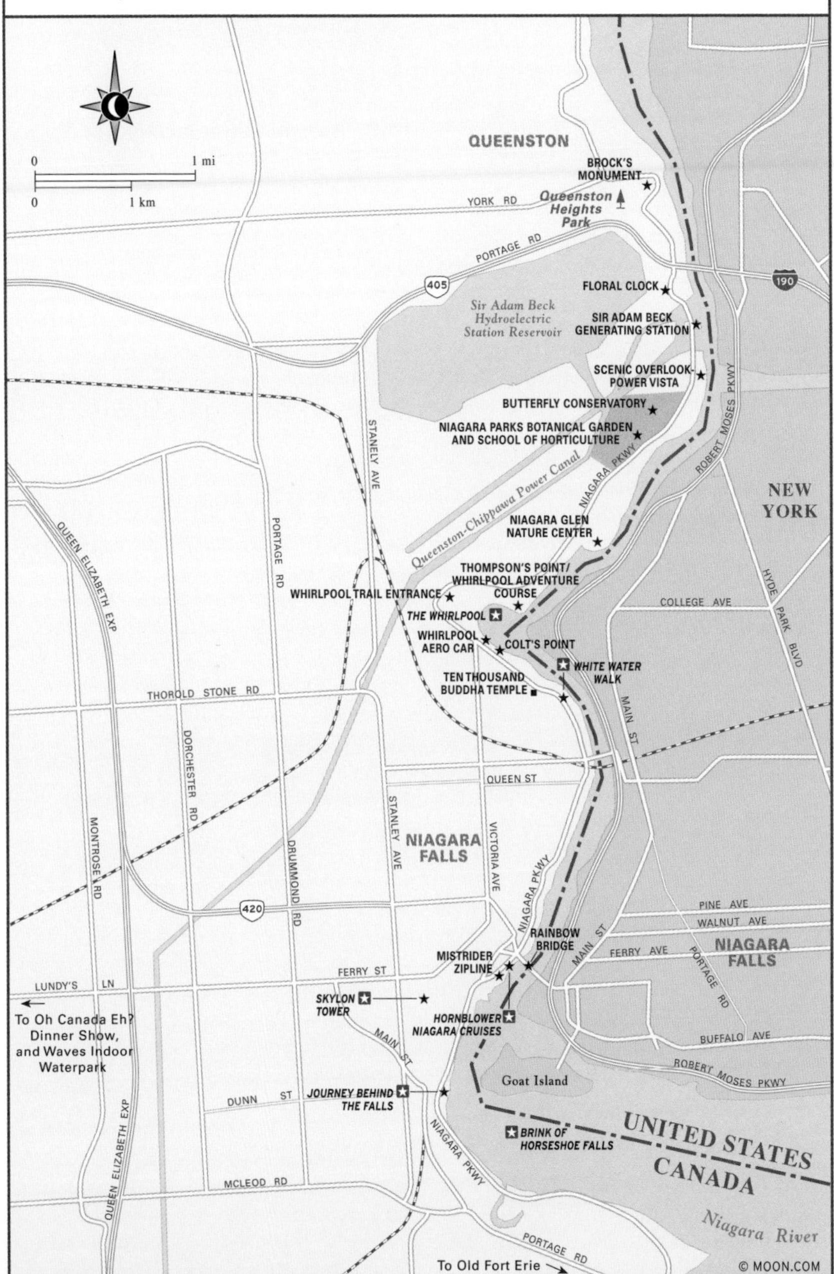
QUEENSTON
0
1 mi
0
1 km
BROCK'S MONUMENT
Queenston Heights Park
YORK RD
PORTAGE RD
405
190
FLORAL CLOCK
Sir Adam Beck Hydroelectric Station Reservoir
SIR ADAM BECK GENERATING STATION
SCENIC OVERLOOK-POWER VISTA
BUTTERFLY CONSERVATORY
NIAGARA PARKS BOTANICAL GARDEN AND SCHOOL OF HORTICULTURE
ROBERT MOSES PKWY
NIAGARA PKWY
Queenston-Chippawa Power Canal
STANLEY AVE
PORTAGE RD
QUEEN ELIZABETH EXP
NEW YORK
NIAGARA GLEN NATURE CENTER
THOMPSON'S POINT/ WHIRLPOOL ADVENTURE COURSE
WHIRLPOOL TRAIL ENTRANCE
THE WHIRLPOOL
WHIRLPOOL AERO CAR
COLT'S POINT
WHITE WATER WALK
TEN THOUSAND BUDDHA TEMPLE
COLLEGE AVE
HYDE PARK BLVD
THOROLD STONE RD
MAIN ST
DORCHESTER RD
QUEEN ST
MONTROSE RD
DRUMMOND RD
STANLEY AVE
NIAGARA FALLS
VICTORIA AVE
NIAGARA PKWY
420
PINE AVE
WALNUT AVE
RAINBOW BRIDGE
MAIN ST
FERRY AVE
NIAGARA FALLS
PORTAGE RD
MISTRIDER ZIPLINE
FERRY ST
LUNDY'S LN
To Oh Canada Eh? Dinner Show, and Waves Indoor Waterpark
SKYLON TOWER
HORNBLOWER NIAGARA CRUISES
MAIN ST
BUFFALO AVE
ROBERT MOSES PKWY
Goat Island
DUNN ST
JOURNEY BEHIND THE FALLS
BRINK OF HORSESHOE FALLS
UNITED STATES
CANADA
QUEEN ELIZABETH EXP
NIAGARA PKWY
MCLEOD RD
Niagara River
PORTAGE RD
To Old Fort Erie
© MOON.COM

cairn with plaques describing the battle and the people who lost their lives and were buried here. Each year on July 5, the anniversary of the conflict, a solemn ceremony commemorates the battle and the 200-plus years of peace that have followed.

BRINK OF THE FALLS

Marineland

Located just five minutes from the falls is **Marineland** (7657 Portage Rd., 905/356-9565, www.marineland.ca, Sat.-Sun. mid-May-June, daily July-mid-Oct., $50.95 adults, $43.95 seniors 60+ and children 5-12), a sprawling theme park with thrill rides, animal shows, and a petting zoo. Visitors of all ages will enjoy the shows in the park's main pool, where beluga whales, dolphins, walruses, and sea lions perform four times daily. You can feed and pet the beluga whales for an additional charge ($8). The aquatic performances are the main attractions here, so plan to attend a show first. The arena, King Waldorf's Stadium, is close to the entry gates; shows start every two hours.

Young children will delight in the petting and feeding pens for land animals, where they can feed deer and view other animals, including elk and bison. The park also features more than a dozen amusement park-style rides for all ages, including Dragon Mountain, the world's largest steel roller coaster.

Families with small children will want to spend a half-day at Marineland. Be prepared to walk. The various attractions are spread out on a campus that is nearly 2 square miles (5 sq km), with no trolley or bus transportation system. The park is in need of cosmetic updates.

The hours of operation vary throughout the year, with the park opening at 9:30am or 10am. Closing hours fluctuate as well, with admission booths closing at 5pm or 6pm. The park attractions remain open until dusk.

International Control Dam Overlook

The **International Control Dam Overlook** (Niagara Pkwy., 2 mi/3.2 km south of Niagara Falls) is an important vista for understanding the natural and developed forces at work in Niagara. The control dam is a concrete structure extending 1,500 feet (450 m) into the Niagara River, upstream of the falls. The dam uses a series of gates that raise and lower to control the flow and dispersion of the water over the falls.

At all times, 50 percent of the water heading down the Niagara River is diverted for hydroelectric power generation before reaching the falls. This dam helps regulate that diversion, but it also serves another important purpose: It spreads the water in an even pattern over the brink of Horseshoe Falls.

As you stand on the grassy area between the river and the parkway, note the gates in the dam—some will be up, others will be down. Look for the semi-submerged concrete weirs running parallel to the shore. The gates and weirs work in concert so that Horseshoe Falls appears to have a uniform wall of water crashing over its brink. Facing south (upstream), you'll see two tall, narrow buildings. These house the gates that also assist in regulating water diverted from the river. Those gates are built over the intake tunnels that feed the Sir Adam Beck Generating Station downstream.

Driving north from Chippawa, you'll see a service road opposite the entrance to the Rapidsview parking complex (7369 Niagara Pkwy.). Park in the Rapidsview complex and walk a few hundred yards to the service road for the best view of the dam. If you park directly at the curb of the service road, the Parks police may ask you to move, as parking is not allowed in this area.

Dufferin Islands

The **Dufferin Islands** (Niagara Pkwy., 1 mi/1.6 km south of the falls, 877/642-7275, www.niagaraparksnature.com, 24 hours daily, free) are a wonderful area, perfect for a picnic or walk. This quiet oasis was built in response to concerns that the area surrounding the falls had lost some of its natural appeal. The park is not on the radar of most tourists, so it offers

Brink of the Falls, Fallsview, and Clifton Hill

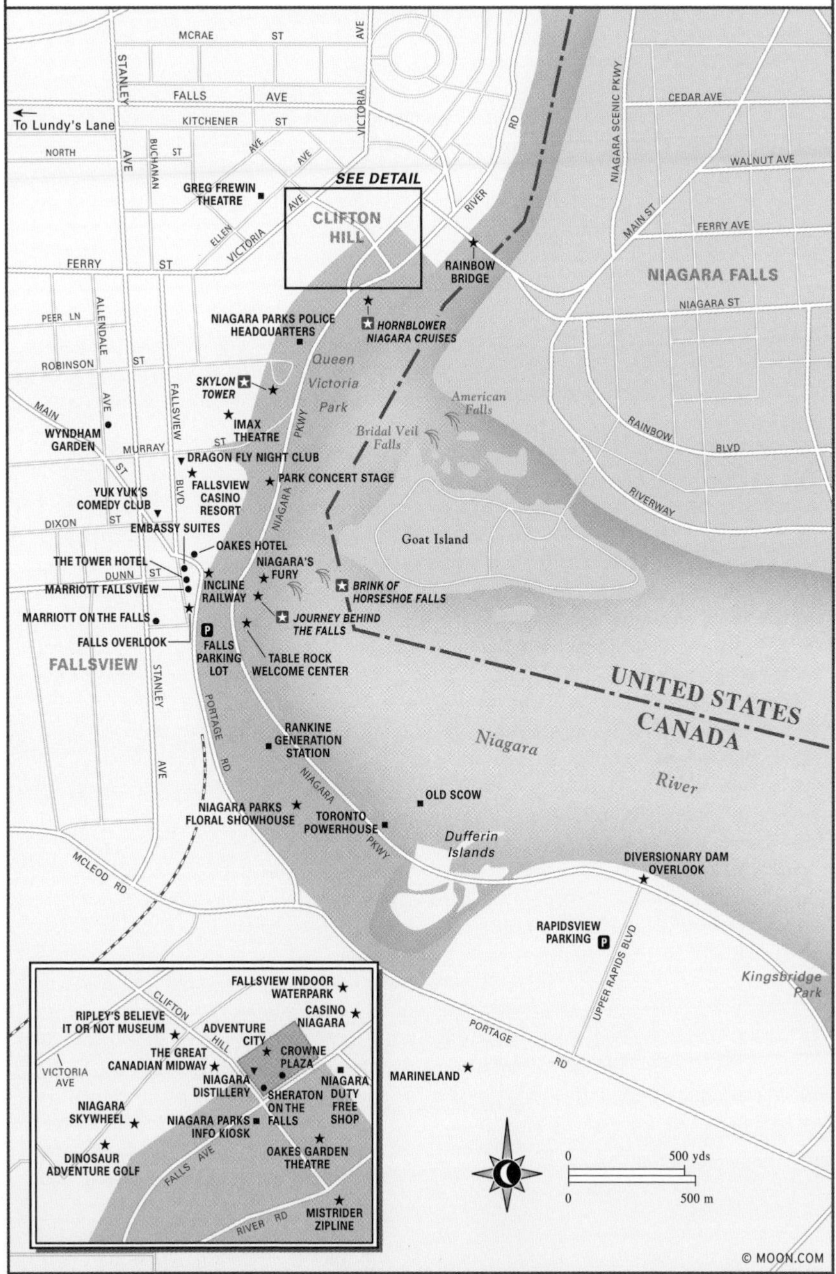
MCRAE ST
FALLS AVE
KITCHENER ST
To Lundy's Lane
NORTH ST
STANLEY AVE
BUCHANAN AVE
VICTORIA AVE
GREG FREWIN THEATRE
SEE DETAIL
CLIFTON HILL
ELLEN AVE
FERRY ST
RIVER RD
RAINBOW BRIDGE
NIAGARA SCENIC PKWY
CEDAR AVE
WALNUT AVE
MAIN ST
FERRY AVE
NIAGARA FALLS
NIAGARA ST
PEER LN
ALLENDALE AVE
NIAGARA PARKS POLICE HEADQUARTERS
HORNBLOWER NIAGARA CRUISES
ROBINSON ST
Queen Victoria Park
SKYLON TOWER
FALLSVIEW BLVD
MAIN ST
WYNDHAM GARDEN
IMAX THEATRE
MURRAY ST
American Falls
Bridal Veil Falls
RAINBOW BLVD
DRAGON FLY NIGHT CLUB
FALLSVIEW CASINO RESORT
PARK CONCERT STAGE
YUK YUK'S COMEDY CLUB
RIVERWAY
DIXON ST
EMBASSY SUITES
NIAGARA PKWY
OAKES HOTEL
Goat Island
THE TOWER HOTEL
DUNN ST
MARRIOTT FALLSVIEW
INCLINE RAILWAY
NIAGARA'S FURY
BRINK OF HORSESHOE FALLS
MARRIOTT ON THE FALLS
JOURNEY BEHIND THE FALLS
FALLS OVERLOOK
FALLS PARKING LOT
TABLE ROCK WELCOME CENTER
FALLSVIEW
UNITED STATES
CANADA
PORTAGE RD
RANKINE GENERATION STATION
Niagara River
OLD SCOW
NIAGARA PARKS FLORAL SHOWHOUSE
TORONTO POWERHOUSE
Dufferin Islands
MCLEOD RD
DIVERSIONARY DAM OVERLOOK
RAPIDSVIEW PARKING
UPPER RAPIDS BLVD
Kingsbridge Park
PORTAGE RD
MARINELAND
FALLSVIEW INDOOR WATERPARK
CASINO NIAGARA
CLIFTON HILL
RIPLEY'S BELIEVE IT OR NOT MUSEUM
ADVENTURE CITY
CROWNE PLAZA
THE GREAT CANADIAN MIDWAY
VICTORIA AVE
NIAGARA DISTILLERY
SHERATON ON THE FALLS
NIAGARA DUTY FREE SHOP
NIAGARA SKYWHEEL
NIAGARA PARKS INFO KIOSK
DINOSAUR ADVENTURE GOLF
OAKES GARDEN THEATRE
FALLS AVE
RIVER RD
MISTRIDER ZIPLINE
0 500 yds
0 500 m

© MOON.COM

an eco-enclave for people to relax and commune with nature.

This 10-acre park features 10 small islands joined by a network of footbridges and trails. The mixture of lightly wooded areas, small green spaces, shallow streams, and trails allows refuge from the crowds and bustle of the nearby tourist areas. While the park is best appreciated on foot, you may also enjoy a slow drive along the paved roads. When driving, look out for geese and ducks using the roads to cross from pond to pond.

During most of the year, the Dufferin Islands are free of crowds. Summer weekends are the most popular times for visitors and locals, who use the park for dog walks and picnic lunches. Catch-and-release fishing and bird-watching are popular activities in the summer. In the winter, animated-light displays for the Festival of Lights are erected in the park. Motorists can drive through the park and make a small donation that benefits the festival organization. The park has a mix of free and paid parking, and offers charging stations for electric cars.

Toronto Power Generating Station and the Old Scow

The **Toronto Power Generating Station** (Niagara Pkwy.) is an abandoned power plant that generated electricity 1906-1974. Looking at the beautiful limestone structure, it's hard to believe it was a power station. When commissioned as a hydroelectric plant, it was an engineering marvel. The plant's owners wanted the exterior to match the importance of the interior, so an Italian Renaissance design was chosen—the first time beaux arts had been used for an industrial structure. Imposing Ionic colonnades flank the stately main portion of the building.

The exterior looks grand but staid, giving it an aura of power and stability. This is no accident. In the early 1900s, some people were concerned about the safety of this new technology. The architecture's grandeur helped assure the public that hydroelectric power was safe and reliable. The building stands along the shore of the river, an elegant reminder of the electric power revolution that was born at Niagara. The interior of the building is closed to the public.

Niagara Parks now owns the station and is weighing how best to repurpose the building. Locals speculate that the grand structure will someday house an interpretive museum. In the meantime, the building has been used for crews shooting movie and television productions.

The grounds immediately adjacent to the station afford the best perspective of the **old scow.** A scow is a type of large boat with a flat bottom and squared-off ends, used primarily for transporting materials like ore or sand in bulk. The old scow was carrying a load of rock when it broke loose, rapidly floated downstream, and became lodged above Horseshoe Falls in 1918. Two men aboard were rescued by the heroics of famed river man Red Hill, Sr. The scow remains grounded in the river, providing a resting spot for gulls and other birds.

You can spot the scow from the parkway while driving, but it's worth a closer examination on foot. The best vantage point is the northern end of the Toronto Power Generating Station. In late 2019, after the scow had been stuck in the same spot for 101 years, exceedingly high water levels in the river pushed it on its side and downstream by 160 feet (50 m).

Floral Showhouse

A few hundred yards from the brink of Horseshoe Falls, the **Floral Showhouse** (7145 Niagara Pkwy., 905/371-0254, www.niagaraparks.com, 9:30am-5pm daily, $7 adults, $4 children 6-12) is a tropical oasis filled with lush foliage and songbirds. The showhouse is an enclosed greenhouse with thousands of flowers and plants chosen for their beauty and fragrance. The main showhouse is a large, airy, indoor space with a waterfall and trapezoid-shaped glass roof. This

1: Dufferin Islands 2: Toronto Power Generating Station

1

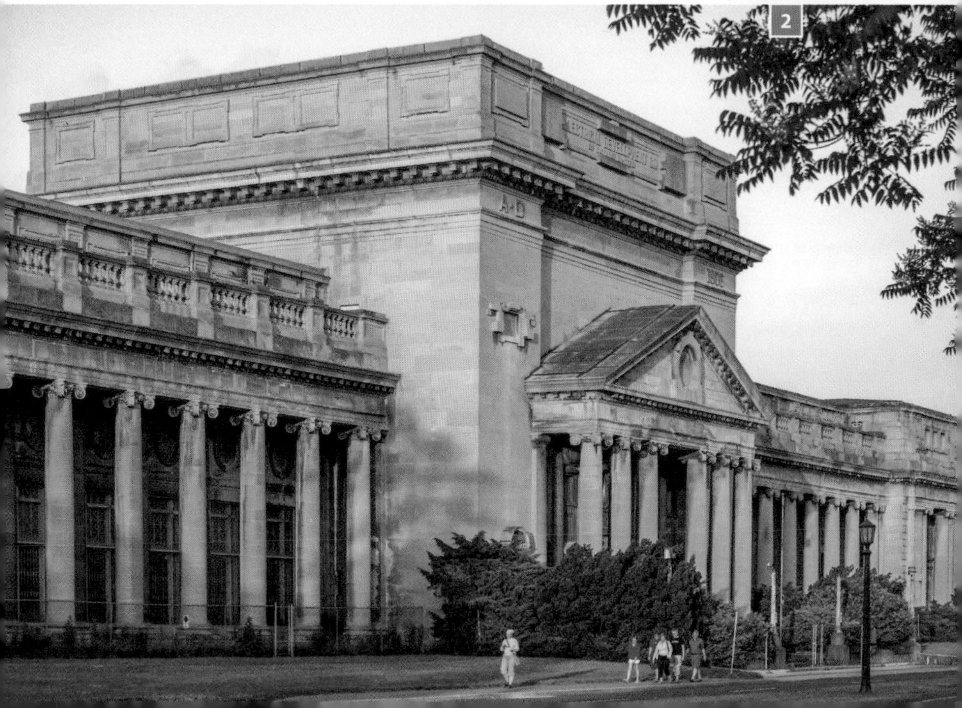

2

spacious area evokes the atmosphere of a tropical forest. Several smaller, rectangular greenhouses are attached to the showhouse, each filled with tropical plants, statuary, and trees.

Of particular interest is the titan arum, the world's largest lily, which grows to 10 feet (3 m) in height. Many people know this plant as the "corpse flower" because it emits a uniquely unpleasant scent when it blooms. The rotting smell is designed to attract insects that will help pollinate the plant. You'll find the Showhouse's corpse flower in the main atrium near the reception desk. Another unique feature of this giant lily is that it will take 8-10 years to bloom for the first time. After that, it may only bloom once every 2-3 years.

The plants on display are changed eight times a year, so there's always something different to enjoy. Easter and Christmas displays are the seasonal highlights. All plants are identified by signs indicating the species name. Although plants are not for sale, you'll find unique gardening-related treasures in the gift shop.

The outdoor gardens surrounding the showhouse consist of a large rose garden, reflecting ponds, and birdhouses, ideal for taking a relaxing afternoon stroll. About 30 minutes is ample time to enjoy this attraction, but flower enthusiasts could easily spend more than an hour. Staff from the Showhouse are responsible for choosing and maintaining the beautiful flowers throughout Victoria Park.

Rankine Generation Station

Heading from the Floral Showhouse toward the brink of the falls, you'll find a handsome building near the entrance to the main parking lot that serves Table Rock. This gorgeous, slumbering giant is known as the **Rankine Generation Station.** From 1905 until 2005, this facility turned the waters of the Niagara into clean, inexpensive electricity. The plant was taken offline because it was too expensive to modernize its system to produce electricity at 60 Hz, which is now the standard in North America.

In 2021, Niagara Parks plans to open the building as a museum to tell the story of how Niagara electrified the world. Each year additional areas are slated to be cleaned up and opened to the public. Visitors will be able to explore the main concourse, featuring 11 large generators that are attached to turbines sunk 180 feet (55 m) below in the bedrock. Today you can see the tunnels where water was returned into the river after generating power at Rankine—look for the two tunnel openings at the base of Horseshoe Falls.

★ Brink of Horseshoe Falls

Arguably one of the most photographed sites in the world, the **brink of Horseshoe Falls** (6650 Niagara Pkwy., 24 hours daily, free) has a view like no other. The brink is a public plaza area behind Table Rock Welcome Centre, which allows you to stand at the crest of Horseshoe Falls. The space is always open to visitors and is integrated into the paved pedestrian pathway that runs all the way to Niagara-on-the-Lake from Fort Erie. Green space, trees, and benches adjacent to the plaza provide convenient places to relax and appreciate the landscape.

It is difficult to fathom how much water spills over the falls. Every second, 680,000 gallons (2,600,000 L) of water pour over the brink, enough to fill the entire Empire State Building in six minutes! The crest line of Horseshoe Falls is 2,200 feet (670 m) wide, joining this spot with Terrapin Point on the U.S. side. On sunny days, the vibrant green water is hypnotic and soothing, until the water slams into the lower river with 2,500 tons (2,200 metric tons) of force.

Mist produced by the thundering waterfall can climb 200 feet (61 m) or more in the air. The wind determines where the mist will fall, and there's always a possibility that standing here, you'll feel some fine precipitation. It's a good idea to carry an umbrella when visiting the brink, as well as a cloth for drying your camera lens.

This area is stunning year-round. During winter, the mist collects on every surface and freezes, creating a crystalline skin on tree branches, guardrails, and light posts that is as beautiful as it is fragile. In autumn, the blazing reds and yellows of the changing leaves bring vibrancy to the gray of the gorge.

The pedestrian area along the brink is always open to visitors, even when the indoor areas of the Table Rock Welcome Centre are closed. Use common sense when taking pictures at the brink and do not climb on top of guardrails or support pillars. Many, many people are vying for a spot along the brink, so take photos, appreciate the vista, and then let another visitor move into your spot. When driving along the Parkway, be advised that some drivers may be more focused on the amazing scenery than the road. Allow yourself a comfortable following distance, as drivers may stop unexpectedly to discharge passengers or just take in the spectacle.

Table Rock Welcome Centre

The **Table Rock Welcome Centre** (6650 Niagara Pkwy., 877/642-7275, www.niagaraparks.com, 24 hours daily, free), the large bronze-and-brown structure at the brink of the falls, houses restaurants, shops, attractions, a first-aid station, and public washrooms. The bathrooms are always open, but hours of operation vary for the attractions, restaurants, and gift shops. The entire complex is being renovated throughout 2021 to replace chain restaurants with venues that reflect local culture. A quick-serve bistro will open on the main floor, complementing new retail space. Aesthetic renovations are also planned for the iconic Elements on the Falls restaurant on the upper concourse.

Paid parking ($10-25) is available across the street from the center, accessible via the crosswalk or pedestrian bridge. The complex is a major hub for the WEGO transportation service. Many visitors park across from the center and then use WEGO buses for their exploration of Niagara. A golf-cart shuttle vehicle in the parking lot assists guests with mobility issues. The service is free, but you'll need to flag down the driver to let them know you need assistance.

★ JOURNEY BEHIND THE FALLS

Journey Behind the Falls (Table Rock Welcome Centre, 6650 Niagara Pkwy., 877/642-7275, www.niagaraparks.com, 9am-11pm daily June-Sept., 9am-5pm daily Oct.-May, $21.95 adults, $14 children 6-12, free for children 5 and under) is, as its name implies, a chance to view Niagara Falls from inside the gorge wall, via a tunnel dug parallel to the face of the falls. The tunnels connect with two portals that allow you to look at the raging sheet of water from behind. The tunnels also lead to an outdoor observation platform at the base of Horseshoe Falls. Included in the cost of admission is a yellow plastic rain poncho. Keep it—it will come in handy later!

The journey starts with an elevator ride 15 stories underground. Upon exiting the elevator, you are immersed in a cool, dim, and dank series of tunnels, with the hum of the falls audible in the distance. The main tunnel slopes slightly downhill, leading to another tunnel on the right. This tunnel is parallel to the face of the falls. Within a few hundred yards, you'll find two portals—windows for viewing the falls from behind.

The portals have no protective glass, just a modest fence separating you from the torrent. The visual aspect of the portals (seeing falling water) is secondary to the *feeling* you experience. The roaring force of the falling water creates a subtle tremor that intensifies as you approach the safety fence. Sheets of water slash at the opening in the rock face, causing dislodged rocks to gather on the floor of the portal. The two portals are identical, so find the one with a shorter line. This portion of your journey should take about 5-10 minutes.

On your way back to the main tunnel, turn right and continue to the observation platform. The platform's upper level is enclosed and offers a protected vantage point of this amazing area at the base of the falls. Away from the sometimes-drenching mist, it provides safe photo opportunities. The open

1
2
3
4

viewing ports give unobstructed views of the falling torrent of Horseshoe Falls.

The lower level of the platform is for the hardy explorer looking for the full monsoon-like experience of Niagara. The difference between the upper and lower levels is like the difference between riding in a regular car versus a convertible with the top down. *What* you see is the same, but *how* you see it is very different.

At the bottom of the stairway is the lower platform, a large patio area. Make certain to wear the rain poncho because you'll likely get soaked. You're now very close to where a 17-story-tall wall of water slams into the river below. The force of this collision generates mist that seems to attack from all sides.

Those looking to minimize their exposure to the wind and mist can seek refuge on the far side of the patio area, where those elements are much lighter. If you're looking for the full experience, though, face the falls and head directly to the safety rail closest to the falls. Depending on weather conditions, the experience can be refreshing or chilling, but it is always satisfying. Before you go out to the lower platform, stow all electronics underneath your poncho, ideally in a protective bag.

The last leg of your journey is the elevator ride back to the top. The line to board the elevators usually requires a 5- to 10-minute wait. Most travelers will spend 60-90 minutes at this attraction. When taking photos in the portals, be sure your camera's flash is activated, as the light coming through the portals provides back lighting.

Portions of this attraction are limited in the winter months. From mid-December through mid-April, the lower observation deck closes for the season, and sometimes the portals are obscured by thick ice. Admission rates are reduced during this part of the season ($15 adults, $10 children 6-12).

1: tunnel opening at the Rankine Generation Station **2:** Journey Behind the Falls viewing platform **3:** Niagara's Fury an indoor 4-D experience **4:** Hornblower Niagara Cruise

NIAGARA'S FURY

Billed as a 4-D experience, **Niagara's Fury** (Table Rock Welcome Centre, 6650 Niagara Pkwy., 905/358-3268, www.niagarasfury.com, 9am-5pm daily, $16.50 adults, $10.75 children 6-12, free for children 5 and under) is a neat attraction, especially for families with smaller children. The experience begins with an eight-minute animation describing the birth of the falls, told through the eyes of woodland creatures. As the cartoon ends, doors open to a 360-degree theater space where a six-minute 4-D movie plays. During the movie, the theater's temperature fluctuates to correspond with the narrative. Water pours down the walls, the floor shakes, raindrops fall from the ceiling, and a simulated snow squall greets you. The choreographed special effects simulate the cataclysmic forces that shaped the geology of this region.

The entire experience is well under 30 minutes. If you'd prefer to stay dry during the 4-D rainfall simulation, stand close to the exits of the theater.

★ Hornblower Niagara Cruises

If you do just one thing in Niagara Falls, Ontario, on your trip, it must be this boat ride. **Hornblower Niagara Cruises Voyage to the Falls Boat Tour** (5920 Niagara Pkwy., 905/642-4272, www.niagaracruises.com, 8am-9:30pm daily May-Oct., $30.50 adults, $20.50 children 5-12, free for children 4 and under) provides boat tours to the base of Horseshoe Falls from the Canadian side of the river. Hornblower uses specially designed catamaran ships to ferry passengers to the base of the falls.

Your admission includes a trip from the top of the gorge down to the dock area aboard a funicular. A funicular transport system uses two trolley cars that are counterbalanced to help them safely and efficiently traverse steep inclines. When one trolley car is at the bottom of the gorge, the other is at the top—the cars are connected by a cable. As one descends the gorge, its weight helps propel the other trolley car to the top. The trolleys accommodate 50

Niagara Daredevils

Niagara has been a magnet for daredevils and thrill seekers for more than 150 years. In the mid-1800s, people began challenging Niagara. Some got inside barrels, attempting to navigate the rapids of the lower river. Soon walking a tightrope over the river became the rage. The most notable tightrope walker was Francois Gravelet (The Great Blondin), who crossed the gorge on numerous occasions—one time while carrying his manager upon his back.

In 1911, Anne Edson Taylor became the first person to go over Niagara Falls in a barrel. She survived the stunt but failed in her attempt to make a living off of it. More than a dozen people have gone over the falls in some type of device, including giant rubber balls, truck-tire inner tubes, kayaks, and a Jet Ski. Five people, including a seven-year-old boy, have survived the 17-story plunge over Horseshoe Falls without the aid of any protective device.

But not every daredevil has survived the plunge. Following the death of a daredevil in 1950, local authorities passed laws making it illegal to attempt "stunting" at Niagara. In fact, people attempting to go over Horseshoe Falls face a fine of nearly $10,000.

Anne Edson Taylor was the first person to survive a plunge over the Falls.

passengers in climate-controlled cars that afford a breathtaking view of the falls as people journey 19 stories down to board the boats.

The ride to and from Horseshoe Falls is pleasant, providing a view of American and Bridal Veil Falls as the boat passes about 500 yards (457 m) from the U.S. shoreline. The calm portion of the ride ends as the boat enters the choppy, roiling waters beneath Horseshoe Falls. Water assaults you from all sides, as wind-whipped mist soaks everything in its path. The ferocious torrent causes the water in the lower Niagara River to resemble a boiling cauldron with numerous whitecaps and eddies surging.

Those on the top deck of the boat receive the most amount of mist. People on the lower deck receive some shelter from the wind-driven water, but everyone should plan on getting wet. If you have a waterproof camera, you'll be able to capture images throughout the journey. Others should stow their camera when the boat is directly under Horseshoe Falls; tucking the camera under your poncho is usually sufficient protection.

Hornblower is looking to top the Maid of the Mist tour, available on the U.S. side, by offering extra services. In addition to the traditional daily 20-minute tours to the base of Horseshoe Falls, Hornblower is providing 40-minute enhanced cruises during the nightly illumination and the summer fireworks shows (9:30pm mid-June-Labor Day, $42.95 adults, $27.95 children 5-12, free for children 4 and under). Hornblower's catamarans offer amenities including washrooms, snack concessions, a deck area protected by retractable glass windows, and a bar.

This attraction is extremely popular, so consider buying tickets online with a predetermined departure time. If you miss your timed departure, you have seven days in which you may redeem your tickets. This flexible date ticketing is perfect for days when it rains and you'd prefer to try the attraction later in your stay. Pre-purchasing your tickets can help avoid waiting in the ticket line, so plan ahead and save a boatload of time!

MistRider Zipline to the Falls

WildPlay's **MistRider Zipline to the Falls** (5847 Niagara Pkwy., 888/263-7073, http://niagarafalls.wildplay.com, 10am-8pm daily early Mar.-Nov., $69.99) is one of Niagara's newer attractions. This thrilling zip line experience starts 220 feet (67 m) above the Niagara River, allowing you to glide to the base of the gorge. The 2,200-foot-long (670 m-long) zip line ride is exhilarating, scenic, and—some would say—brief. It is a ride of a lifetime as you zoom at speeds of more than 40 miles per hour (64 kph), suspended from the wire cable by your safety harness.

To avoid delays on-site, register online and make certain to complete your waiver in advance. Riders must be at least seven years of age and weigh between 50 and 300 pounds (22-136 kg). The zip line also accommodates people who use wheelchairs. After gearing up and completing a safety demonstration, you'll be attached to the zip line via a pulley device. Eventually you reach the launching position, which is 20 stories above the green waters of Niagara. Brave riders will find that spreading your arms out like a starfish will increase your speed. Be prepared for a solid but safe bump as you engage the braking system at the bottom of the line—your feet are quite likely to be temporarily tossed above your shoulders! You return to the top of the gorge via a passenger van.

The only cameras allowed while you're using the zip line are mounted GoPros or devices with a wrist strap. Be advised that sometimes adverse weather conditions, such as high winds, may prevent operation of the zipline. Also note that guests must wear the safety helmet supplied by the venue. For guests with turbans or religious head coverings, this mandatory safety rule could present an issue.

Nighttime zip line rides (8pm-9:45pm mid-May-Oct., $79.99) are also offered. These rides give guests a unique perspective on the brilliant colors of the nightly illumination of Horseshow Falls. The zip line is closed a few minutes before 10pm, when seasonal fireworks are launched from a nearby platform along the Canadian shore of the lower Niagara River. Early riders can save a few bucks by choosing the Early Bird Zipline experience (8am-9:40am daily June-Labor Day, $59.99).

Tours

There are several options for visitors seeking a guided experience of Niagara. If you are seeking a smaller, more intimate tour, **See Sight Tours** (pickup at your hotel, 888/961-6584, www.seesight-tours.com, daily) is the way to go. The company uses a fleet of late-model minivans for tours, which means your group will never be more than seven people. The Best of Niagara Falls tour is four hours and includes admission to a Hornblower Cruises ride, Journey Behind the Falls, and the Skylon Tower ($119 adults, $89 children 5-12, $10 children 4 and under; prices are in U.S. dollars). Feeling a little brave and a bit hungry? The Ultimate Falls Tour ($254 adults, $169 children 3-12, $10 children 2 and under; prices are in U.S. dollars) adds a helicopter flight and lunch at the Skylon Tower.

Hop aboard a vintage British bus for great views of the falls and Victoria Park. **Double Deck Tours** (Corner Falls Ave. and Clifton Hill (905/374-7423, www.doubledecktours.com) features beautiful and authentic 1950s double-decker buses to explore Niagara. The Hop-On Hop-Off Tour (10am-6pm mid-June-Labor Day, $31.08 adults, $26.28 children 6-12) takes you through a 90-minute loop of the area, with stops at major attractions including Table Rock and the Whirlpool Aero Car. A certified guide entertains you with the story of Niagara as you complete the circuit at your own pace. The Niagara Falls Bucket List Tour (11am and 12:15pm daily May-Labor Day, $104.14 adults, $63.42 children 6-12) is a 3.5-hour guided tour that includes admission to Journey Behind the Falls, a Hornblower Niagara Cruises ride, and the Whirlpool Aero Car.

Air-conditioned motor coaches are the choice of transport for **Magnificent Tours** (pickup at most hotels, 888/614-8687, www.magnificentniagarafallstours.com, daily), a company that bills itself as Niagara's "Largest Tour Company." The company's Best Tour (9:30am and 2pm, $130 adults, $65 children 6-12; prices are in U.S. dollars) includes a Hornblower Niagara Cruises ride, Journey Behind the Falls, and a stop at the Whirlpool Observation Deck. The Niagara Wine Tour (9:45am, $105 adults, $25 children 6-12; prices are in U.S. dollars) is a wonderful way to visit a minimum of three wineries, a chocolate shop, and Niagara-on-the-Lake during a guided six-hour tour.

Take flight over Niagara aboard a tour with **Niagara Helicopters** (3731 Victoria Ave., 905/357-5672, www.niagarahelicopters.com, 9am-sunset daily, $149 adults, $92 children 3-12). Tours fly year-round and last about 12 minutes. Niagara Helicopters uses four choppers, so waiting time at the launch area is minimal even in high season. The experience is second to none and takes you above the whirlpool, rapids, Rainbow Bridge, and magnificent Horseshoe Falls. Helicopters can accommodate groups of seven guests. Service is dependent on weather conditions, so call ahead on windy or rainy days.

Outdoor Gardens

As you walk north from the brink of the falls, you can see across the gorge to Niagara Falls. From there, turn 180 degrees and look across the Niagara Parkway, where you'll find the outdoor gardens of **Queen Victoria Park** (Niagara Pkwy. from Table Rock to Clifton Hill, www.niagaraparks.com, 24 hours daily, free). This park is a meticulously groomed landscape with lush green lawns, rock gardens, fountains, and trees. Plants have been chosen so that something is always blooming in the spring, summer, and autumn. Park benches and verdant, grassy areas are perfect for a rest and have panoramas of the gorge and falls.

The **Oakes Garden Theatre** (Niagara Pkwy., www.niagaraparks.com, 24 hours daily, free), immediately across Clifton Hill from Queen Victoria Park, is a hidden gem that is easily overlooked because it appears to be part of a private attraction or hotel. It was once the site of the grand and historic Clifton Hotel, the meeting place for both Union and Confederate representatives discussing diplomatic matters during the American Civil War. Today the Oakes Garden is the setting for many special events, including live music and festivals. The gardens feature a beautiful curved walkway adorned with pillars and built into small hills that overlook a raised stage area. The falls supply a lovely backdrop to the fan-shaped stage. The Oakes is one of the best spots to view the fireworks displays over the falls at 10pm on Fridays and Sundays in summer.

FALLSVIEW

Overlook

One of the best views of the falls is from an overlook not marked on any maps and without a name. It's near the intersection of Livingstone Street and Fallsview Boulevard, just in front of the Marriott on the Falls Hotel. From this humble perch, you can see Table Rock Welcome Centre, Horseshoe Falls, and the upper rapids of the Niagara River. You can also get a good sense of the distance between the Diversionary Dam, Toronto Power Generating Station, and the brink of the falls.

Very few people know about this overlook, so it isn't crowded, and it's a short walk from all the major high-rise hotels and the casino. Walk south on Fallsview Boulevard until you reach the end of the road. If you're driving, park along the curb on Fallsview Boulevard. Look for the WEGO bus shelter across from the taxi stand and you'll be at the right spot.

★ Skylon Tower

The most iconic built landmark in Niagara Falls is the **Skylon Tower** (5200 Robinson

---

1: MistRider Zipline to the Falls **2:** Oakes Garden Theatre **3:** White Water Walk **4:** The Whirlpool

1
2
3
4

St., 905/356-2651, www.skylon.com, 8am-midnight daily May-mid-Oct., 11am-9pm mid-Oct.-Apr., main level free). Since 1965, the concrete structure has towered 52 stories above the city, allowing for a 360-degree view of the region. On clear days, the skylines of Toronto and Buffalo are visible beyond the falls.

The main level of Skylon Tower features several gift shops, a Starbucks, and a ticket counter. The top of the tower provides fine dining in the Revolving Dining Room as well as family-style fare at the Summit Style Buffet. Above it all is the observation deck, with some of the best panoramas of Niagara.

The **elevator ride** ($16.24 adults, $10.44 children 3-12, free with purchase of meal at upper restaurants) to the top of the tower is a breathtaking 52-second trip in a glass-enclosed capsule. The brief trip is a prelude to the vista that greets you on the observation deck. The indoor observation area is enclosed in glass and climate-controlled. Decals on the windows identify points of interest that appear in the distance. If you are staying more than one day in the region, consider the Tower's Day and Night Pass ($20.88 adults, $12.76 children 3-12). It allows you to ascend to the Observation Deck twice within a 24-hour period. Some travelers will enjoy this option to appreciate the view twice—once during the day, and then at night during the fireworks display.

In the outdoor observation area, a wire enclosure keeps you safe, while allowing enough space for your camera lens to poke through and capture unobstructed images of the landscape.

Depending on weather conditions, plan on spending 20-30 minutes on the outdoor observation platform. Most people will spend a majority of their time looking east at the falls and the lower Niagara River, 775 feet (234 m) below. Looking north, you may be able to glimpse Toronto (40 mi/64 km away) and its CN Tower, which is roughly twice as tall as the Skylon Tower.

If you are looking for a unique camera shot, face the windows of the enclosed observation area with your back to the landscape. Use the camera to capture your reflection in the windows with the panorama in the background.

The observation deck is a great place to experience the nighttime beauty of the falls. The view of the nightly illumination from this perch is without parallel. During summer's nightly fireworks shows, viewers in the tower watch the display from above, as the fireworks explode beneath the level of the observation deck. You'll need to arrive by 9:30pm and stake out a place along the eastern edge of the platform for the best view.

Kids are drawn to the Family Fun Centre, an arcade in the lower concourse level of the tower with dozens of interactive amusements and small coin-operated rides. Several fast-food restaurants and bathrooms are also on this level. Upon exiting the building from the concourse level, you'll find the entrance for the 3-D/4-D movie theater that is part of the Skylon complex. The movie, theater, and 4-D effects are somewhat dated, so spend your limited touring time elsewhere.

Clifton Hill

Historically, Niagara Falls has always had circus-like attractions for tourists. Years ago, private museums intrigued visitors with Egyptian mummies, two-headed calves (still on display at Ripley's Believe It or Not!), reconstructed skeletons of large animals, and memorabilia like Sitting Bull's moccasins. Today, that spirit of carnival and weirdness is found along the street known as Clifton Hill, home to numerous arcades, creepy fun houses, mini-golf courses, and wax museums. For those traveling with children, Clifton Hill is a good place to spend an afternoon.

Find **Adventure City** (4915 Clifton Hill, 905/374-4446, www.adventurecityniagarafalls.com, 10 am-9 pm daily, free admission, game prices vary) at the base of Clifton Hill near the Rainforest Cafe. Kids and adults can enjoy more than 125 arcade-style games. The complex also houses a

4-D theater, indoor mini-golf course, bumper cars, and an interactive Super Hero Laser ride. On a rainy day, the All Access Pass ($21.99) could be a value—it gives admission to all the previously mentioned attractions plus some arcade tokens.

The **Great Canadian Midway** (4950 Clifton Hill, 905/358-3676, www.cliftonhill.com, 9am-2am daily, free admission, game prices vary) is a spacious, loud, energetic arcade with more than 300 of the latest interactive games, as well as some old-school amusements like Skee-Ball. Games operate with tokens purchased at the front desk or automated exchange kiosks. Advertising flyers with discount coupons for tokens are in racks on the walkway into the midway complex.

Take a relaxing ride and enjoy a spectacular view on the **Niagara SkyWheel** (4950 Clifton Hill, 905/358-4793, www.cliftonhill.com, 9am-2am daily, $12.99 adults, $6.99 children 12 and under). This gentle giant of a Ferris wheel is as tall as Niagara Falls—about 175 feet (53 m). Rides in the fully enclosed, climate-controlled gondolas last about 12 minutes. The safety and comfort of the gondolas ensure a good ride for the entire family, including those uncomfortable with heights. Take your camera along, as this is one of the best perches to snap images of the falls. Each gondola carries up to six people and provides an excellent 360-degree view of the falls, Clifton Hill, and beyond. The best time to enjoy this attraction is during the day or during the twice-weekly summer fireworks display.

Tee off at **Dinosaur Adventure Golf** (4960 Clifton Hill, 905/358-3676, www.cliftonhill.com, 10am-midnight daily, $10.99 adults, $6.99 children 12 and under). Navigate two 18-hole courses with a prehistoric theme. Many of the 50 dinosaur statues will growl at you along the course. Try to keep your concentration as a 50-foot-high (15-m-high) volcano erupts periodically, sending smoke and flames into the air.

Oddities abound in **Ripley's Believe It or Not!** (4960 Clifton Hill, 905/356-2238, www.ripleysniagara.com, 10am-10pm daily, $18.99 adults, $12.99 children 6-12). You can easily spend 90 minutes or more in this museum with more than 800 items on display, including shrunken heads and bizarre artifacts. This attraction is best for children who can read or have someone read to them.

Lundy's Lane

Lundy's Lane is a major corridor that leads to the Fallsview area and is known for its numerous hotels, restaurants, and shops. Once the site of the bloodiest battle in Canada's history, it now has a wonderful heritage museum.

The **Niagara Falls History Museum** (5810 Ferry St., 905/358-5082, www.niagarafallsmuseums.ca, 10am-5pm Tues.-Wed and Fri.-Sun., 10am-9pm Thurs., $5 adults, $4 children 6-19) is small but packed with interesting displays telling the story of the falls. Kids can try on military uniforms, shoulder replica muskets, and lift cannonballs from the War of 1812 era. There's also a "feet-on" interactive exhibit that allows you to attempt to walk a simulated high wire. Take 60-90 minutes to appreciate this wonderfully interactive history museum. There's a special rate ($15) for families of up to five people.

Before you leave the museum, grab a free walking map of Drummond Hill Cemetery and walk two blocks west to experience **Lundy's Lane Battlefield** (6110 Lundy's Lane, 905/358-5082, www.visit1812.com, dawn-dusk daily, free). On this spot during the War of 1812, 6,000 British and American soldiers clashed in fighting that lasted five hours. Casualties were high, with each side recording about 800 dead, injured, or missing. The Battle of Lundy's Lane is regarded as the bloodiest day of battle in that war, yet when the smoke cleared, neither side could claim victory.

Following the War of 1812, visitors arrived to commemorate the battle, with soldiers from the war acting as guides. Observation towers, formal monuments, and grave markers were dedicated. As time passed, the battlefield transitioned into a cemetery.

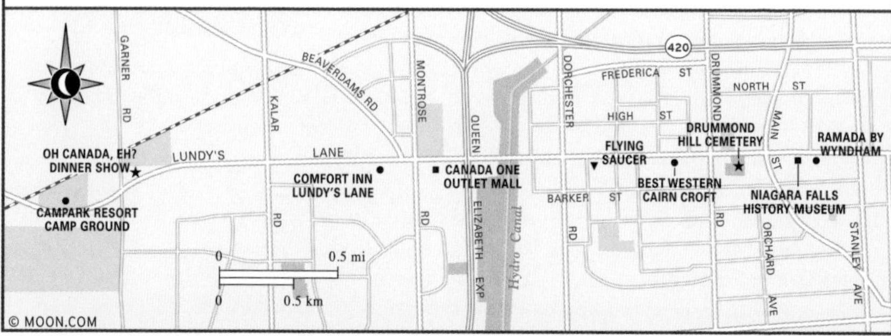

Today the cemetery and battlefield are peaceful reminders of the sacrifices of that battle. Using the walking map, you can find many interesting places, including the area where a funeral pyre was hastily constructed to incinerate the dead. The grave of Canadian heroine Laura Secord is here as well. Secord survived a 20-mile (32-km) walk through enemy territory during the war to alert the British of an impending American attack. The round-trip walk from the museum and the tour of the battlefield takes 60-90 minutes.

PARKWAY NORTH

When Winston Churchill visited Canada in August 1943, he called the stretch of the Niagara Parkway heading north from Niagara Falls "the prettiest Sunday afternoon drive in the world." The 6-mile (10-km) portion joining the falls to the Floral Clock runs along the edge of the gorge and reveals many natural wonders as you head toward Niagara-on-the-Lake. Although Mr. Churchill preferred to drive in a car, guests are encouraged to make the journey on foot, by bike, or by scooter. A paved bike path runs the length of the Niagara River from Fort Erie to Lake Ontario.

★ White Water Walk

Following the Niagara Parkway north, you'll find the **White Water Walk** (4330 Niagara Pkwy., 877/642-7275, www.niagaraparks.com, 10am-4:30pm daily Apr.-mid-June and Sept.-mid-Oct., 9am-7:30pm mid-June-Aug., $16.50 adults, $10.75 children 6-12) about 1.5 miles (2.4 km) past the Rainbow Bridge. The White Water Walk gives you the opportunity to safely stroll alongside the turbulent waters of the lower rapids without getting wet.

After descending more than 200 feet (61 m) in an elevator, you'll walk along a quarter-mile (0.4-km) stretch of the Niagara River's edge that has some of the most awe-inspiring portions of the lower rapids. In this narrow part of the gorge, water surges at 30 miles per hour (48 kph), slamming against giant rocks along the riverbed, creating constant waves ranging 9-15 feet (3-5 m) high. This raging white water is the backdrop for a scene in the film *Superman II,* in which Lois Lane is saved by quick-thinking Clark Kent.

Stroll at your own pace on the White Water Walk, pausing to read the informative signs. The walkway is raised, providing a safe, child-friendly, and dry way to see the rapids. The boardwalk is wheelchair-accessible; however, two attached viewing platforms require the use of stairs. Most visitors complete the walk in 30 minutes, but photographers and others fascinated by the roar of white water could easily spend an hour here. This attraction is a WEGO stop (green line, White Water), but you can also park curbside along Niagara Parkway.

Ten Thousand Buddha Temple

Directly across from the White Water Walk is the **Ten Thousand Buddha Temple**

(4303 River Rd., 905/371-2678, www.chamshantemple.org, 9am-5pm daily, free), also known as the **Cham San Monastery.** The complex is an oasis of calm and peace in an otherwise bustling tourist area. This stunning pagoda and serene three-acre campus are home to a group of Buddhist monks dedicated to spreading peace and the understanding of dharma philosophy. The focal point inside the seven-level pagoda is a magnificent 40-foot (12-m) Buddha statue. The public area of the temple is open daily; free tours of the entire shrine (including the main pagoda) are offered on weekends June-October.

Park in the free lots surrounding the campus. The temple is perfect for quiet meditation or for learning more about Buddhism. Visitors are asked to remove their shoes to view some indoor areas of the temple; photography is not permitted inside the temple.

★ The Whirlpool

Three miles (5 km) downstream from the falls, the Niagara River takes an abrupt right-hand turn. This area of the river forms a **whirlpool** that is violent and magnificent to behold. The whirlpool is a remnant of an ancient waterfall basin filled with loose rocks. As the Niagara River receded over the past 12,000 years, it intersected this bowl of loose rock and the course of the river changed.

Looking down at the river, note how the water enters the whirlpool and slams into the far gorge wall, turning counterclockwise. The water is forced to cross under the main flow and bubbles up on the other side. It is this force that creates the ever-churning vortex known as the whirlpool. Over the years, this has proven to be the most dangerous stretch of the Niagara, where everything caught in the river collects before heading downstream or disappearing forever.

The river is generally about 30-40 feet (9-12 m) deep. The whirlpool's depth is more than 100 feet (30 m). It has swallowed objects that are never seen again. The swirling eye of the whirlpool is always moving and dangerous, and should be avoided. Prior to the jet boats (pages 91 and 145), an attraction using Zodiac vessels plied the whirlpool, ending with tragic results during its first season of operation.

There are two main ways to safely view the whirlpool on the Canadian side of the gorge. The **Whirlpool Aero Car** (3850 Niagara Pkwy., 877/642-7275, www.niagaraparks.com, 10am-5pm daily mid-Mar.-June and Sept.-Oct., 9am-8pm daily July-Aug., $16.50 adults, $10.75 children 6-12) allows passengers to glide over the whirlpool aboard an aerial tram. The aero car departs from Colt's Point on its slow journey to Thompson's Point, on the far side of the whirlpool. The 10-minute ride transports passengers 210 feet (64 m) above the whirlpool, affording excellent views of the gorge and surging water below. The aero car's capacity is 40 people (standing room only); it is not wheelchair-accessible.

Ticket sales end 30 minutes before closing time. Sometimes service may be interrupted due to high winds, so call ahead if you are visiting during bad weather. The staff member traveling onboard can take a group photo with your camera, if requested. A café and public restrooms are available at the gift shop. Parking is free.

The second way to see the whirlpool is at **Thompson's Point** (Niagara Pkwy., dawn-dusk daily, free), a spot unknown to many tourists. Thompson's Point affords a great view of the Niagara River as it drops 50 feet (15 m) in elevation, creating awe-inspiring rapids. It is the perfect perch to see the counterclockwise flow of the water as the river enters the whirlpool, crosses underneath itself, and then starts to completes its trip to Lake Ontario.

Thompson's Point has many of the same views as Colt's Point (where the aero car departs from) but is less crowded and more panoramic. Thompson's Point is positioned so that you can better observe the river as it enters and exits the whirlpool. From here, you have a better sense of the entire natural system that creates the counterclockwise vortex. If the aero car is operating, stand on the left side of the platform to feel the vibration of the

1
2
NIAGARA PARKS

cable car's mechanism beneath your feet. The aero car pauses for a moment at Thompson's Point before returning to Colt's Point.

Thompson's Point is easy to miss. Driving north on the Niagara Parkway, slow down as you near the entrance for the Whirlpool Golf Course and Restaurant. Look for a small sign for Thompson's Point just before a service road on your right, which leads to free parking. Take a short walk to the observation area.

Whirlpool Adventure Course

Niagara's newest eco-attraction, the **Whirlpool Adventure Course** (3500 Niagara Pkwy., 800/263-7073, http://niagarafalls.wildplay.com, 11am-3pm Sat.-Sun. Apr.-mid-June, 9am-7pm daily mid-June-mid-Sept., 10am-4 pm Sat.-Sun. mid-Sept.-Oct., $14.99-29.99 admission based on course selection) is an amazing collection of suspended obstacle courses, zip lines, and aerial games. Put on your helmet, strap into your harness, and experience tightrope walking, wobbly bridges, rope swings, and cargo nets.

You have a choice of three courses; each is self-paced so you can advance as your ability allows. The park's construction gives you a stunning view of the swirling whirlpool as you navigate the various obstacles and conquer your fears. A true "high"-light is the "What's to Fear Jump," where brave participants leap from a platform 40 feet (12 m) and land safely on the ground, thanks to an elastic tether.

Plan on spending at least 90 minutes to complete a course. In order to participate, guests must be at least 5 years old and more than 4 feet, 8 inches (142 cm) tall. Save time by completing a liability waiver online and expect a safety demonstration prior to beginning the course.

Water Park

The **Fallsview Indoor Waterpark** (5685 Falls Ave., 800/234-8413, www.fallsviewwaterpark.com, 10am-9pm daily, $37.99 and up) offers three acres of watery fun year-round. The park is nine stories above the ground and has 16 waterslides to keep everybody engaged and entertained. There's a splash pad for little ones, as well as two hot tubs for adults. Round out your stay enjoying an indoor and an outdoor pool, a wave pool, and a playground with a 1,000-gallon (3,785 L) tipping bucket that drenches guests several times an hour. If you're visiting the falls in the winter or you're traveling with children, this could be a good option for you. The water park is attached to three hotels, and you may purchase a hotel package or a day pass.

Niagara Parks Botanical Gardens and School of Horticulture

No matter what season you visit the **Niagara Parks Botanical Gardens and School of Horticulture** (2565 Niagara Pkwy., 905/356-8554, www.niagaraparks.com, dawn-dusk daily, free), you'll find something in bloom. This 100-acre campus is home to Canada's only residential horticultural school.

A creative and artistic perennial garden with seasonal plants in hanging baskets greets you at the campus entrance. There are more than 3,000 species of flowers and plants, including a Victorian rose garden with more than 2,400 rose plants. Horticulture enthusiasts could easily spend an entire afternoon wandering the grounds, exploring the herb, rock, shrub, lily, and vegetable gardens. Tree species include crab apples, dogwoods, Japanese maples, and conifers including spruces.

A limited number of students are admitted to this prestigious college, and their hard work and passion are evident in the lush, beautiful landscapes throughout the campus. Roaming the grounds is free; parking for the gardens is $5.

Butterfly Conservatory

Relax and watch the butterflies flutter by at the **Butterfly Conservatory** (2565 Niagara Pkwy., 905/358-0025, www.niagaraparks.

1: Butterfly Conservatory 2: Floral Clock

com, 10am-7pm daily July-Aug., 10am-5pm daily Sept.-June, $16.50 adults, $10.75 children 6-12). Take a break from the roaring power of the falls by enjoying the delicate beauty of more than 2,000 butterflies housed in the conservatory.

Start by viewing a brief, informative video on the lives of these colorful creatures. Stroll indoors at your own pace, stopping to observe dozens of species of butterflies in this lush tropical environment. Sometimes the butterflies will investigate you, landing on your arms, shoulders, and head. Bring your camera and remember to dress appropriately, as the conservatory is kept warm and humid year-round.

The conservatory experience should take about one hour to complete. Note that the pathways can be congested by other visitors with strollers—this is an attraction where you should relax and take your time. There's a gift shop and café. The WEGO bus stops here; parking is $5.

Floral Clock

Flower fans should find time to stop at the **Floral Clock** (14004 Niagara Pkwy., www.niagaraparks.com, dawn-dusk daily, free), a 40-foot-wide (12-m-wide) outdoor clock with a face made of thousands of plants organized in a beautiful design. The design is changed twice a year and typically uses more than 15,000 bedding plants. During daylight hours, you can stroll behind the clock, where a door leads to a small room with images of all the designs over the years. Those with green thumbs will want to take photos and explore a bit more than most visitors, who will be satisfied with a five-minute stop here.

Recreation

PARKS

There is no shortage of green spaces in Niagara Falls. The city maintains 96 parks, many of which are community parks with baseball diamonds, soccer fields, a shelter, benches, and playgrounds.

Two large parks are not operated by the city. Niagara Parks Commission is responsible for **Queen Victoria Park,** the green space immediately along the rim of the gorge from the brink of the falls to Clifton Hill, and **Niagara Glen Park** (3050 Niagara Pkwy., www.niagaraparks.com, dawn-dusk daily, free). Niagara Glen has ample free parking and dozens of picnic tables and grills, as well as a large pavilion with additional tables. This park is also home to the trailhead for the Niagara Glen hiking trails. At Glen Park, check out the **Niagara Glen Nature Centre** (905/354-6678, www.niagaraparks.com, 10am-5pm daily June-Aug., 10am-5pm Sat. Sept.-Oct., free), a treasure trove of information on the parks system and the hiking trails, animals, and plants in the Glen. Park naturalists can guide you to the best hiking trails in the Glen for your skills and experience.

HIKING

The city has 20 walking/hiking trails (www.niagarafalls.ca) within its limits, most of which are well under 2 miles (3.2 km) and generally flat.

The best hiking in this region is in two areas along the gorge, the Whirlpool Trail and the Niagara Glen Paths, but note that these are quite dangerous for inexperienced hikers. Trails here lead to stretches of the Niagara River including the whirlpool and lower rapids. Trying to wade or swim in these stretches can lead to injury or death.

All Niagara Parks trails are open year-round, but they are not maintained in winter. It is up to the individual hiker to determine if snowfall affects the trails to the degree that they are not passable.

Hiking Rules

Here are some of the guidelines issued by Niagara Parks for hikers:

- Pack out trash.
- Stay on the marked trail.
- No fires are permitted.
- Respect wildlife; appreciate animals from afar. Do not approach animals.
- Use common sense—trails are not maintained during winter months and present extra hazards.

Niagara Parks hiking guidelines are in compliance with **Leave No Trace** (www.leavenotrace.ca). Check the website for information on ethical hiking.

The best source of information on local hiking trails is the **Niagara Glen Nature Centre** (3050 Niagara Pkwy., 905/354-6678, www.niagaraparks.com, 10am-5pm daily June-Aug., 10am-5pm Sat. Sept.-Oct.). Staff at the center can answer questions about trail locations and conditions, as well as the level of difficulty.

Whirlpool Trail

The **Whirlpool Trail** (off Niagara Pkwy., just north of the Whirlpool Aero Car, 905/354-6678, www.niagaraparksnature.com, dawn-dusk daily) is a challenging hike. It starts with more than 300 wooden stairs down the slope of the whirlpool wall. From the stairs, it's about 1 mile (1.6 km) to the water's edge. You'll encounter steep drops as you walk through a mature ravine forest.

At the bottom of the trail, the massive, swirling whirlpool unfolds before your eyes. As you look up, you may see the aero car quietly hovering over the water. Occasionally the din of the water's movement is interrupted by a jet boat filled with soaked but exhilarated passengers. Walking clockwise along the shore (downstream), you'll eventually meet up with the River Path, which connects to the Niagara Glen Paths. This point is 1.5 miles (2.4 km) from the trailhead. At this point, many hikers choose to return to the beginning of the Whirlpool Trail. Those who want to keep exploring the Niagara Glen Paths may want to start at the trailhead of the Niagara Glen system, rather than from the Whirlpool Trail.

To find the Whirlpool trailhead, proceed north along Niagara Parkway, passing the aero car attraction. After the next intersection at Whirlpool Road, look for a small parking lot on the right side of the road. Park and look for the stairwell.

Niagara Glen Paths

Within Niagara Glen Park lies the trailhead for the **Niagara Glen Paths** (3050 Niagara Pkwy., 905/354-6678, www.niagaraparks.com, dawn-dusk daily). The paths consist of seven trails that add up to a robust 5 miles (8 km). Individual paths are named and blazed with the following color codes: Terrace Path (red), Cliffside Path (white), Trillium Path (light blue), Cobblestone Path (purple), Woodland Path (yellow), Eddy Path (green), and River Path (blue).

Starting from the 55-foot-tall (17-m-tall) steel staircase, take the trail north to the Cliffside Path. Following this path, you'll intersect with the Terrace Path. Head down (turn left), and you'll encounter stone stairs and amazing boulders. The Terrace Path ends when you reach the River Path that runs along the river's edge. This portion of the Glen Paths reveals the splendid Carolinian Forest with its beech and tulip trees.

As you head upstream along the River Path, you'll see the green water and the steep wall of the gorge on the U.S. side of the river. This relatively flat terrain contains sumac, sassafras, and cedar trees. Eventually you will reach the Eddy Path, which reconnects you to the Cliffside Path. End the hike by returning to the steel staircase and trailhead in Niagara Glen Park. Head down the grassy hill toward the large pavilion. Continue to the rim of the gorge and you'll find the stairs.

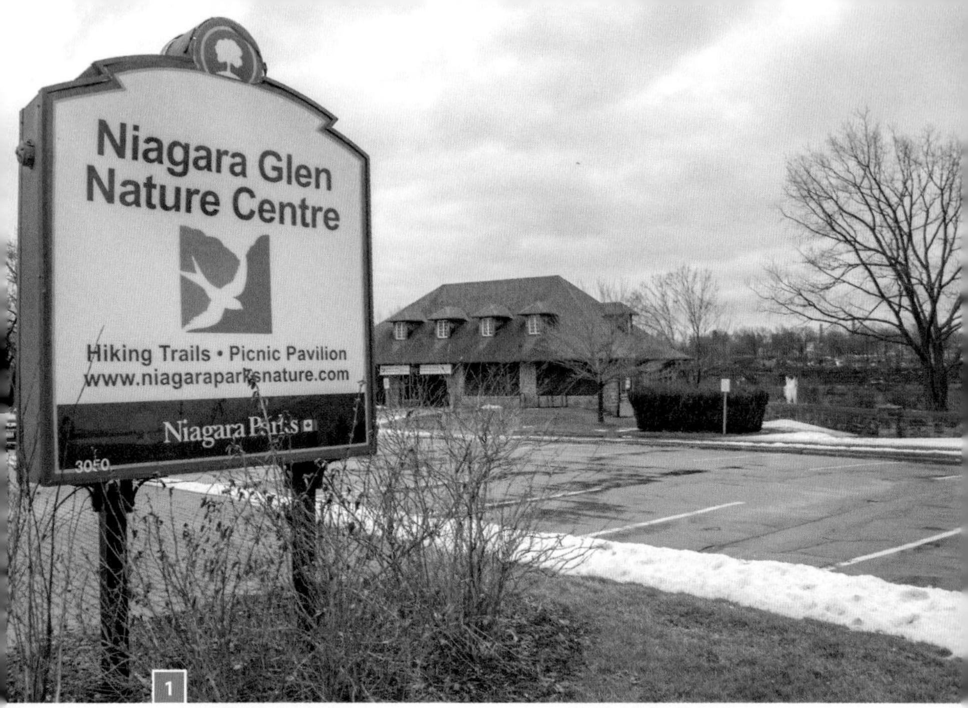

Niagara Glen
Nature Centre
Hiking Trails • Picnic Pavilion
Niagara Parks
1
2

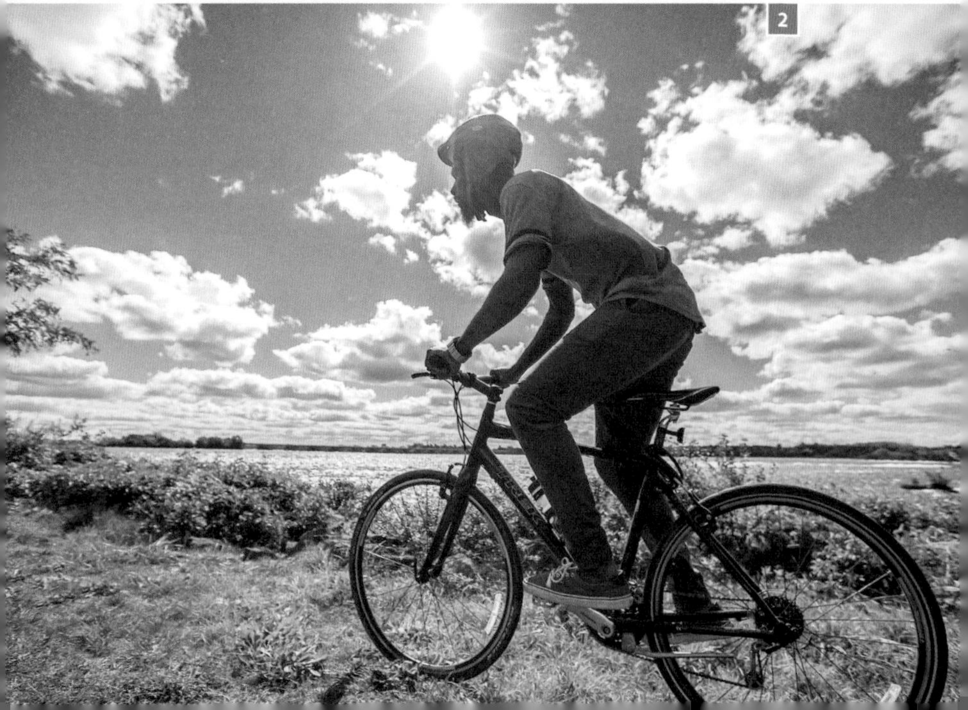

Worried about rockslides? So is the Parks Commission. Geologists routinely assess the gorge, looking for rockslide hazards. When a trouble spot is identified, workers will proactively address the potential problem and safely remove the rock.

BICYCLING

Biking is quickly gaining in popularity in the Niagara region. The **Niagara Recreational Trail** (www.niagaraparksnature.com) provides a safe, paved 35-mile (56-km) path along the Niagara River from Lake Erie to Lake Ontario.

In the Niagara Falls area, two shops offer bike rentals. **Snap E-Bike Rentals & Experiences** (4239 Park St., 905/651-1951, www.snapebike.com, 9am-8pm daily, $50 and up) exclusively rents electric bikes. These fat-tired vehicles are battery powered but can also be pedaled if the rider desires. The primary benefit of these bikes for Niagara visitors is that they are a safe, realistic way to complete the 25-mile (40-km) round-trip ride from the falls to Niagara-on-the-Lake.

Guests receive training, a helmet, a bike lock, and advice on where to go and what to see. Each bike comes with a saddlebag for gear storage. It can even hold a bottle of wine, should you purchase one during your journey. The shop offers a four-hour Adventure Tour (10am, 2pm, and 3pm daily, $120) that explores the downtown, Fallsview, and Queenston regions. Renters must be over the age of 16 and taller than 5 feet, 2 inches (157 cm). The shop is conveniently located a few blocks from the bus and train station.

Zoom Leisure (431 Mississauga St., 866/811-6993, www.zoomleisure.com, 8:30am-7pm daily Apr.-Oct., $20 and up) has 11 bike-share locations along the Niagara Recreational Trail. Helmets, locks, and maps are included in rentals. Drop-off and pickup service is available, and is free if you're within 5 miles (8 km) of one of their shops. In addition to bike rentals, Zoom also offers **bike tours** of various destinations, guided by a staff member. Guided tour packages ($69-119) include meals, wine sampling, and more.

ICE-SKATING

Skating and ice hockey are popular year-round in Niagara Falls. There are two city ice arenas: the **Gale Center** (4171 4th Ave., 905/356-7521) and the **Willoughby Memorial Arena** (9000 Sodom Rd., 905/295-6554). Both have public skating times and equipment rentals. Information on ice time availability for both arenas changes frequently, so call ahead or check online (www.niagarafalls.ca).

Entertainment and Events

NIGHTLIFE

Clifton Hill is very lively after the sun sets. It erupts with noises and flashing lights, calling people to its arcades, restaurants, bars, museums, and attractions. Much of the area is geared to families with kids. Clifton Hill is a spectacle in stark contrast to the natural beauty of the falls, but there is some charm in the kitsch, the wax museums, haunted houses, funky bowling alley, and food stands, all of which create an artificial glow, like a small slice of Las Vegas.

Clubs

The young beautiful people hang out at **Dragonfly Night Club** (6380 Fallsview Blvd., 905/356-4691, www.dragonflynightclub.com, 10pm-3am Fri.-Sun., 19 years and over, $5 and up entry fee), which is adjacent to the Fallsview Casino. This stunning, Asian-themed dance club caters to the well-heeled, hip crowd under 30. If you are looking for an upscale, cosmopolitan experience, this is

1: Niagara Glen Nature Centre **2:** cycling along the Niagara Recreational Trail the only club in town for you. Do check out the LED video screen that covers the ceiling over the dance floor. Expect a waiting line, crowded dance floor, and numerous groups inside, such as bachelorette parties.

For a good laugh, try **Yuk-Yuks Comedy Club** (6455 Fallsview Blvd., 800/899-9136, www.yukyuks.com, Thurs.-Sat., $25 and up) inside the Four Points Hotel attached to the Casino complex. The headliner talent here is top-notch and skews to showcasing Canadian comics. Shows are at 9pm Thursday and Friday, 8pm and 10:30pm Saturday. You must be 18 or over to attend. Parking is free with paid admission. Just advise the valet along Stanley Street that you are attending a comedy show, and he or she will direct you to free parking.

Casinos

When **Casino Niagara** (5705 Falls Ave., 905/374-3598, www.casinoniagara.com, 24 hours daily) first opened in 1996, it was meant as a temporary location while a larger, permanent casino was being built. Once the permanent casino, Fallsview Casino Resort, was complete and operating, the Ontario government decided to keep Casino Niagara open. It's much smaller than Fallsview but still has a lot for gamers, including 2,700 slot machines, 40 tables for gaming, and poker rooms. There are four restaurants and free live music 9pm-1:30am on weekends on the main gaming floor.

The **Fallsview Casino Resort** (6380 Fallsview Blvd., 888/325-5788, www.fallsviewcasinoresort.com, 24 hours daily) is Canada's largest gaming facility. This casino primarily attracts Toronto residents and draws a sizable crowd no matter the time of day. Billed as the largest gaming resort in Canada, this world-class casino has 3,000 slot machines and more than 130 gaming tables. From penny slots to high-limit VIP rooms, it's a safe bet that you'll find something to wager on.

The 1,500-seat Avalon Ballroom Theatre at the Fallsview is designed for intimate performances—all seats are within 100 feet (30 m) of the stage, and the venue hosts more than 250 performances a year. The venue routinely attracts performers such as Jay Leno, Keith Urban, Roger Daltry, and musical revue acts. Live music from regional bands is played on weekends at Club 365, a lounge bar on the main gaming floor. Gamers and those attending performances at Ontario casinos must be at least 19 years old.

Performances

Another Las Vegas-style nightlife attraction is found at the **Greg Frewin Theatre** (5781 Ellen Ave., 905/356-0777, www.gregfrewintheatre.com, shows 7:30pm Fri.-Sat., seasonal weekday shows, tickets $34.95-54.95). World-renowned illusionist Greg Frewin will astound you with his magic show featuring music, dancers, and tigers. The entertainment is perfect for families, couples, and groups, and it will leave you marveling at Frewin's magical acts. Frewin is available at the end of each show for autographs and pictures. Sometimes the theater hosts tribute bands on weekdays. Ellen Avenue runs parallel to Victoria Avenue and is joined by Clifton Hill. Parking is free.

If you have an appetite for dinner theater, consider the **Oh Canada, Eh? Dinner Show** (8585 Lundy's Lane, 800/467-2071, www.ohcanadaeh.com, 6:15pm Mon.-Sat. mid-Apr.-mid-Oct., $59.95-79.95). Set in a rustic log cabin, the show features your servers as its stars. More of a musical than a comedy, it has songs that celebrate and satirize Canadian culture.Tickets include a family-style dinner, which allows second helpings. The show is appropriate for all ages and accessible for everybody, not just those from the Great White North. Gratuities are not included in the ticket cost. If you are not hungry for dinner, tickets for the show only ($30) are also available. During the off-season, November through March, the venue hosts various dinner performances such as murder mysteries and musical comedy revues.

CRAFT BREWERIES AND DISTILLERIES

Visiting a craft distillery is great, but what if that distillery was also a brewery and a barbecue rib joint? **Niagara Distillery** (4915 Clifton Hill, 905/374-4444, www.niagaradistillery.com, 1pm-10pm Sun.-Fri., noon-midnight Sat.) offers all three in a convenient location at the foot of Clifton Hill. All spirits and beers are made using water that has plunged over the falls—or at least that is their claim. The distillery creates vodka, rum, and whiskey on-site, so why not try the Sangria Fresca cocktail (vodka, white wine, mango, blueberry, elderflower, and lemon) for a refreshing break on a hot summer day. Enjoy it on the open-air patio as you people-watch.

The on-site brewery features a rotation of four craft beers. Amber Eh! is a wonderful amber ale served from the tap or for purchase in a four-pack of cans. If it's on the seasonal menu, do try the Ice Wine beer, which is created with local ice wine grapes, yielding a 9.7 percent alcohol content. While enjoying a drink, you're likely to be tempted by the large barbecue grill that infuses the complex with the mouthwatering smells of slow-cooking ribs and chicken. The combination of creativity, craft, and convenience here is hard to beat.

THE ARTS

The **Mount Carmel Chateau Park Art Centre** (7021 Stanley Ave., 905/371-3922, www.chateaupark.ca, 9am-4pm daily, tours $4.95-12.95, reservations required) is an oasis of tranquility and reflection immediately adjacent to the buzz of Fallsview. The art center is part of a larger retreat campus and monastery operated by the Carmelite Friars of the Mount Carmel Monastery. The monastery is a work of art, built in 1894 and surrounded by 12 acres of gardens, lawns, and statues. The gallery offers an impressive number of paintings, sculptures, and pottery by contemporary Canadian artists. If you take the self-guided tour ($5), allot one hour to view the art gallery and another hour to appreciate the building and grounds. The chapel's stained-glass windows are truly magnificent.

Another gallery emphasizing the works of Canadian artists is the **Niagara Falls Art Gallery** (8058 Oakwood Dr., 905/356-1514, www.niagarafallsartgallery.ca, 1pm-4pm Mon.-Fri. July-Aug., noon-4pm Sat. Sept.-June, $5). The permanent collection features many paintings by William Kurelek, who captured the lives of Canadians in the 20th century on the country's great prairies. The John Burniak collection of falls-related art is a must-see: It tells the stories of Niagara through the eyes of artists from the 1700s through the present day. A Children's Museum on-site focuses on engaging youngsters with hands-on art projects. Take the McLeod Road exit (No. 27) off the Queen Elizabeth Way (QEW) heading east. Oakwood Drive is the first right turn after the exit. The gallery is about seven minutes from the Fallsview area.

FESTIVALS AND EVENTS

The most popular nighttime activity in Niagara is watching the **illumination of the falls.** Every night, hundreds of high-efficiency LED lamps illuminate all three of Niagara's waterfalls, starting just after dusk. From October through April, the illumination ends at 1am; during the rest of the year, the lights stay on until 2am.

The lights project soft colors onto the falls, creating an amazing, shimmering, surreal effect. The best place to appreciate the illumination is along the gorge rim, from the brink of the falls to the Rainbow Bridge. The slowly changing colors are visible from different vantage points, as well as from the Skylon Tower and Niagara SkyWheel. Light patterns reflect holiday themes, including red and white lights on Canada Day; red, white, and blue lights on July 4th; and green lights on April 22, Earth Day. Funding for the illumination is a cross-border effort. The cities of Niagara Falls in the United States and Canada, and the parks on both sides of the Niagara River, pitch in to keep the lights on.

1
2

Another nighttime tradition is the **fireworks display** over the falls (10 pm weekends mid-May-mid-June, Sept. and Oct., daily mid-June-Aug., free). You can watch the pyrotechnics from the same places as the illumination. Particularly good vantage points are the Skylon Tower, the lawn near the Parks Police Headquarters, and the Rainbow Bridge. The fireworks last five minutes and also occur on holidays such as Canada Day and July 4th.

Adding to the experience are **free music concerts** that rock the stage in Victoria Park on weekends and holidays, starting in late June and running through the first week of September. Musical acts are regional bands playing rock and pop favorites. Each concert culminates at 10pm with the fireworks over the falls—an entertaining and free attraction perfect for families and couples. Bring a blanket, stretch out on the well-manicured grass of the park, and stay for the fireworks.

Each year, the biggest festival in Niagara Falls is the **Festival of Lights** (citywide, www.wfol.com, mid-Nov.-Jan.). More than one million tourists visit the falls during the festival to view 120 animated light displays at the Dufferin Islands. There are religious and cultural displays, as well as those with seasonal scenes and Disney characters. The festival is best explored on foot or by car. The park is transformed into a winter wonderland of lights as you slowly drive on the main road. At the park exits, volunteers collect donations—typically, people give $5-10 per car—which help fund the festival.

Put on your blue suede shoes and boogie over to the **Elvis Festival** (5781 Ellen Ave., 905/356-0777, www.gregfrewintheatre.com, third weekend of Apr., $30 and up). This four-day festival pits competing Elvis impersonators against each other. The king of performers is announced on the Sunday of the event. The festival is hosted in the falls area because Canada is the only country outside of the United States in which Elvis Presley performed.

Canada Day (Queen St., 905/356-7521, www.niagarafalls.ca, July 1, free) is celebrated along Queen Street, which is 2 miles (3.2 km) north of the falls. This patriotic holiday, celebrated on July 1, commemorates the unification of the Canadian provinces, which eventually led to sovereignty. The festivities include a parade along Queen Street, entertainment on the main stage at City Hall, food vendors, and a car show. The evening culminates in a fireworks display over the falls at 10pm. Traffic can be heavy with tourists and locals enjoying the fireworks.

Shopping

NIAGARA FALLS FARMERS MARKET

For more than 50 years, some of the freshest food in Niagara Falls has been found year-round at the **Niagara Falls Farmers Market** (5943 Sylvia Pl., www.niagarafalls.ca, 6am-noon Sat.). A modest indoor area hosts a handful of sellers, while more than a dozen vendors set up shop in the adjoining lot. You'll find whatever is in season at the market, including tomatoes, corn, beans, mushrooms, strawberries, apples, and peaches. Some vendors sell baked goods and homemade canned goods. To locate the farmers market, find the Niagara Falls History Museum on the corner of Ferry Street and Sylvia Place; the market is behind the museum in the public parking lot on Sylvia Place.

MALLS

In general, retail prices for clothing and other goods tend to be higher than those in the United States. Residents of southern

1: beautiful nightly illumination of Horseshoe Falls
2: fireworks display

Frozen Falls?

Do the falls freeze?

It can become quite cold in the Niagara region during the winter. But have the falls ever frozen over? No, not completely.

During extremely cold winters, mist from the falls will settle on the lower Niagara River, accumulating into a mountain of ice that obscures the face of the American and Bridal Veil Falls. The ice formations are lovely, and usually a natural ice bridge will form in the lower Niagara River, joining the U.S. and Canadian shores. In the 1800s and early 1900s, tourists used to gather on the ice to experience the frozen river. But people have not been allowed to venture onto the ice bridge since February 1912, when the bridge suddenly crumbled and three tourists lost their lives.

While ice may form along the crest lines of the falls, the water usually continues to flow. The one exception was in March 1848, when ice caused the falls to run dry. Strong winds created a natural ice dam to form at the mouth of the Niagara River. For one day, water slowed to a trickle over Niagara Falls until the winds shifted, moving the ice dam and allowing water flow to resume.

Ontario often travel across the border to the United States to purchase clothing, shoes, and accessories. However, there are name-brand stores and bargains at the **Canada One Outlet** (7500 Lundy's Lane, 905/356-8989, www.canadaoneoutlets.com, 10am-9pm Mon.-Sat., 10am-6pm Sun.). Among the 40 stores are Roots, Coach, Tommy Hilfiger, Guess, Nike, and Levi's. The mall is conveniently located on Lundy's Lane near the QEW overpass.

Some big box retailers are close to the falls. **Canadian Tire** (6840 McLeod Rd., 905/358-0161, www.canadiantire.ca, 8am-9pm Mon.-Fri., 8am-6pm Sat., 8am-5pm Sun.) is a discount retailer with an automotive shop, handy in the event of car trouble. Less than a half-mile west on McLeod Road is **Walmart** (7481 Oakwood Dr., 905/371-3999, www.walmart.ca, 7am-11pm daily), with groceries, clothing, and a pharmacy.

More than a dozen convenience stores and pharmacies are in Niagara Falls, many of them clustered along the Lundy's Lane corridor. **Nicholbys** (5613 Victoria Ave., 905/356-6103, www.nicholbys.com, 24 hours daily) is a clean, reasonably priced convenience store in the heart of the Fallsview area.

Food

DINERS AND BUFFETS

Breakfast for under $3 and authentic alien decor? Look no farther than the **Flying Saucer Drive-In** (6768 Lundy's Lane, 905/356-4553, www.flyingsaucerrestaurant.com, 6am-3am Mon.-Fri., 6am-4am Sat.-Sun., $12). The Saucer sports a distinctive 1950s spaceship motif served tongue-in-cheek with a little kitsch on the side. This local diner legend is known for its ambience, portion sizes, and late-night hours. The Canadian Burger with three-quarters of a pound of beef, jack cheese, and back bacon is out of this world. Earthlings 12 and under can choose from entrées on the kids' menu, priced under $7.

For good value and an even better view, head to the ★ **Grand Buffet** (Fallsview Casino Resort, 6380 Fallsview Blvd., 888/325-5788, www.fallsviewcasinoresort.com, 8am-11pm daily, $25) in the Fallsview Casino Resort. It has everything you'd expect at a casino buffet—a wide variety of main dishes and over-the-top desserts—and a great view of the falls. There's a discount of $4 if you sign up for a player's card. You cannot enter the restaurant unless you are 19 or over, per casino regulations.

GASTROPUBS

The Syndicate (6863 Lundy's Lane, 289/477-1022, www.syndicatebrewery.ca, 11:30am-11pm daily, $24) sources its ingredients locally, including meat, so the menu changes based on their availability. The meal price includes a soup or salad, an entrée, and dessert, an exceptional value. Pair your meal with wine or one of the craft beers available on tap. This eatery affords a real break from the chain restaurants. Reservations are strongly recommended.

FINE DINING

Regarded by many as Niagara's top fine-dining establishment, ★ **AG** (5195 Magdalen Ave., 289/292-0005, www.agcuisine.com, 5:30pm-9:30pm Tues.-Sun., $41) earns its reputation by using locally sourced, seasonal ingredients. The restaurant adds a touch of class to a town with many chain restaurants catering to price-conscious travelers. Consider ordering an ice wine martini to complete your meal.

At ★ **Elements on the Falls** (6650 Niagara Pkwy., 905/354-3631, www.niagaraparks.com, 11:30am-9:30pm daily, $38), the food is as good as the view. Conveniently located in the Table Rock Welcome Centre, Elements provides casual fine dining with an emphasis on "Taste of the Place," which means ingredients in many dishes are locally sourced. Niagara Parks operates this restaurant, and they've kept the best dining view of the falls for themselves. Element's location provides an excellent romantic spot for viewing the fireworks over the falls or the nightly illumination. The menu is eclectic, featuring gourmet fish, steak, veal, and vegetarian selections. If you've never had ice wine—which is made from grapes that were frozen while still on the vine—choose any of the local ice wines served here to pair with the warm apple barge dessert.

ITALIAN

Niagara Falls is blessed with several good Italian restaurants, and **Casa Mia Ristorante** (3518 Portage Rd., 905/356-5410, www.casamiaristorante.com, 11:30am-2:30pm and 5pm-10pm Mon.-Fri., 5pm-10pm Sat.-Sun., $42) may be the best. Casa Mia serves authentic Italian meals prepared by the same family that started the business in 1988. If you appreciate homemade sauces and pasta, you'll dine happily here. The restaurant is about a 10-minute drive from downtown, but well worth the trip.

Since 1962, tradition has been served up with every dish at the **Napoli Ristorante**

(5485 Ferry St., 905/356-3345, www.napoliristorante.ca, 4pm-10:30pm daily, $40). Reservations are suggested, but if you don't make them, you can enjoy a glass of local wine at the bar while you wait. The pasta is homemade, but there's so much more to enjoy—all of it made to order and known for the freshness of ingredients such as tomatoes, basil, and cheeses. Dishes are truly old-school Italian, so expect the pizza to be thin crust.

ASIAN

Find the best of two Asian food styles at the **Wind Japanese and Thai Restaurant** (7241 Lundy's Lane, 905/371-3888, www.windrestaurant.com, 11:30am-10pm daily, $40). Make reservations if visiting on a Friday or Saturday evening, as this restaurant is popular. Wind is an all-you-can-eat establishment, but it's not a buffet. As you are seated, you are given a computer tablet on which to place your orders. The menu is diverse and the portions are small, so you can order as much as you desire during your two-hour dinner; perfect for experimentation. For dessert, consider trying the fried ice cream and coconut cheesecake.

CANADIAN/ LOCAL CUISINE

Step away from the tourist zone and eat at **The Moose and Pepper Bistro** (4740 Valley Way, 289/296-8858, www.mooseandpepper.com, 4pm-9pm Mon.-Sat., $28), where the locals dine. The venue's humble exterior belies the warm, comfortable Canadian interior. The menu is Canadian with an Italian accent, plus gluten-free and vegan entrées. Start the warm mushroom salad, a generously sized starter with lemon-infused mushrooms and dried cranberries. The bison burger with blueberry barbecue sauce is best paired with the avgolemono soup. Saturdays have live jazz music, and Wednesday is date night, when a three-course meal for two with a bottle of wine is value priced ($70).

Looking for an honest, unsophisticated, and local early meal in Niagara Falls? The **Easy Street Grill** (8240 McLeod Rd, 289/296-2328, 8am-2pm, $9) doesn't have a website, but it may have the best breakfast in the city. You won't find more Canadian-inspired dishes than the breakfast poutine platter and the bacon cheeseburger omelet served here. The Grill is unpretentious and has a lot of local charm, but it is only open for breakfast and lunch. It's a few minutes outside of the main tourist drag but worth the trip for stick-to-your-ribs food at reasonable prices.

Speaking of authentic Canadian restaurants, you may want to "check" out **The Blue Line** (4424 Montrose Rd., 289/296-8785, www.bluelinediner.com, 8am-2pm Tues.-Fri., 8am-1:30pm Sat.-Sun., $12) a hockey-themed breakfast and lunch diner. A big draw is that former National Hockey League All-Star Marcel Dionne is involved in the restaurant's ownership and is often on the premises for pictures and autographs.

Portions are generous and prepared quickly. This diner's menu is exactly what you'd expect, featuring omelets, eggs, and pancakes in a space decked out in hockey memorabilia. Favorites include the eggs Benedict and the Hall of Famer omelet (bacon, ham, and sausage). A little hockey trivia: Marcel Dionne scored more than 100 points in 8 of his 18 seasons playing in the NHL. Only Wayne Gretzky and Mario Lemieux are ahead of Dionne for this accomplishment.

MEXICAN

The excellent "Fresh-Mex" fare at **Frijoles** (3465 Portage Rd., 289/296-3999, 11am-8pm Mon.-Wed. and Sat., 11am-9pm Thurs.-Fri., $8) is Mexican-inspired food with a touch of Southern California. Burritos, rice bowls, and tacos are made to order with your choice of beef, pork, chicken, fish, vegetables, beans, or everything mixed together. The restaurant is revered for its 10 homemade sauces—the hottest sauce is named Chuck Norris's Tears. Complete your burrito by choosing from 15 fresh toppings including pineapple salsa, tangy pickled cabbage, and guacamole.

STEAK HOUSES

You will walk away from **Prime Steakhouse** (5685 Falls Ave., 905/374-4444, www.primesteakhouseniagarafalls.com, 6pm-8:30pm Sun.-Thurs., 5:00pm-10pm Fri.-Sat., $45) completely satiated. First, the view: The restaurant is on the 10th floor of the grand Crowne Plaza Hotel near the foot of the Rainbow Bridge. Tables along the windows reveal the American Falls and the Horseshoe Falls in the distance. Next, the food: Generously sized portions of beef, pork, and lamb are crafted to perfection. Prime is regarded by many as the best steak house in the downtown area and has burnished that reputation with tempting sides that include maple-smoked bacon and green bean poutine with mushroom gravy. Save room for the "10-Storey" chocolate cake, baked with 10 levels of decadence including Nutella pudding and hazelnut cookie crumb.

Accommodations

FALLSVIEW AREA

As you are booking accommodations in Niagara Falls, Ontario, note that several additional fees are not reflected in advertised rates. The largest of these fees is the Harmonized Sales Tax (HST) of 13 percent. Other fees may include the Municipal Accommodation Tax, a Daily Mandatory Charge, and parking fees. Ask for the price including fees so that you can make the best decision.

The **Crowne Plaza Niagara Falls Fallsview** (5685 Falls Ave., 905/374-4447, www.niagarafallscrowneplazahotel.com, $188) is a hotel with history. The Crowne Plaza is unique among the Fallsview area high-rise hotels in that it retains much of its nostalgic charm (it was built in 1927). A recent renovation means that it has all the modern amenities that you need as well. The best rooms face the gorge and an excellent view of the American Falls. This hotel is closer to Clifton Hill than the brink of the falls, but all the major sights are within walking distance.

The **Sheraton on the Falls** (5875 Falls Ave., 905/374-4445, www.marriott.com, $255) is a 669-room high-rise hotel in the heart of the tourist area, the base of Clifton Hill. For guests with children, this location can be an advantage because the property is adjacent to the massive, three-acre indoor water park. Amenities are top-notch here, especially the Christienne spa, which features an infinity hydrotherapy tub that overlooks the American Falls. The in-house Massimo's Italian Restaurant and the Fallsview Buffet are both delightful.

The **Wyndham Garden Niagara Falls Fallsview** (6141 Fallsview Blvd., 844/926-0751, www.wyndham.com, $219) is a property offering good value. There's a heated indoor pool, a good-sized fitness center, and free high-speed Internet. The WEGO bus stops just outside the hotel. The Skylon Tower and the brink of the falls are within reasonable walking distance.

Floor-to-ceiling windows with unobstructed views of the falls are a draw at **The Tower Hotel** (6732 Fallsview Blvd., 866/325-5784, www.niagaratower.com, $319). This boutique hotel is designed for romantics and has an in-house wedding chapel. The 42-room hotel, renowned for its unobstructed views of the falls, is atop a tower close to the casino and the incline railway. The circular shape of the tower forced designers to create oddly shaped rooms that tend to be small (refrigerators and microwaves are in the closet). The Fallsview rooms have the best view but are smaller than the city view rooms. During summer, it's worth splurging for the Fallsview rooms. In the off-season, reserve a city view room and ask for an upgrade at check-in. The staff is very friendly. There's no self-parking, but the valet service ($20/day) allows unlimited in-and-out access at no extra charge.

Stay in the middle of the action at the ★ **Fallsview Casino Resort** (6380 Fallsview Blvd., 888/325-5788, www.fallsviewcasinoresort.com, $319). If you like the convenience of being close to gaming and world-class entertainment while still being close to the falls, this is your hotel. All 374 guest rooms are large in comparison to other properties in the area. Suites feature large whirlpool tubs and extra space for relaxation. Ask for a room with a view of the falls, preferably on the 12th floor or higher; corner suites offer the best opportunity to see American and Horseshoe Falls from your room. If you bring a car, signing up for the casino's perks card can earn you reduced-cost or free parking. If a show at the casino is sold out, check the box office at noon; some unclaimed comp tickets may still be available.

The fireplaces in the rooms of the ★ **Sterling Inn and Spa** (5195 Magdalen St., 289/292-0000, www.sterlingniagara.com, $349) may put a spark in your romantic getaway at the falls. This boutique hotel provides couples with a special experience. Rooms are spacious, and most are equipped with whirlpool tubs. Have a warm breakfast delivered to your room for a special treat.

If you're keen on staying in a room with a beautiful view of the falls, you'll have to choose a chain hotel. Choose the ★ **Marriott Niagara Falls Fallsview Hotel & Spa** (6740 Fallsview Blvd., 866/576-5456, www.marriott.com, $290) because it's in the heart of everything, just a few blocks from the casino, and very close to the incline railway that takes you down to Table Rock. Make sure to reserve a room facing the falls (the higher the floor, the better). There are two Marriott hotels on Fallsview Boulevard—check your hotel's address so you don't register at the wrong property.

Clean, cheap, and close: That's the best way to describe the **Rex Motel** (6247 McLeod Rd., 905/354-4223, www.rexmotel.com, $109). This no-frills, family-owned gem is five minutes away from the glitz of Fallsview. The owners greet all guests and provide suggestions for area attractions. The rooms include fresh towels folded into swan shapes, and the motel has free Wi-Fi and free parking.

LUNDY'S LANE

Lundy's Lane hotels are farther away from the falls but generally have lower prices. The **Best Western Cairn Croft Hotel** (6400 Lundy's Lane, 800/568-8520, www.bestwestern.com, $254) is a solid value with 165 rooms and a beautiful indoor courtyard area and pool. Parking is free, and the hotel is a stop on the WEGO route.

The **Ramada by Wyndham, Niagara Falls** (5706 Ferry St., 800/536-1211, www.wyndhamhotels.com, $115) is neat and clean. Prices for this 190-room hotel are a good value, especially since it has an indoor pool and free parking. The only drawback is that motor coach groups use the hotel, so there can be congestion at checkout times and at breakfast in the restaurant.

Comfort Inn Lundy's Lane (7514 Lundy's Lane, 855/973-7216, www.choicehotels.com, $128) lives up to its name by providing decent accommodations at a reasonable price. The main portion of the hotel is open year-round; courtyard rooms are available during the summer season. The main hotel offers recently renovated rooms and an indoor pool with hot tub. This property is adjacent to the historic Lundy's Lane Cemetery.

If you're camping, the **Campark Resort** (9387 Lundy's Lane, 877/226-7275, www.campark.com, $55 campsite, $78 cabin) is a good option. It has 400 campsites, including traditional sites for tents and large RV sites with water, power, and cable TV connections. Modern cabins with beds, kitchenettes, and other amenities can be rented year-round. A large outdoor pool, hot tub, splash pad, and playground offer a welcome respite after a long day of touring. If you don't want to drive your RV into town, daily shuttle-bus service is provided.

PARKWAY NORTH

As you drive north from the falls, there is a cluster of family-operated bed-and-breakfasts. Among the best values is the **Chestnut Inn** (4983 River Rd., 905/374-7623, www.chestnutinnbb.com, $198). Enjoy the panorama of the Niagara Gorge from the sweeping front porch of this property. Robin, your host, serves your breakfasts and welcomes you to your room, which includes a private bath, fireplace, and balcony. The B&B is near the White Water Walk attraction and is close to a WEGO bus stop. Robin is also open to sharing her recipe for the sumptuous French bread toast.

The **Greystone Manor Bed & Breakfast** (4939 River Rd., 905/357-7373, www.greystone-manor.ca, $148) sets the standard for service in this region. It features four rooms, each with a private bath. If you desire even more privacy, reserve the Topaz Room, a renovated carriage house with its own private entrance and balcony. The gracious host, Rob, offers outstanding customer service and attention to detail, whether you have dietary restrictions or you require a late check-in after being delayed at the border. With lower room prices than most hotels, the Greystone is highly recommended.

The **Butterfly Manor** (4917 River Rd., 905/358-8988, www.butterflymanors.com, $300) has recently updated all five of its rooms. Expect new pillow-top mattresses to ensure a good rest after a day of touring. Each room has its own private bathroom. Hosts are flexible about breakfast times, so you may set your own schedule. This property is perfect for guests using public transportation, as it's walking distance to the bus and train station and close to the WEGO bus stop.

Children will absolutely love their stay at the ★ **Great Wolf Lodge** (3950 Victoria Ave., 888/878-1818, www.greatwolf.com, $339). Prices are not cheap, but they include admission to the world-class, indoor water park (available to guests only). The park features numerous waterslides (one goes uphill), a wave pool, a splash area for the little ones, and a whirlpool hot spa for adults only. The hotel provides a nightly story hour that gives parents time to relax. This facility is safe, clean, and a joy for kids year-round.

Information and Services

Niagara Falls, Ontario, is a midsize city of 82,000 residents. Although many government signs and notices are bilingual (English and French), English is the official language of Ontario.

The U.S. and Canadian dollars fluctuate in relative value. Sometimes the currencies are at par, while at other times, there is a significant difference. To obtain the best rate for your dollars, exchange them at a bank before your trip. Better yet, use a credit card that does not charge fees for processing purchases made in Canada.

Crime is low in Canada, especially in the tourist areas of Niagara Falls. Niagara Parks has its own police department. Many of its officers use bikes to monitor traffic and keep rubbernecking tourists moving along the parkway. The City of Niagara Falls and the Province of Ontario have their own police forces as well. For an emergency, dial 911, just as in the United States.

Getting There and Around

AIR

There is no airport in Niagara Falls, although smaller regional airfields are nearby. Many visitors to the falls are day-trippers from New York City who land at the **Buffalo Niagara International Airport** (BUF, 4200 Genesee St., Cheektowaga, 716/630-6000, www.buffaloairport.com), rent a car there, and then drive 20 miles (32 km) to Niagara Falls and cross the border. Taxis and rideshares are plentiful at the Buffalo airport, 24 hours a day. A taxi ride to the falls costs $90.

CAR

The usual mode of transport for visitors to Niagara Falls is by automobile. One international bridge joins Niagara Falls, Ontario, with Niagara Falls, New York—the **Rainbow Bridge.** Border inspection wait times at the bridge are difficult to predict, but updates are available via the **Niagara Bridge Commission** website (www.niagarafallsbridges.com).

Do yourself a favor and check the Bridge Commission website for real-time updates before you arrive at the border. You may save time by opting to use the Lewiston-Queenston Bridge to the north or the Peace Bridge to the south. Hourly updates are also available by calling 800/715-6722. In general, the bridge is busier during traditional morning and evening commute times because hundreds of people cross the border to work each day. Many factors can cause an extended wait to clear customs, such as security issues, border guard shift changes, and the volume of motor coaches.

If you are driving across the border at the Rainbow Bridge, the toll is US$4 or C$5.25.

Driving in Ontario is virtually the same as in the United States, except that speed limit signs use the metric system. Pedestrians always have the right of way within a designated crosswalk—motorists must stop. When driving along the scenic Niagara Parkway, keep in mind that many drivers are visitors to the region and may be paying more attention to the scenery than to other cars or traffic lights.

The main thoroughfare in southern Ontario is the Queen Elizabeth Way, known as the QEW. The QEW joins Niagara Falls to Toronto.

A flashing green light at an intersection indicates that it is safe to make a left-hand turn (equivalent to a green arrow light).

Parking is expensive in Niagara Falls. Prime tourist lots operated by Niagara Parks charge up to $24 per day.

BUS

The **WEGO** (www.wegoniagarafalls.com) bus system is simple and easy to use. Passes good for 24 hours are $9 for adults and $6 for children ages 6-12. The system uses four color-coded routes to cover the tourist area of Niagara Falls. You must purchase a pass before boarding the bus. Passes are available at more than 30 falls-area hotels (look for the "We Sell WEGO" signs in your hotel's lobby) and at the four official welcome centers operated by Niagara Parks.

Bus schedules are available on the WEGO website, bus shelters, or at Niagara Parks' welcome centers. WEGO buses are accessible and also feature a rack on the front of each bus that can accommodate two bicycles.

TRAIN

Traveling by rail from Toronto to the falls is easy. **GO Transit** (www.gotransit/com) trains leave from Union Station in Toronto for the **Niagara Falls train station** (4267 Bridge St.) twice daily. The one-way cost is $21.15. The train station at the falls is also on the WEGO purple line. **Amtrak** (www.amtrak.com) trains coming across the border from the United States, on the Maple Leaf route, stop at this station twice daily. The trip from the Buffalo station to the station in Niagara Falls, Ontario, is 90 minutes, with fares starting at $22 for a standard coach seat. As this is an international crossing, have your passport available when you obtain your ticket.

A cab ride from the train station to the Fallsview area is under 3 miles (5 km) and costs less than $15. A taxi stand is located directly outside the train station. Cab drivers know the train schedule, so you shouldn't have a hard time finding a cab once your train arrives.

INCLINE RAILWAY

The **Falls Incline Railway** (Portage Rd. near Main St., www.niagaraparks.com, 10am-6:30pm daily with increased hours in summer, $5.31 round-trip, free for children 5 and under) is an easy way to traverse the 100-foot-tall (30-m-tall) ridge that separates the Fallsview area of hotels from Table Rock Welcome Centre. Each tramcar holds 40 passengers and is fully enclosed for year-round comfort.

The railway is located off Portage Road, one block from Main Street. Pedestrians can use a footbridge that connects the railway with the Embassy Suites and Marriott Hotels and crosses over Portage Road. Round-trip fare is $5.31 and an all-day pass is $6.19. If you don't want to use the railway, you'll have to take Murray Hill Road to travel from Table Rock Welcome Centre to the Fallsview area.

WALKING OR BICYCLING

It is possible to cross the border on foot or by bike. The journey is gorgeous, as the bridge is a great spot from which to behold the American Falls, Bridal Veil Falls, and distant Horseshoe Falls. Those who are walking can stop midway over the bridge, see the flags of both countries, and stand on the international border line! The cost for pedestrians to cross the bridge is US$1 or C$1. Cyclists are treated the same as cars, and you must stay on the car lanes—do not be tempted to hop your bike over the guardrail and use the sidewalk. You are expected to proceed and wait in the lanes leading up to the inspection booths as a car would. The fare for cyclists to cross Rainbow Bridge is US$4 or C$5.25. Pay with cash or credit card and, as always, have your documentation ready. In addition, remove your sunglasses during customs inspection.

Niagara Falls, New York

The charm of the U.S. side of Niagara Falls lies in its natural splendor. It once was regarded as *the* destination for the region. Curious travelers from around the world flocked to Niagara Falls, New York, to embrace the natural beauty and power of the falls—and still do today, as a once-in-a-lifetime experience to check off the bucket list. The U.S. side provides many opportunities to see the rainbows, feel the mist, and hear the roar of rushing water of the falls.

The park at Niagara Falls is the oldest state park in the country and has retained much of its natural beauty since opening in July 1885. America's preeminent landscape architect, Frederick Law Olmsted, designed the park— which underwent a $70 million renovation—to maximize access to all of Niagara's many moods. It is on the U.S. side

Highlights

Look for ★ to find recommended sights, activities, dining, and lodging.

★ **Cruise into the mist:** Any trip to the falls must include the **Maid of the Mist.** This boat tour cruises into the heart of Niagara's awe-inspiring power (page 67).

★ **Explore the Cave of the Winds:** Walk beneath one of Niagara's mighty cascades (page 72).

★ **Take in the view from Terrapin Point:** This is the best land-based observation area (page 73).

★ **Island hop:** Get up close to the raging upper rapids of the Niagara River on the beautiful **Three Sisters Islands** (page 73).

★ **Revisit history at Old Fort Niagara:** Over 300 years old, this fort once protected the gateway to the New World (page 91).

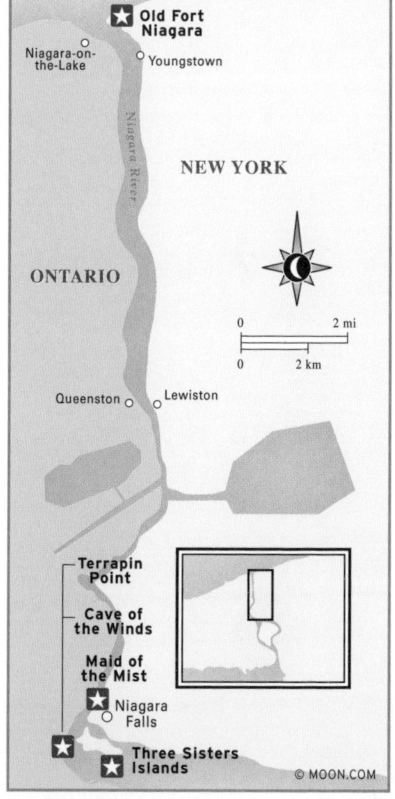

that the Class VI white water of the upper rapids will leave you in awe. Here, too, the deceptively gentle flow of the water near Luna Island draws you in for reflection. On Green Island, you can enjoy an intimate and quiet, lush green picnic spot protected from the raging rapids nearby.

While the best panoramic view of Niagara Falls is from the Canadian side, the natural wonder of the falls is best experienced on the U.S. side, where you can reach out and touch Bridal Veil Falls. The water roaring over the falls at 70,000 gallons a second creates a thrill you won't soon forget.

The treasures of the Niagara region are also found beyond the falls. North along the gorge is Lewiston, a beautiful and historic town nestled at the base of the ridge where the falls began 12,000 years ago. Lewiston is a place where the arts and culture flourish, with a Norman Rockwell-ian main street that leads to the river and spectacular sunsets. Farther north, Old Fort Niagara, the longest continually occupied military structure in North America, stands sentinel as it has for over 300 years, guarding the confluence of the Niagara River and Lake Ontario. Here, reenactors bring to life the history of the gateway to the New World, the scene of bloodshed among Native American, French, British, and American combatants.

HISTORY

To the native peoples who lived here, Niagara Falls was a mystical place. Although none of the tribes in the area left written records, their oral traditions tell of gods who lived behind the mighty waterfall. By the time the British expelled the French from this region in 1759, the Iroquois Confederacy was trading, working with, and fighting for (and against) the European settlers. The Iroquois are also known as the Haudenosaunee, which translates to "People of the Longhouse." Until the American Revolution, the Iroquois kept most white settlers out of the area; however, the Iroquois sided with the British during the conflict and were eventually forced from their lands for their opposition to the American cause.

The Europeans who settled here were awed by Niagara's beauty but also saw the raging Niagara River as a source of power. Prior to being named Niagara Falls, New York, this settlement was known as Manchester. Local folk imagined the economy paralleling that of Manchester, England, a prosperous mill and manufacturing city. As a result, industrial mills marred Niagara's shoreline for many years as manufacturing and tourism competed against each other. Tourism prevailed after New York State purchased the land surrounding the falls from private owners, finally creating the park that exists today. More than 150 buildings, including factories, hotels, and mills, were removed to return Niagara to a more natural state. Frederick Law Olmsted designed the park and set guidelines that direct the stewardship of the park to the present day.

In July 1885, the Niagara Reservation Park opened, making it the oldest state park in the United States. The history of the city of Niagara Falls is as turbulent as the water coursing through the upper rapids. The lure of cheap and plentiful electric power brought many industries to the area, and the city's population grew to 102,000 by 1960. At present, the city has fewer than 50,000 inhabitants; its decline mirrors that of other northeastern U.S. cities that experienced a loss of manufacturing and jobs during the 1970s.

The area immediately surrounding the state park is clean and safe, and is experiencing new development. New programs featuring live music, themed activities, and increased vendor opportunities are rejuvenating the city streets adjacent to the park. In addition, New York State has provided funding

---

Previous: Bridal Veil Falls; Maid of the Mist boat tour; Old Fort Niagara in Youngstown.

Niagara Falls, New York

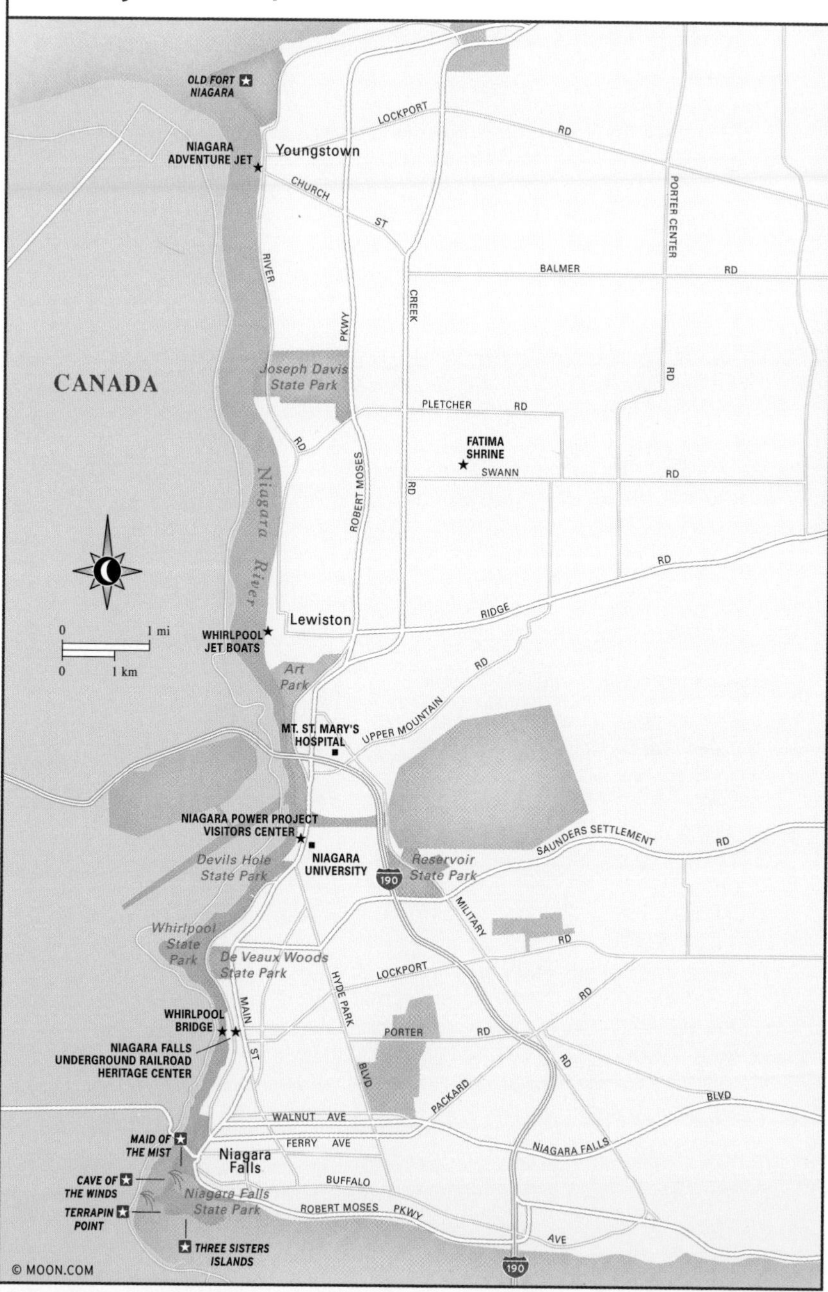

for important enhancements to major attractions within the park.

PLANNING YOUR TIME

Niagara Falls is an ideal one-day destination and a good base for several additional day trips in the surrounding region. Plan on visiting the major attractions—Maid of the Mist and Cave of the Winds—early in the day, when waiting times are short. Reserve some time in the evening to view the nightly illumination of the falls and, in summer, fireworks. If your travel plans require crossing the border, give yourself plenty of time. It can sometimes take more than an hour for customs and immigration inspection.

One of the most popular day trips is a visit to Lewiston and to Old Fort Niagara in Youngstown. These attractions are best appreciated together because of their proximity; Lewiston is about 7 miles (11.2 km) north of the falls, and the fort is another 6 miles (9.6 km) beyond. Seeing both towns involves a five- to six-hour day with a mix of driving, walking, and sightseeing.

ORIENTATION

The city's **downtown** area is immediately adjacent to Niagara Falls State Park, with hotels, restaurants, and attractions all within walking distance of the park. The epicenter is Old Falls Street, which runs from the Seneca Niagara Casino to the pedestrian entrance of the park.

Little Italy is about 1 mile (1.6 km) from the park, along Pine Avenue. Here you'll find small shops, authentic Italian restaurants, and a sense of what the city was like at its zenith in 1950. Pine Avenue becomes **Niagara Falls Boulevard** and morphs from a walkable neighborhood into a four-lane thoroughfare with accommodations and retail stores, including the nearby Fashion Outlets of Niagara Falls USA, one of the region's largest shopping centers. The boulevard is known for its value-priced hotels and family-operated motels, and it provides access to I-190.

Traveling on I-190 north from the city brings you to the village of **Lewiston** and **Old Fort Niagara in Youngstown.** These two destinations are more pastoral and historic than urban Niagara Falls. Beyond the fort, on state Route 18, a scenic drive along Lake Ontario leads into the hamlet of Olcott, which includes a quaint shopping district along the water and a small, old-fashioned amusement park perfect for the kids, the Olcott Beach Carousel Park.

Sights

NIAGARA FALLS STATE PARK

Each year, more than eight million people journey to **Niagara Falls State Park** (Prospect St., 716/278-1796, www.niagarafallsstatepark.com, 24 hours daily, parking $10), drawn by its 400 acres of unparalleled beauty and splendor. Although many waterfalls are taller than Niagara, none is more prodigious. Visitors come here to feel the power of nature and experience a boat ride on the chaotic, roiling waters beneath the world's most famous waterfall. There are developed diversions here, but make no mistake: The main attraction is the 750,000 gallons per second of water hurtling over American Falls, delivering 2,700 tons of force into the river below. Within the boundaries of the park are the famed Maid of the Mist boat tour, the Cave of the Winds, Terrapin Point, Luna Island, and Three Sisters Islands.

At the entrance to the park, walkways, hedges, and signs will direct you toward the visitors center, which houses an information desk with maps and brochures, as well as clean bathrooms. The lower level of the visitors center has a gift shop, restaurant,

Niagara Falls State Park

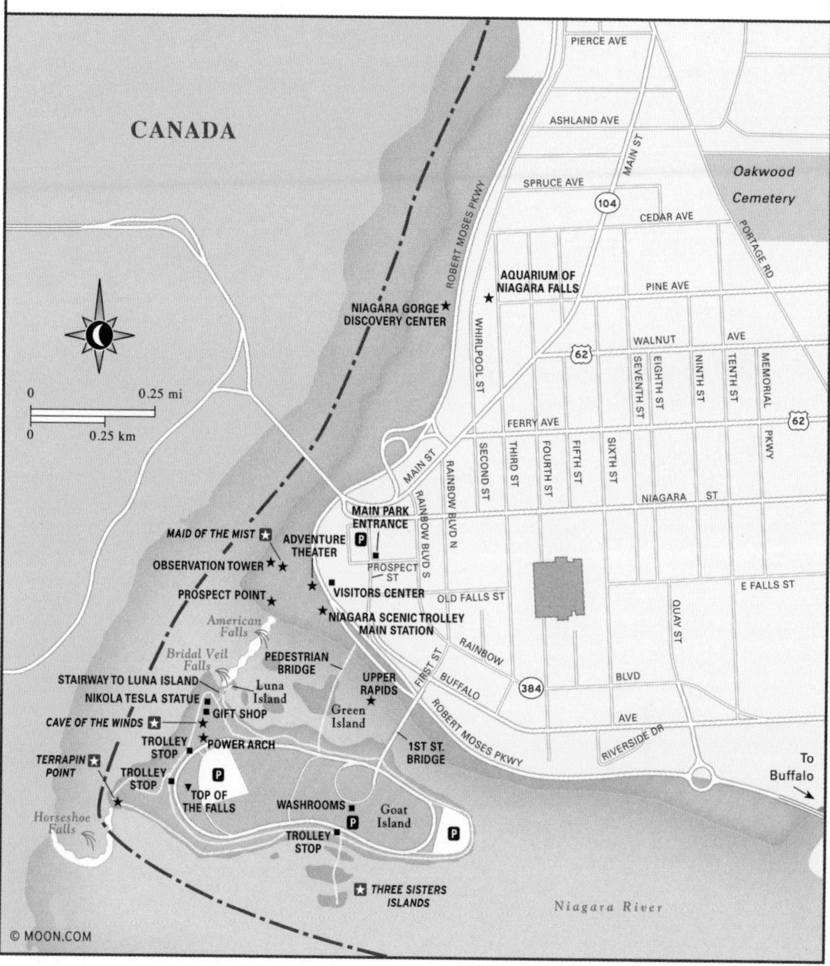

interpretive historical displays, and the **Niagara Adventure Theater.**

The Niagara Adventure Theater shows a 40-minute film with highlights of Niagara's history as well as stunning helicopter shots of the gorge and falls. It depicts the stories of the mythical "Maid of the Mist," a Native American woman who threw herself over the falls (supposedly either to save her tribe or to avoid a forced marriage), along with early European explorers and daredevils who challenged Niagara. The 275-seat theater is comfortably air-conditioned. The main entrance for the park is along Prospect Street, across from the Hard Rock Cafe.

★ Maid of the Mist

There are few experiences like the **Maid of the Mist** (Niagara Falls State Park, 716/284-8897, www.maidofthemist.com, 9am-5pm Mon.-Fri., 9am-6pm Sat.-Sun. Apr.-mid-May and Sept.-early Oct., 9am-6pm Sun.-Fri.,

Discovery Pass

One of your first considerations when touring Niagara Falls State Park is the decision to purchase the Discovery Pass (www.niagarausadiscoverypass.com, $49 adults, $38 children 6-12), which allows you to visit five major attractions with one voucher; it also includes the trolley. Purchasing the pass will save you more than 30 percent compared with purchasing each attraction separately.

INCLUDED IN THE DISCOVERY PASS

Attraction	Adult	Child 6-12	Child 5 and under
Maid of the Mist	$22.25	$13	Free
Cave of the Winds	$19	$16	Free
Niagara Adventure Theater	$12	$9	Free
Niagara Gorge Discovery Center	$3	$2	Free
Trolley (day pass)	$3	$2	Free
Aquarium of Niagara	$14.95	$10.95 (ages 3-12)	Free (2 and under)

If you intend to spend an entire day in the park, the pass is the way to go. However, if you are planning to spend a few hours at the park and just want the highlights, then try going à la carte. In either event, the trolley is an inexpensive way to make your way through the park.

9am-8pm Sat. mid-May-late June, 9am-8pm daily late June-early Aug., 9am-7:30pm daily early Aug.-late Aug., 9am-5pm daily early Oct.-late Oct., $22.25 adults, $13 children 6-12, free for children 5 and under with an accompanying adult). What begins as a gentle, 20-minute boat ride suddenly transforms into a journey into the heart of the falls. From the safety of the vessel, you are buffeted by heavy mist. It's awe-inspiring to see the 17-story-high, thundering wall of water that slams into the lower Niagara River. Since 1846, this ride has thrilled millions of tourists; it's the top attraction in Niagara. The touring company recently deployed a new fleet of battery-powered, emissions-free electric boats, replacing the diesel-powered boats that had operated for decades.

Once you're aboard the boat, relax and enjoy the view. After the boat pulls away from the dock, it passes American Falls. Notice the stairs along the left (north) side of the falls. This is part of the Crow's Nest, which can be accessed after the boat ride.

As the boat moves onward, you'll approach Bridal Veil Falls, flowing between Luna Island and Goat Island. You'll see brave folks underneath this waterfall, experiencing the Cave of the Winds. Next, there's a deceptively calm stretch of water, the quiet before the storm. Thousands of waterfowl can be seen resting or building nests in the rocky ledges of the gorge.

The chatter of the birds gives way to the ominous din of Horseshoe Falls. As the boat enters the basin beneath the falls, water thunders down from a precipice 17 stories above. Wind whips mist from all sides as the boat bobs on what looks like a boiling cauldron of water. For five intense minutes, the boat fights the surging waters, and the unpredictable wind dictates visibility.

Riders on the upper deck or in the lower bow area receive the brunt of the mist. People looking to avoid getting soaked can find limited shelter on the lower deck in the middle of the boat. How wet you get depends mostly on the wind's velocity and direction, so there's no guarantee that you'll stay dry. The poncho provides sufficient protection for your camera and phone during the heaviest periods of misting.

As the boat travels back to the dock, consider heading to the rear of the lower deck. The boat's stern provides an excellent vantage point for capturing the panorama of the gorge. The Maid of the Mist boat ride affords a rare opportunity to photograph the falls and gorge from water level in the lower Niagara River.

The ticket booths are near Prospect Point, about 500 yards (457 m) from the visitors center. Board the boat via the elevators at the base of the Observation Tower. Avoid a long line for the Maid of the Mist tour by arriving before 11am, though you won't usually wait longer than 20 minutes (except on U.S. holidays like Independence Day and Labor Day). If you plan to visit both sides of the border, there are advantages to taking the tour on the U.S. side. It is less expensive, and there are usually shorter lines.

After exiting the boat, continue past the elevators and you'll see the **Crow's Nest.** The Crow's Nest is an excellent natural observation deck at the base of American Falls, set atop giant boulders that are the remnants of a massive rockslide. The stairs that lead to the Crow's Nest are somewhat steep, but safe, and they permit an up-close view of American Falls. Keep your rain poncho from the Maid of the Mist if you plan to visit the Crow's Nest. At the entrance to the Crow's Nest are park benches (a great place to catch your breath) and bathrooms. Buying a ticket for the Observation Tower ($1.25) will also gain you access to the Crow's Nest, if you aren't riding on the Maid of the Mist.

OBSERVATION TOWER

The **Observation Tower** (9am-10:30pm daily Apr.-late Oct., 10am-4:30pm daily late Oct.-Mar., included in Maid of the Mist ticket, à la carte $1.25 when the Maid of the Mist operates, free admission otherwise) serves two primary functions: to provide a panoramic view of the three waterfalls that comprise Niagara, and to house the elevators that lead to the docks of the Maid of the Mist. From afar, the tower resembles an incomplete bridge; its platform extends more than 200 feet (61 m) from the gorge wall. The views here are among the best on this side of the border. If you stand atop the metal benches on the platform, you can get a great photo of your loved ones as they stand along the guardrail, with the falls in the background.

The Observation Tower is among the best bargains in all of Niagara. Admission is included in the cost of the Maid of the Mist ticket or can be purchased à la carte ($1.25). The tower is closed during foul weather or high winds.

Prospect Point

Prospect Point is located at the brink of American Falls, near the Observation Tower Platform. It affords an excellent view of the entire American Falls crest line and the upper rapids of the Niagara River. The upper rapids form as the riverbed drops more than 55 feet (16.7 m) in elevation while the river runs east around Goat Island. A pedestrian bridge 300 yards (274 m) upstream from Prospect Point has the best view of the churning, frothy white water of the upper rapids. At night, lights along the shoreline illuminate the upper rapids, a surreal spectacle to behold.

Goat Island

Goat Island, between Horseshoe Falls and Bridal Veil Falls, has perhaps the most visceral on-land experience of Niagara on the U.S. side of the border. The island parts the river in two, creating different areas for the water to channel its moods. The island is home to the best sightseeing in the park, as well as walking paths, woods, picnic areas, and concessions. Visitors often spend most of their time in the park on Goat Island. The major attractions here are Terrapin Point, the Cave of the Winds, and the Tesla Statue. Goat Island is also the gateway to Luna Island and the Three Sisters Islands.

The island is named for the goats kept on the island by a British settler in the late 1700s. Subsequent attempts to name it Iris Island

Maid of the Mist Tips

- You are issued a disposable rain poncho before you board the boat. When you're wearing the poncho, your neckline, shins, and feet are exposed. Wear sandals, shorts or capris, and V-neck tops to avoid getting exposed clothing and shoes soaked.
- After receiving your poncho, resist the urge to put it on immediately. Stopping on the pathway to the boat to figure out how to wear the poncho causes a chain reaction pileup behind you. You don't need the poncho until well after the boat leaves the dock. Wait until you board the boat to don your raincoat, especially on hot days.
- The boat does not have seats, so all passengers stand throughout the journey. No matter where you stand, you are going to get wet. If you want the full experience, stand in the front of the boat or on the top level. If you want to stay drier, choose a spot on the lower deck in the middle of the boat.
- If you choose the upper level, opt for a space along the rail closest to the exit space. You can save a lot of time by being among the first guests to exit the boat from up top.
- After exiting the boat, you will see the large blue plastic bins in which you may place your poncho for recycling. Keep your poncho if you are going to climb the stairs along American Falls before heading back up the elevators to the observation deck.
- The majority of the journey is dry. You'll have plenty of warning to put cameras, phones, and tablets under your poncho as you approach the falls. Use common sense and your electronics will survive the voyage.
- If you've experienced the Cave of the Winds earlier in the day, continue to wear the souvenir sandals you received at that attraction. This will save you from getting your footwear wet when aboard the Maid of the Mist.

(after the goddess of rainbows) failed, and the name Goat Island has stubbornly stuck.

To drive onto Goat Island, use the bridge at the foot of First Street. On the island, there are two parking lots ($10) for vehicles, including campers). On foot, Goat Island is accessed via the pedestrian bridge that joins the mainland portion of the park, Bath Island, and Goat Island.

POWER ARCH

In 1896, the world's first commercial hydroelectric power plant, Adams Power Plant, sent electricity from Niagara Falls to Buffalo, signaling a new age in long-distance power transmission via Nikola Tesla's alternating current design. Though the plant was eventually demolished, the **Power Arch** was left intact. This three-story-tall stone arch served as the facade of the plant's main building. It was moved to Goat Island from the southern part of the city in 1967 to serve as a memorial to Niagara's important industrial heritage. It's located about 200 yards (183 m) away from the Cave of the Winds ticket office.

TESLA STATUE

Although Tesla's engineering designs and discoveries impact our lives to this day, many people look quizzically at the **statue of Nikola Tesla** on Goat Island. He was a genius with more than 300 patents to his name, responsible for inventing alternating current, fluorescent lighting, wireless communication, and remote control devices. The bronze statue, by sculptor Frano Kršinić, was dedicated in 1976, a gift to the park from the Yugoslavian government. The statue depicts

1: Nikola Tesla statue by Croatian sculptor Frano Krsinic **2:** Luna Island between Bridal Veil Falls and the American Falls **3:** Maid of the Mist tour boat

NIKOLA TESLA
INVENTOR
JULY 10 1856 SMILJAN YUGOSLAVIA
JANUARY 7 1943 NEW YORK

1

2

3

MAID OF THE MIST

a contemplative Tesla looking down at notes in his lap. Like Tesla, the statue overlooking the falls is larger than life—about 10 feet (3 m) tall.

LUNA ISLAND

Luna Island is a small scrap of land that separates American and Bridal Veil Falls. It offers spectacular views of both the falls and the gorge, and several spots allow close access to the menacing brink of Niagara.

Take a moment to stand in the south corner of Luna Island, immediately next to the brink of Bridal Veil Falls. The green water flows rhythmically, providing a sense of peace. But a peek over the brink exposes the thundering, falling water, which reveals the duality of Niagara, where beauty and force contrast sharply. You'll experience this contrast most intensely on the U.S. side, where you can get close to the water and don't have to fight the crowds on the Canadian side.

Many consider Luna Island to be the best place to experience the **fireworks display** over the falls during the summer season. Arrive 30 minutes early for a good viewing spot along the rail. When the fireworks have ended, linger behind and enjoy the beautiful nightly illumination of the falls instead of waiting in traffic.

To reach Luna Island, walk down the flight of steps at the northernmost tip of Goat Island, then cross the small bridge.

★ CAVE OF THE WINDS

The **Cave of the Winds** (Niagara Falls State Park, 716/278-1730, www.niagarafallsstatepark.com, 9am-9pm Sun.-Thurs., 9am-10pm Fri.-Sat. mid-May-early Sept., 9am-7pm Sun.-Thurs., 9am-9pm Fri.-Sat. early Sept.-mid-Oct., 9am-5pm daily mid-Oct.-late Oct., $17 adults, $14 children 6-12) is a self-guided tour along a series of decks leading to the foot of Bridal Veil Falls. The Hurricane Deck is the last of these, located directly under Bridal Veil.

Standing on the Hurricane Deck takes courage and stamina, since you're saturated by cascading water; the souvenir rain poncho provides little protection. Children often find this attraction equal to, if not better than, the Maid of the Mist. On a hot summer day, this torrent of water can be refreshing.

If you have a camera or cell phone, place them in the plastic bag provided and let someone hold it while you stand out on the deck. Visitors who want to stay dry on the tour can stay on the upper decks and simply enjoy the dramatic view of the falls from there.

Included in the cost of admission is **The World Changed Here Pavilion,** a newer (2017) interactive exhibit space that precedes the trip into the gorge and showcases the massive transformation that took place when the state reclaimed industrialized lands near the cataracts and created Niagara Falls State Park in the 1880s. The pavilion experience concludes with a film that highlights how Frederick Law Olmsted's pioneering vision for the park and Nikola Tesla's harnessing of the falls' power through alternating current each changed the course of history. A park guide then picks you up from a pavilion waiting area to proceed down into the gorge.

In recent years, this attraction has grown in popularity and frequently has wait times for purchasing tickets—though a timed ticketing program during high season has eased overcrowding. The best strategy is to experience the Cave of the Winds early or late in the day.

Purchase tickets on Goat Island at the main ticket area (near the Power Arch). You'll be given a plastic bag, rain poncho, and sandals that are suggested for safety reasons. Place your street shoes in the plastic bag, then proceed to the large stone building that houses the elevators going down to the attraction. Recycling bins are available for your rain poncho and sandals following the tour. The souvenir sandals are rather spiffy! You can recycle them, but why not keep them or at least use them for your wet journey aboard the Maid of the Mist?

The best-kept secret of Niagara Falls may be that the Cave of the Winds also offers a **Winter Experience** (9am-3pm daily in the winter months when conditions permit, \$7 adults, \$5 children 6-12). This abbreviated tour still includes an elevator trip down the gorge to see the American Falls in all its icy, wintry glory. While winter weather and shifting ice necessitate the removal of most of the attraction's decks, an observation area still provides a spectacular, unique view at the base of the winter falls that few people have experienced. It also keeps visitors much drier than the summer version of the attraction. The viewing area can become very icy in the winter, so the park offers optional cleat rentals that are included in the cost of admission.

★ TERRAPIN POINT

Terrapin Point is the westernmost point of Goat Island and forms the brink of Horseshoe Falls. It provides the most dramatic views of the falls from the U.S. side. Terrapin Point is downhill from the main body of Goat Island. You'll enjoy sweeping views of the upper rapids of the Niagara River, the brink of Horseshoe Falls, and the tumult of the lower Niagara River at the base of the giant waterfall. Renovations to the sloped entrance to Terrapin Point have made the area more accessible for seniors and people with mobility issues. Please stay on the paved paths and refrain from cutting across the grassy areas, as such activity damages the natural beauty of this most beautiful and delicate place.

Terrapin Point is an amazing natural area with a microclimate that changes quickly with the wind. One moment, it's sunny and clear, with a double rainbow over the gorge. The next minute, a cooling blanket of ultrafine mist blows in, generated by the force of the water hurtling over the 175-foot (53-m) precipice. The thickness and height of the mist plume are a function of the temperature difference between the water and the air. The greater the difference, the larger the mist plume. The vagaries of the wind determine where the mist falls. Bring your camera and an umbrella.

The point is accessed via stairs and a paved path, about 300 yards (984 m) away from the Top of the Falls restaurant. For safety reasons, Terrapin Point is closed to visitors during the winter season, usually starting in December, due to hazardous accumulations of snow and ice. Its reopening date is determined by the spring thaw.

★ Three Sisters Islands

Many tourists overlook **Three Sisters Islands,** which jut out from the southern side of Goat Island into the upper rapids of the Niagara River. The islands—Celinda, Angelina, and Asenath—are named after the children of Parkhurst Whitney, a distinguished officer in the War of 1812 and a local hotelier. These small, lightly wooded, and enchanting islands are about 0.5 mile (0.8 km) upstream from Terrapin Point. Paved pathways with guardrails give visitors a chance to get close to the raging upper rapids of the river. Signs warn against leaving the designated paths, but some curious visitors explore the water's edge on the island farthest out into the rapids.

Niagara Gorge Discovery Center

The **Niagara Gorge Discovery Center** (701 Whirlpool St., 716/278-1070 www.niagarafallsstatepark.com, 9am-5pm Sat.-Sun. late Apr.-late June and early Sept.-late Oct., 9am-5pm Sun.-Thurs., 9am-7pm Fri.-Sat. late June-early Sept., \$3 adults, \$2 children 6-12) is a rock-solid attraction for visitors interested in the geology that shaped the gorge. Opened in 1971, the facility is circular and designed to resemble a hydroelectric water turbine. Rock hounds and geology geeks could easily spend 45 minutes here enjoying the interactive exhibits, movies, and the virtual elevator ride, all of which illuminate the ancient forces of nature that shaped the Niagara Gorge. The rock-climbing wall and the video detailing the collapse of the Schoellkopf Power Plant are some of the most popular exhibits. Even visitors with only a passing interest in geology will find these exhibits engaging, educational, and accessible.

1
2

The center is part of Niagara Falls State Park; park for free at the lot on Whirlpool Street. Pedestrians can walk here by using the paved path along the rim of the gorge. From Prospect Point, continue north and then pass under the Rainbow Bridge.

Niagara Scenic Trolley

The **Niagara Scenic Trolley** (716/278-1730, www.niagarafallsstatepark.com, 9am-10pm Sun.-Thurs., 9am-11pm Fri.-Sat. mid-June-early Sept., 9am-8pm Sun.-Thurs., 9am-10pm Fri.-Sat. early Sept.-mid-Oct., 9am-6pm daily mid-Oct.-early Jan., $3/day adults, $2/day children 6-12) transports visitors to the state park's attractions, with hop-on, hop-off service. It navigates a 3-mile (4.8-km) course around the park, stopping at key points including the visitors center, Niagara Gorge Discovery Center, Goat Island, and all parking lots. The trolley is an attraction in itself, with live narration provided by knowledgeable park employees.

AQUARIUM OF NIAGARA

The **Aquarium of Niagara** (701 Whirlpool St., 716/285-3575, www.aquariumofniagara.org, 9am-5pm daily, $14.95 adults, $10.95 children 3-12) is small but makes the most of its size. Most of the activity is inside the aquarium and centers on the large main tank where harbor seals and sea lions perform. The aquarium has made a number of recent updates to its facility, including the Penguin Coast exhibit with adorable Peruvian penguins in a state-of-the-art habitat (feedings at 10am and 2pm daily), and the Aliens of the Sea exhibit that showcases an up-close and personal look at four jellyfish species. The Shark and Ray Bay exhibit, a new habitat for sharks, stingrays, and a variety of invertebrates, will debut in 2020. Numerous smaller tanks contain saltwater and freshwater fish, including seahorses, electric eels, and sturgeons.

The exhibits and animals are well cared for by the cheerful staff. Check the online schedule for hourly demonstrations with penguins, harbor seals, and sea lions. The aquarium is good for families with small children, who can expect to spend about 90 minutes here.

1: Cave of the Winds **2:** Aquarium of Niagara

NIAGARA FALLS UNDERGROUND RAILROAD HERITAGE CENTER

Opened in 2018, the **Niagara Falls Underground Railroad Heritage Center** (825 Depot Ave. W., 716/300-8477, www.niagarafallsundergroundrailroad.org, 10am-6pm Tues.-Sat., 10am-4pm Sun., $10 adults, $8 seniors 62+ and students 13+ with ID, $6 children 6-12) retells in dramatic fashion the city's role as the final stop for escaped enslaved people before they crossed the Niagara River to freedom in Canada. Housed in an 1863 Customs House attached to the city's train station, the center unearths stories of bravery by enslaved people who risked everything in pursuit of freedom. It also presents information about the Niagara Falls residents who hid and protected them in their final hours of peril before escape. Through dynamic illustrations and voice-over animation, the center brings to life a critical period in the region's—and the country's—past, told from the perspective of those who lived it. While the museum is small and can be seen in under an hour, its quality and depth make it a must-visit to fully understand the history of the region.

DOWNTOWN NIAGARA FALLS

Downtown Niagara Falls is bordered by Niagara Falls State Park to the south and west, Niagara Street to the north, and 4th Street (and the casino) to the east. This tourist area is safe, clean, and lively—especially during summer. Visitors can get regional information and advice at the **Niagara Falls USA Official Visitor Center** (10 Rainbow Blvd., 716/282-8992, www.niagarafallsusa.com, 8:30am-7pm daily May 15-Sept. 15, 8:30am-5pm daily Sept. 16- May 14). For the most official, up-to-date

NIAGARA GORGE DISCOVERY CENTER
1
2
Freedom is gained by appreciating difference and finding common ground
NIAGARA FALLS RAILROAD DEPOT

Downtown Niagara Falls

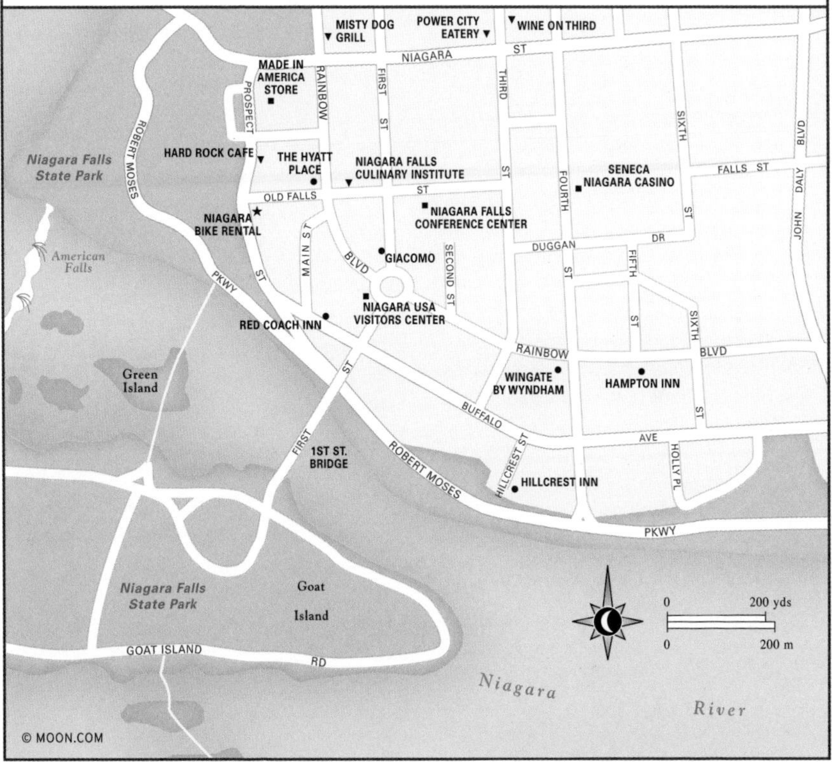

information on events and attractions, the visitors center should be your first stop. The center also offers a host of maps and brochures, assistance with trip and itinerary planning, and a gift shop filled with falls souvenirs.

Seneca Niagara Resort & Casino

At 26 stories tall, the glistening **Seneca Niagara Resort & Casino** (310 4th St., 877/873-6322, www.senecaniagaracasino.com, 24 hours daily) towers over the downtown area. This full-service casino welcomes gamers with more than 4,000 slot machines and 100 gaming tables, as well as smoking and nonsmoking areas. Ongoing renovations—including $40 million in recent updates—keep the gaming areas and hotel rooms looking fresh.

Nationally acclaimed entertainers perform at the 2,400-seat Event Center and the 440-seat Bear's Den. In winter, when many downtown restaurants are closed or have restricted hours, the casino's nine restaurants are open, some 24 hours daily.

The casino is nearly impossible to miss from any vantage point in downtown. Look for the tall, metallic-blue building. You must be 21 to play the slot machines or enter the gaming floor. The casino lobby and restaurants are open to patrons of all ages.

1: Niagara Gorge Discovery Center **2:** Niagara Falls Underground Railroad Heritage Center

SIGHTSEEING TOURS

Tours of Niagara Falls can add a great deal of enjoyment to your visit. However, most of the major attractions are clustered, reducing the need for transportation. Most private tour operators include only two paid attractions (Maid of the Mist and Cave of the Winds), which account for less than half of a tour's typical $100 price tag.

The price may be worth it, though, because these tours are guided and provide transportation, with most operators offering hotel and campground pickups that save you parking fees. Before purchasing a tour, inquire whether all guides are properly licensed and if they escort guests throughout the tour or simply drop them off at attractions with return pickup times. **Bedore Tours** (800/538-8433, www.bedoretours.com) provides pickups at all hotels, motels, and campgrounds in the area. **Over the Falls Tours** (716/283-8900, www.overthefallstoursniagara.com) offers tours on both sides of the border.

Niagara Falls Adventure Tours (716/432-8543, www.niagarafallsadventure.com, $76) is the only company offering walking tours of the falls. Included in your tour package is the Niagara Falls State Park Discovery Pass. Lead guide Nick Hurd is a veteran licensed guide who provides an overview of the history of the park and answers any questions you may have about the region. After the one-hour walking tour, you can enjoy the rest of the day in the park at your own pace, using the Discovery Pass for admission to various attractions.

Those who want to see the falls on two wheels should consider **Bike the Falls Tours** (1 Prospect St., 716/463-7453, www.bikethefallstours.com, $40 adults, $37 seniors 65+ and students up to college). The twice-a-day tours, offered May-October at 10am and 2pm, last 2-3 hours and traverse the islands of Niagara Falls State Park. These tours provide a new perspective and reach areas typically not seen with a car.

It's hard to beat the view a few hundred feet over the falls, and that's exactly what you get at **Rainbow Air Helicopters** (454 Main St., 716/284-2800, www.rainbowairinc.com, daily 9am-dusk, weather permitting, $125). Tours are 10-12 minutes long and get you closer to the American Falls than the Canadian choppers. The ride is thrilling, exhilarating, and everything you'd expect!

Recreation

HIKING AND BICYCLING

Niagara Falls has several biking and hiking paths. The entire state park is designed to promote access by foot and bike, and some trails for cyclists and hikers stretching north of the Niagara Gorge Discovery Center provide stunning views of Niagara's other wonder—the **Niagara Gorge**—and its churning, roaring rapids.

Gorge Rim Trail

Just outside the Niagara Gorge Discovery Center is the **Gorge Rim Trail** (716/278-0820, www.niagarafallsstatepark.com, dawn-dusk daily, free) trailhead. This easy hike stretches from the state park to the Robert Moses Power Plant, a one-way distance of 6.2 miles (10 km). The multipurpose trail goes along the top of the gorge and is mostly paved. As you proceed north, there are excellent views of Canada, the rapids, and the whirlpool. Rest stops have interpretive signs describing the industrial heritage of the area. This trail feeds into others that descend into the gorge for views of the rapids and whirlpool. A kiosk at the trailhead has good informational posters and brochures about the

1: Rainbow Air Helicopter **2:** the Gorge Rim Trail

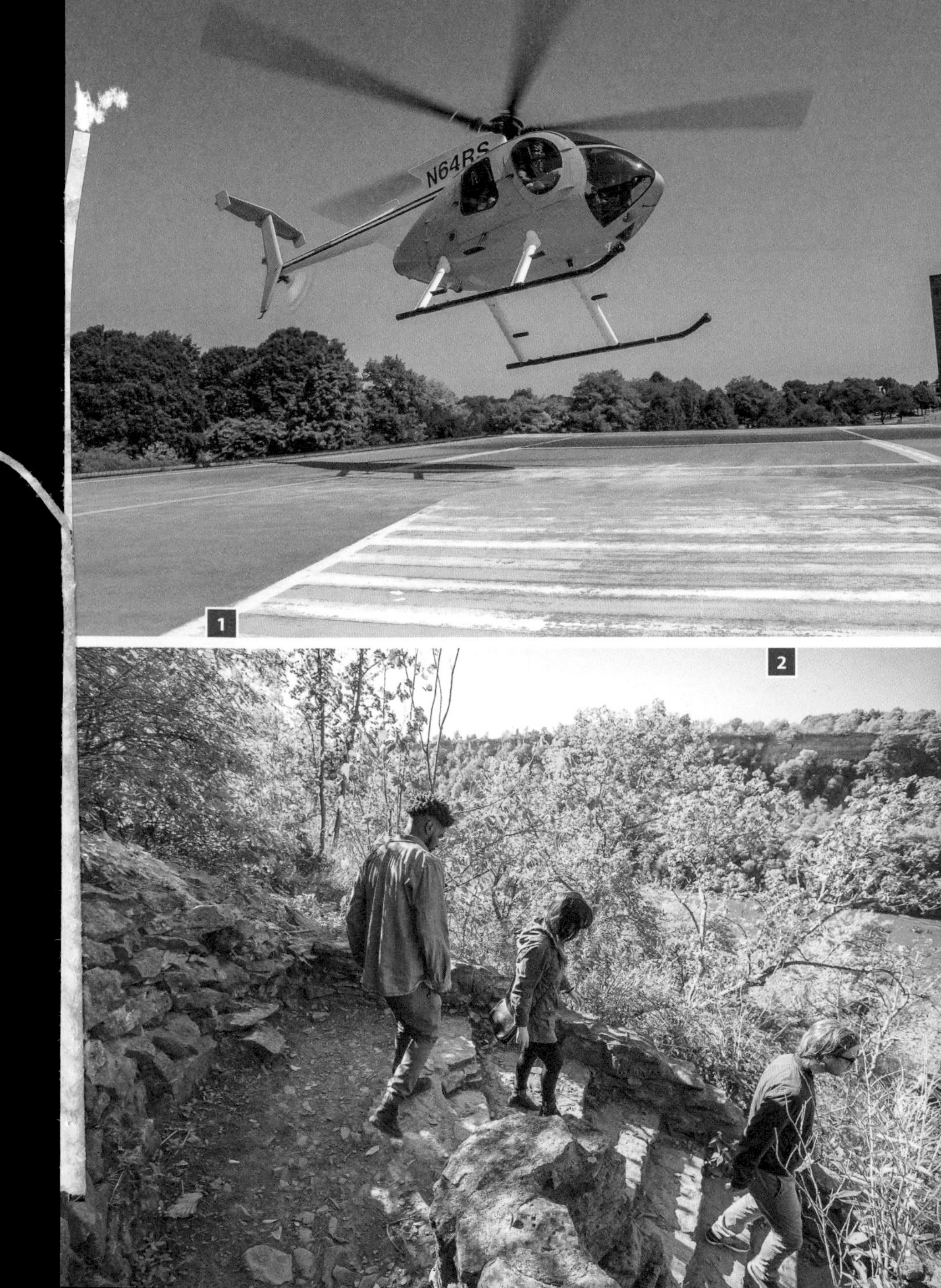
N64RS
1
2

entire 15 miles (24.1 km) of trails that extend north from the falls toward Lake Ontario.

Bicycle Rental

Niagara Bike Rental (Old Falls St. and Prospect St., 716/345-5446, 10am-9pm Mon.-Thurs., 10am-11pm Fri.-Sun. mid-May-mid-Sept.) equips you with everything needed for a two-wheel adventure, including helmets, baskets, and bike locks. Also included are maps with bicycle-friendly routes to explore. Rentals start at $10 an hour or $25 for an all-day rental. This centrally located kiosk rents wheelchairs, mobility scooters, strollers, and wagons, too.

A bikeshare program, **Reddybikes** (716/407-7474, www.reddybikeshare.socialbicycles.com, $3 for a 2-day pass plus $0.10/minute when riding), seasonally circulates dozens of bicycles placed at a host of docking stations in neighborhoods throughout the city; download the app on their website to identify a nearby station and to unlock a bike.

Entertainment and Events

NIGHTLIFE

After a long day of communing with rocks and water, you might be ready for some rock and roll at the **Hard Rock Cafe** (333 Prospect St., 716/282-0007, www.hardrock.com, 11am-10pm Sun.-Thurs., 11am-11pm Fri.-Sat.). The Hard Rock has continuous music videos, a reasonable selection of beers, and a ton of cool rock and roll memorabilia affixed to the walls. Look for the sketch by Jim Morrison, Jimi Hendrix's guitar, and the pair of Bono's signature sunglasses. The Hard Rock hosts live music with no cover charge every Friday evening.

You'll find entertainment daily at the **Seneca Niagara Resort & Casino** (310 4th St., 716/299-1100, www.senecaniagaracasino.com, 24 hours daily). Waitstaff will serve drinks while you're gaming, or you can sit at the bar in **Stir** and enjoy free live music on weekend evenings.

Within stumbling distance of downtown is **The Craft Kitchen and Bar** (223 Ferry Ave., 716/600-2337, www.thecraftnf.com, 4pm-close Wed.-Sat., noon-close Sun.). Since opening in 2017, The Craft has become Niagara Falls' go-to craft beer bar, with two dozen different brews on tap, including a host of locally produced varieties and many more bottled options. The Craft also has a solid pub grub menu of burgers, poutine, chicken fingers, and more.

THE ARTS

There is something for everyone at the **Niagara Arts and Cultural Center** (NACC, 1201 Pine Ave., 716/282-7530, www.thenacc.org, 9am-5pm Mon.-Fri., noon-4pm Sat.-Sun., free). NACC features works from more than 70 local artists, including paintings, sculpture, and crafts, and displays change frequently. NACC is a converted high school building with 60 artists' studios, two theaters, two galleries, and a TV production soundstage. Check the NACC's online events calendar for the most up-to-date information on gallery exhibits.

Art Alley (425 3rd St.) is a public art project featuring 19 murals spread across an alleyway that connects 3rd Street's bars and restaurants with a public parking lot. The "Greetings from Niagara Falls New York" mural makes for a perfect Instagram opportunity.

FESTIVALS AND EVENTS

Daily entertainment is a regular occurrence downtown, specifically along the **Old Falls Street, USA** cobblestone corridor. This three-block area runs from the Seneca Niagara Casino to the pedestrian entrance of the state park. During the summer, daily events include exercise classes, movie screenings, music concerts, and family activities. A current schedule is online (www.fallsstreetusaom).

The top nighttime activity in Niagara Falls is the **illumination of the falls** (dusk-1am daily Jan.-Mar., dusk-2am daily May-Dec.). The falls are bathed in softly colored light each evening by hundreds of energy-efficient LED lights stationed on the Canadian side. Though the illumination is difficult to see from the U.S. side, there are a few places with a good view. Terrapin Point (Apr.-Nov.) is the best spot during summer and fall. During winter, the best vantage point is also in Niagara Falls State Park, at Stedman's Bluff, the point on Goat Island that overlooks Luna Island.

During the high season (late May-Sept. 1), **fireworks** light up the skies over Niagara Falls on select nights each week as well as on major U.S. and Canadian holidays; visit www.niagarafallsstatepark.com for a schedule. The five-minute displays are a wonderful climax to a day of sightseeing. They can be seen almost anywhere along the rim of the gorge in the park. The top two vantage points are Luna Island and the Observation Deck, with the Rainbow Bridge pedestrian walkway as a good alternative.

The **Niagara Falls Blues Festival** (www.niagarafallsbluesfest.org, free) focuses on the "Three Bs"—blues, barbecue, and beer. Thousands of people gather at Old Falls Street in September for two days of blues music performed by nationally acclaimed artists. Dozens of food vendors sell tasty barbecue delights. Typically, the entertainment begins at 5pm Friday and 1pm on Saturday. Bands play until 11pm nightly. The festival is usually held the second weekend in September, but that can vary, so check the website.

Shopping

The area immediately surrounding the park has many nearly identical souvenir shops. A refreshing alternative is **Made in America** (1 Niagara Center, 2nd floor, 716/304-3622, www.madeinamericastore.com, 9am-5pm daily Apr.-Oct.). Set in the tall blue-glass building adjacent to the main entrance of the state park, the store sells souvenirs with an authentic American flavor, along with clothing.

For non-touristy shopping, you'll need to travel outside of the downtown area. A little more than 5 miles (8 km) from downtown is the **Fashion Outlets of Niagara Falls USA** (1900 Military Rd., 716/297-2022, www.fashionoutletsniagara.com, 10am-9pm Mon.-Sat., 10am-6pm Sun.). There are more than 150 retail stores, such as Coach, Ralph Lauren, Hugo Boss, and Eddie Bauer. Many Canadian shoppers cross the border to find a better selection, lower prices, and lower taxes on clothing and electronics. This complex is adjacent to a **Walmart** (1549 Military Rd., 716/298-4484, www.walmart.com), which, in turn, leads to Niagara Falls Boulevard and another corridor of big-box retail stores.

DOWNTOWN

For a great meal with a ton of ambience, dine at the ★ **Red Coach Inn** (2 Buffalo Ave., 716/282-1459, www.redcoach.com, 7:30am-9:30pm Sun.-Thurs., 7:30am-10:30pm Fri.-Sat., $25). The cuisine is American, while the decor is reminiscent of an English Tudor manor. Entrées are satisfying and desserts are decadent, with one serving usually perfect for two adults. In winter, call ahead and ask for a table near the large open-hearth fireplace. In warmer months, dine on the open patio overlooking the upper rapids of the Niagara River.

The **Power City Eatery** (444 3rd St., 716/299-0124, www.powercityeatery.com, 7:30am-3pm Mon.-Fri., 9am-3pm Sat., 9am-1pm Sun.) is a great breakfast or lunch option near downtown. This coffeehouse features homemade breads and baked goods and specialty sandwiches like a house-cured pastrami on rye.

Wine on Third (501 3rd St., 716/285-9463, www.wineonthird.com, 3:30pm-10pm Sun.-Thurs., 3:30pm-11pm Fri.-Sat., $25) is an upscale café, perfect for a romantic dinner with wine. The cuisine is contemporary American, and the wine list is good. When the weather permits, eat outside along 3rd Street and people-watch.

For good food fast, the ★ **Misty Dog Grill** (431 Main St., 716/285-0702, 11am-10pm Sun.-Fri., 11am-11pm Sat. Apr.-Oct., $8) can't be beat. In the heart of downtown (look for the giant ice-cream cone on Main Street near Niagara Street), this take-out stand has a surprisingly large menu, great for families on a budget. They have kid-friendly food such as hot dogs, burgers, and fries, plus plenty of other choices, including wraps, sandwiches, and salads. If you want to try authentic chicken wings and cannot travel to Buffalo, try them here. Walk next door for the best hard ice cream in town.

The odds are good that you'll find something for every appetite at the **Seneca Niagara Resort & Casino** (310 4th St., 716/299-1100, www.senecaniagaracasino.com). The best steak in town is at **The Western Door Steakhouse** (877/873-6322, www.senecaniagaracasino.com, 5pm-10pm Sun.-Fri., 5pm-midnight Sat., $45). Reservations are recommended. The **Koi Restaurant** (877/873-6322, www.senecaniagaracasino.com, 5pm-9:30pm Sun.-Tues., 5pm-10:30pm and 11pm-3am Fri.-Sat., $30) serves traditional and contemporary Asian dishes. At the **Blues Burger Bar** (877/873-6322, www.senecaniagaracasino.com, 11am-9pm Sun.-Thurs, 11am-10pm Fri.-Sat., $15), you enjoy a satisfying burger along with a side dish and drink at the restaurant, or you may order your meal for takeout.

LITTLE ITALY

The venerable ★ **Como Restaurant** (2220 Pine Ave., 716/285-9341, www.comorestaurant.com, 11:30am-9pm daily, $18) allows you to dine where the mob did. If you like home-style Italian food, with huge portions served in an old-school restaurant atmosphere, then the Como is for you. This restaurant features red sauce staples like chicken parmesan, baked lasagna, and cheese manicotti and will give you an authentic glimpse into the world of Niagara Falls in the 1960s, when Mafia don Stefano Magaddino frequently ate at the Como.

No food tour to Niagara Falls is complete without a stop at **DiCamillo Bakery** (1700 Pine Ave., 716/284-8131, www.dicamillobakerybuffaloniagara.com, 7am-7pm Mon.-Sat., 7am-5pm Sun.), which has been in business since 1920. DiCamillo's peanut sticks (fry cakes covered in chopped peanuts) are the stuff of legend in Western New York, and their pizza slices (a steal at $2) showcase their homemade dough. DiCamillo's has several locations; the Pine Avenue store is a fine stop on the way to other restaurants in Little Italy like Fortuna's and La Hacienda.

1: Little Italy **2:** The Giacomo hotel

1

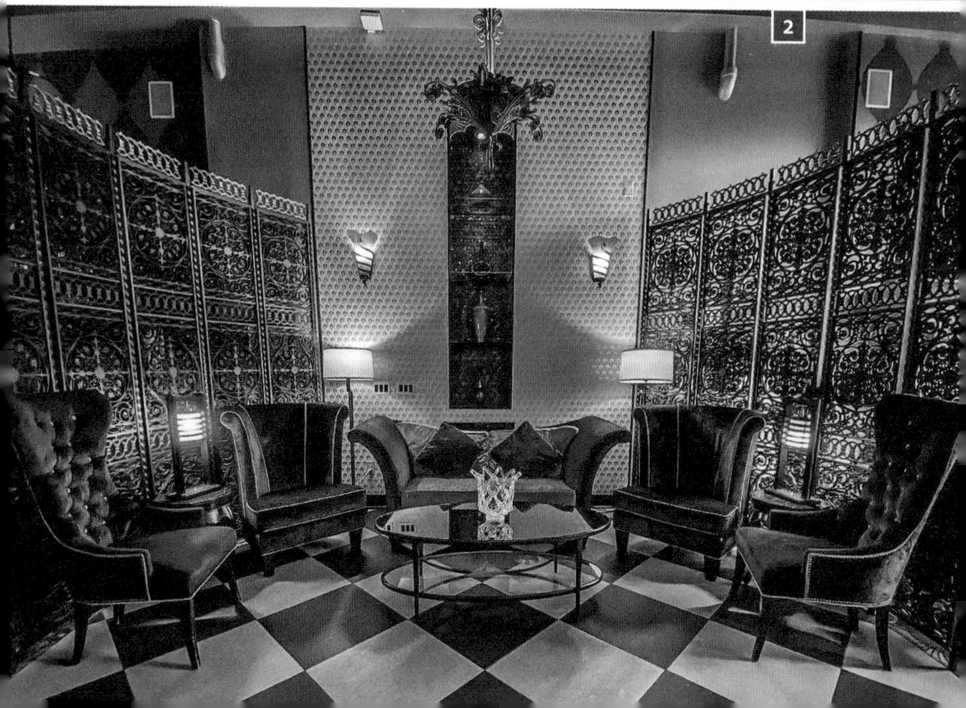

2

An Offer You Can't Refuse

For many years, the U.S. Mafia controlled the city of Niagara Falls. Running the organization was Stefano Magaddino, an old-school Sicilian American mafioso known for his brutality and cunning. As Prohibition enforcement forced legitimate distillers and distributors to stop alcohol production, Magaddino filled the void. Moving from Buffalo to Niagara Falls, he profited from bootlegging owing to the proximity of Canada to his turf.

Magaddino earned the nickname "the Undertaker" because he operated a chain of funeral homes in the area. Smuggling operations expanded into labor union racketeering, extortion, gambling, loan sharking, and narcotics. Magaddino was influential on the national stage as well, becoming a member of the mob's "commission" of top dons. The Undertaker eschewed the limelight, choosing to run his Niagara Falls operation from the shadows. He survived at least two assassination attempts and died of natural causes in 1974. Interfamily rivalry went on to rip the local mob apart, reducing its influence in the area.

Accommodations

Niagara Falls hotels are in two geographic regions—downtown and Niagara Falls Boulevard. Downtown properties are typically more expensive, as they are within walking distance of the state park. Niagara Falls Boulevard hotels are less expensive, but they are older and require a 5-mile (8-km) drive to the falls. Hotels earn most of their revenue during summer, so don't expect any bargains then. In winter and early spring, some hotels are willing to negotiate rates. Rates listed here reflect high season costs.

DOWNTOWN

As tall as Niagara Falls, ★ **The Giacomo** (222 1st St., 716/299-0200, www.thegiacomo.com, $300) towers over the other lodgings in the falls region. Setting the standard for service in the area, this boutique hotel is in a restored art deco building just two blocks from the state park. Rooms are large and comfortable, and the complimentary breakfast is excellent. Visit the lounge on the top floor for its view of American Falls and the rapids.

The **Seneca Niagara Resort & Casino Hotel** (310 4th St., 716/299-1100, www.senecaniagaracasino.com, $205) is the largest hotel in the state outside New York City, with more than 600 rooms and suites. There's a large indoor pool and spa, and nine restaurants are on-site. The hotel is just three blocks from the state park.

Find historic B&B lodgings at the **Park Place Bed and Breakfast** (740 Park Pl., 716/796-8782, www.parkplacebb.com, $139). This stately home is on the historic registry and reflects the Arts and Crafts style of the early 1900s. Choose from five suites, including one that has a private porch overlooking the well-kept garden. Suites all have private bathrooms, although some are not within the suite. Free Wi-Fi, private parking, and a library room are other amenities at this cozy B&B.

If you're looking for a hotel for your family, look no further than the **Hampton Inn Niagara Falls** (501 Rainbow Blvd., 716/285-6666, www.hamptoninn3.hilton.com, $227). Everything you want is in a clean and safe, family-friendly hotel that is walking distance to the falls. Of course breakfast, parking, and an indoor pool are included.

One of Niagara Falls' newest properties may also be among its best placed. **The Hyatt Place** (310 Rainbow Blvd. S., 716/285-5000, www.hyatt.com, $300) is just one block from Niagara Falls State Park and steps from the restaurants and entertainment of Old Falls Street. The park and mist from the falls are viewable from the outdoor patio on the hotel's top floor, a perfect spot on a summer night.

Another newer property is the **Wingate by Wyndham Niagara Falls** (333 Rainbow Blvd., 716/285-4000, www.wyndhamhotels.com, $170). This property is fresh and is two blocks away from the southern end of Niagara Falls State Park. The pool and fitness center are great, but the included breakfast could use a little more selection.

Ever wanted to stay in a former chocolate factory? Opened in 2017, the **Courtyard by Marriott Niagara Falls** (900 Buffalo Ave., 716/284-2222, www.marriott.com, $237) is a new hotel built in an old industrial building on the edge of Niagara Falls State Park. The property is modern and comfortable but retains some of its industrial touches, especially in the lobby.

NIAGARA FALLS BOULEVARD

Many motels in Niagara Falls harken back to the 1950s, when thousands of families and honeymooners drove to the falls from throughout the northeastern United States. The **Falls Motel** (5820 Buffalo Ave., 716/283-3239, www.fallsmotel.com, $108) is among a handful worth staying at. Rooms are small, well kept, and clean. The family owners take pride in making sure that your stay is comfortable and satisfying. The front desk can provide up-to-date information on seasonal attractions, weather, and transportation.

The **Best Western Summit Inn** (9500 Niagara Falls Blvd., 716/297-5050, www.bestwesternnewyork.com, $161) has clean rooms and free Internet access. It is close to the Fashion Outlets of Niagara Falls USA and provides a complimentary continental breakfast that's actually worth waking up for.

Information and Services

The downtown area has a handful of souvenir shops and hotel gift shops that sell basic items like toothpaste and aspirin. Expect high prices, a limited selection, and limited store hours. The closest 24-hour convenience store is **7-Eleven** (402 Niagara St., 716/285-4497, 24 hours daily), across from the casino.

Visitors can get regional information and advice at the **Niagara Falls USA Official Visitor Center** (10 Rainbow Blvd., 716/282-8992, www.niagarafallsusa.com, 8:30am-7pm daily May 15- Sept. 15, 8:30am-5pm daily Sept. 16- May 14) Many regular commercial souvenir shops display the internationally known blue sign with a question mark, purporting to be a tourist information center. Niagara Falls USA provides unbiased information about the falls and the outlying areas.

Getting There and Around

AIR

The **Buffalo Niagara International Airport** (BUF, 4200 Genesee St., Cheektowaga, 716/630-6000, www.buffaloairport.com), the region's largest airport with the most airlines and daily flights, is a 25-minute drive from Niagara Falls. Expect to pay $70-80 for a cab ride or ride-share from the airport to downtown Niagara Falls. Taxi service providers at the airport are generally reliable and safe, with no advance reservations required.

CAR

If your hotel is in the downtown area, you don't need a car to visit Niagara Falls State Park. Downtown hotels are within walking distance, and the park is best explored on foot or via the hop-on, hop-off **Niagara Scenic Trolley** (716/278-1730, www.niagarafallsstatepark.com, 9am-10pm Sun.-Thurs., 9am-11pm Fri.-Sat. mid-June-early Sept., 9am-8pm Sun.-Thurs., 9am-10pm Fri.-Sat. early Sept.-mid-Oct., 9am-6pm daily mid-Oct.-early Jan., $3 adults, $2 children 6-12). If your hotel is outside the downtown area, drive to the park. Parking is plentiful at numerous private lots ($5 and up) or within the state park ($10) main lot and the lots on Goat Island. You can pay and park at the main lot, then move your car to the Goat Island lot for no additional charge, as long as you show your receipt at the parking attendant booth. During winter, when there are few tourists, parking at the state park is sometimes free, especially on Goat Island.

Municipal parking lots and garages are plentiful and cost $30 per day Friday-Sunday and $20 per day Monday-Thursday May-October, and $10 per day November-April. One of the most convenient municipal garages is just one block from the state park, at 365 Rainbow Boulevard. Street parking costs $5 per hour May-October and $3 per hour November-April. Motorists parking on the street can pay at nearby kiosks or by downloading the Whoosh! app to their phone. A downloadable map of municipal parking areas in downtown Niagara Falls can be found at www.niagarafallsusa.com.

Private parking lots are convenient but have their downsides. Private lot attendants sometimes wear clothing similar to Parks Department uniforms and use orange flags to draw tourists into their parking lots, then lure them into adjacent souvenir stores with the promise of a free prize, map, or information, followed by a sales pitch for tours. These lots are close to the park, however, and can save you a few bucks.

BUS

Trailways (www.trailwaysny.com) and **Greyhound** (www.greyhound.com) bus lines pick up and drop off passengers daily at the **Quality Hotel & Suites** (240 1st St., 716/282-1212, www.qualityniagarafalls.com).

The **Discover Niagara Shuttle** (716/222-0729, www.discoverniagarashuttle.com) may be the easiest and best way to experience all that the Niagara region has to offer—and it's free. The service operates May-October and connects more than a dozen attractions and points of interest in Niagara County, from the Niagara USA Visitor Center to Old Fort Niagara. The shuttle buses run every 35-40 minutes 9am-6pm daily, with additional service every 45-60 minutes 6pm-midnight on Fridays and Saturdays. Visit the website to download the Discover Niagara Shuttle app, which provides real-time schedule information and a complete list of stops.

Niagara Frontier Transit Authority (716/855-7211, www.metro.nfta.com) provides local bus service. Routes 55 and 55T pick up passengers in the downtown area and serve key areas of the city, such as the Pine Avenue business district. Fares are $2 each way for both routes; the Trolley Route (55T) is free for guests staying at participating hotels (ask at your hotel's front desk for a trolley pass).

TRAIN

Amtrak (www.amtrak.com) stops at the **Niagara Falls train station** (825 Depot Ave. W.) twice daily via the Empire route, and once daily via the Maple Leaf route. From Buffalo, the train ride takes about an hour (on either route). Fares start at $13 each way. The Empire route terminates at Niagara Falls, New York, while the Maple Leaf continues across the border and stops at Niagara Falls, Ontario, terminating in Toronto. You can take the train from the Canadian side to visit Niagara Falls State Park, but be prepared to use a taxi to get from the train station to the park, and vice versa—or wait for the next Discover Niagara Shuttle, which stops at the station May- October.

From the train station, you'll need to take a taxi or ride-sharing vehicle (Uber and Lyft are ubiquitous here) 2.5 miles (4 km) to reach the park and downtown area ($8-10). Taxis wait at the train station during scheduled stop times, so you shouldn't have trouble getting a cab once you arrive.

North of the Falls

The Niagara region's beauty does not end at Niagara Falls, and neither should your travels. Following the river north, you'll find outstanding hiking, history, and other attractions. Along the 15 miles (24 km) of the lower Niagara River, you'll see a deadly whirlpool, an imposing power plant, an outdoor arts campus, and a 300-year-old military fort.

Lewiston is a historic village with gorgeous hills, fertile plains, and a beautiful waterfront. In December 1813, during the War of 1812, the town was raided and destroyed by British soldiers and Native American warriors bent on revenge for American atrocities committed during the war. The picturesque village is now a tourist destination in summer and fall, thanks to its quiet beauty and the quaint shops that line Center Street.

Old Fort Niagara, at the place where the river ends and Lake Ontario begins, is the longest continually occupied military structure in North America. Surrounding the fort is the village of **Youngstown,** a launching point for excellent boating and fishing, and site of beautiful sunsets.

SIGHTS

Whirlpool State Park

Less than 3 miles (4.8 km) north of the falls is one of the most amazing natural features of the entire region: the whirlpool. A great way to appreciate it is from **Whirlpool State Park** (off Niagara Scenic Pkwy., 716/284-4691, www.nysparks.com, dawn-dusk daily, free). The views of the raging river below are beautiful and breathtaking.

When you arrive at the park, pass through the stone shelter and take the paved path to the left, which will lead you to the rim of the gorge. Once there, you'll grip the guardrail as you glimpse the rapids at the bottom of a sheer, 200-foot (61-m) drop. The Class VI white water churns menacingly down the narrow river, surging headlong into the massive whirlpool. The whirlpool basin is a relic from a waterfall that existed long before the last ice age. The Niagara River tears through this basin and makes a sharp right-hand turn as it heads downstream toward Lake Ontario.

When the river water level is high, the water slams into the far wall of the gorge and circles counterclockwise, passing on its journey to Lake Ontario. This phenomenon forms a whirlpool, perhaps the most dangerous stretch of the river. The ever-moving vortex is more than 200 feet (61 m) deep and tosses floating objects such as tree trunks

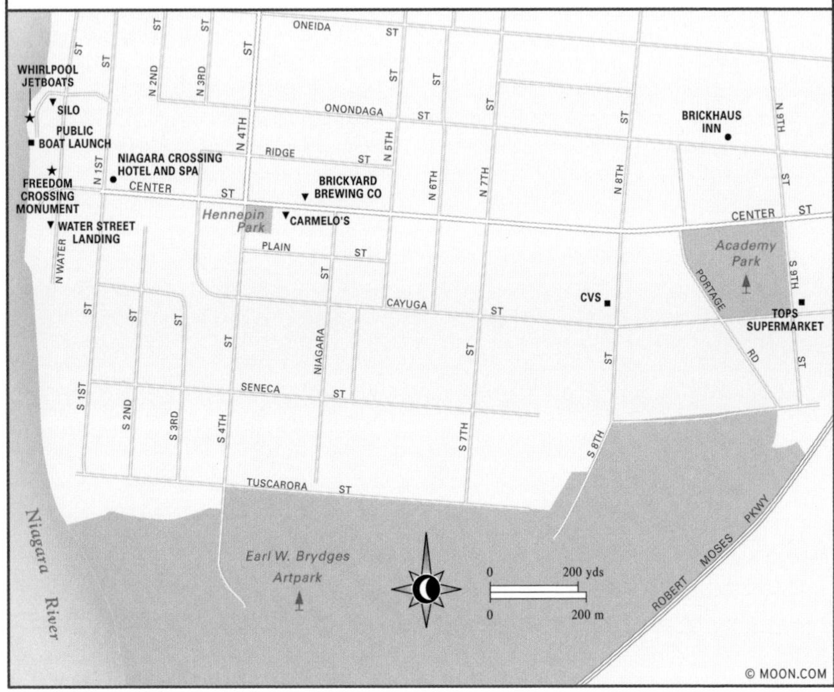

like matchsticks. Even the modern, superpowerful jet boats do not cross this section of the river, but instead turn to avoid the capricious power of the whirlpool.

As you travel along the rim of the gorge, be aware of your footing. Some spots have washed out and present a hazard. Keep children close by, as the gorge is steep and unforgiving. At the path's end, you have a view of the more serene part of the river as it flows north toward the power plants and eventually Lake Ontario.

The path completes a circuit (0.3 mile/0.5 km), leading you back to the shelter where you started. There are picnic tables and grills here, along with interpretive materials, signs, restrooms, and a water fountain. You'll find Whirlpool State Park an ideal place to picnic and enjoy a wonder of nature.

Devil's Hole State Park

The ominously named **Devil's Hole State Park** (Niagara Scenic Pkwy. and Rte. 104, 716/284-5778, www.nysparks.com, dawn-dusk daily mid-May-Nov., free) is a partly wooded, 42-acre park. It sits on the remnants of an ancient stream that poured over the wall of the gorge, creating a small waterfall. The stream is now a mere seasonal trickle down the gorge wall. It was here, in September 1763, that more than 100 British soldiers and civilians were killed during a Native American ambush meant to sever the settlers' portage route around the falls.

The park is primarily a starting point for hikers and others who descend the 400 stairs down the gorge to enjoy the view of the rapids and power plant, or to try their luck at fishing for trout and salmon. There is ample parking and several tables with grills for picnicking.

Niagara Power Vista

Adjacent to Devil's Hole State Park is the **Niagara Power Vista** (5777 Lewiston Rd., Lewiston, 716/286-6661, www.nypa.gov/niagarapowervista, 9am-5pm daily, free), the visitors center of the Niagara Hydroelectric Power Plant. It is difficult to fully grasp the size of this massive facility until you enter. Built into the side of the Niagara Gorge, this plant produces clean, inexpensive energy transmitted throughout New York State. The portion of the plant open to visitors has displays and interactive, kid-friendly exhibits that explain how the Niagara River is harnessed to generate electricity.

The visitor center has a 4-D Power Up simulator that takes you on an entertaining ride as you trace the creation of hydroelectricity from molecules of running water to electrons at your wall outlet. Also of note is a Van de Graaff generator demonstration that will make your child's hair stand on end. There's no better place in the region to spark your child's interest in science.

While at the Power Vista, be sure to visit the platform for fishing at the base of the power plant. Access the platform from Hyde Park Road, turning right onto Power Authority Service Road and parking at the bottom. The anglers will be glad to show the impressive trout and steelhead on their stringers.

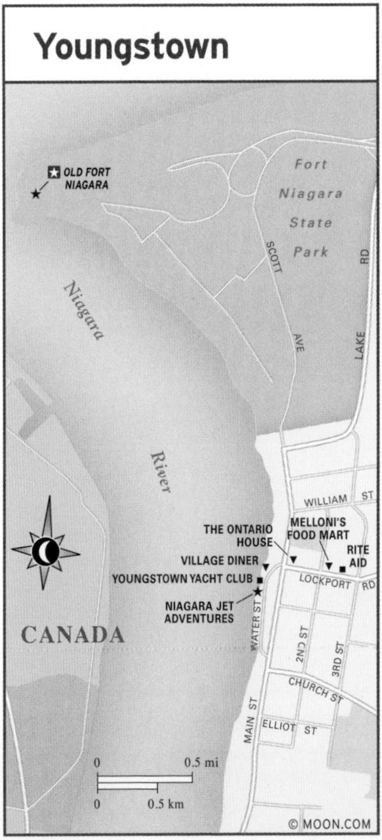

Youngstown

Artpark

The most popular attraction in Lewiston is **Earl W. Brydges Artpark** (450 S. 4th St., 716/754-4375, www.artpark.net, dawn-dusk daily, free), a sprawling, 150-acre complex dedicated to the enjoyment of all art forms. It features two large performance venues: an indoor stage with seating for 2,400 and an outdoor amphitheater for 10,000 people. The amphitheater is an amazing space for a concert because the stage backdrop is the Niagara River Gorge. Check out the Tuesdays in the Park summer concert series, where you can see major acts like Chicago, the Doobie Brothers, and Lynyrd Skynyrd.

In addition to musicals and dramatic performances, Artpark provides weeklong classes (known as "camps") for young people to explore drama, music, and graphic arts. Nature's artistry is on stage here as well. Artpark has picnic shelters and connects to the Niagara Gorge's hiking trails, with excellent shoreline fishing in the lower Niagara River.

Jet Boats

A thrill ride found several miles downstream from the falls is as memorable as the Maid of the Mist. **Niagara Jet Adventures** (555 Water St., Youngstown, 716/745-7121, www.niagarajet.com, $69 adults, $51 children 12 and under) is a rock-and-roll ride through the white water of the Niagara River. Departing from a marina in the shadow of Fort Niagara,

1
2
3
4

these specially designed boats use three Cadillac engines (combined thrust of 1,800 horsepower) to slash over, under, and through the most treacherous parts of the Niagara.

Enjoy this white-knuckle ride in the comfort of a dry, climate-controlled cabin. Captains are knowledgeable and capable, and add humor to the experience. A steward keeps the action moving by adding narration, and there's a bit of audience participation including some dancing. If you want to get drenched, reserve seats on the open-air wet deck for a thoroughly saturating experience. This attraction is a 20-minute drive from Niagara Falls and well worth it. The ride lasts about an hour, the memories a lifetime.

The **Whirlpool Jet Boats** (115 S. Water St., Lewiston, 888/438-4444, www.whirlpooljet.com, $62.95 adults, $39.95 children 12 and under) provide an adventuresome, 45-minute ride through the lower rapids of the Niagara River. Prepare to get wet! This attraction promises thrills—and delivers—as boats slash through the rapids during its 9-mile (14-km) round-trip. Bring extra clothes and a towel, and consider wearing a bathing suit during the ride. The ride is available in two options: wet or dry. For the "wet jet" ride, sit in the front row. The dry ride (in a glass-enclosed boat known as the Jet Dome) is wonderful, but not as thrilling.

This attraction can also be accessed from two locations on the Canadian side of the border in Niagara-on-the-Lake (61 Melville St. and 55 River Frontage Rd., 888/438-4444, www.whirlpooljet.com, $72.95 adults, $44.95 children 12 and under). The Melville Street location is farther downstream, so it requires an extra 15 minutes in the jet boat. However, the exciting, adventure-filled portions of the ride are identical from all locations.

Freedom Crossing Monument

Lewiston's **Freedom Crossing Monument** is a dramatic yet uplifting monument that pays tribute to the courage of fugitive enslaved people, as well as to the people of Lewiston who helped transport them to Canada via the Underground Railroad. The bronze statue portrays a family as they board a rowboat for the journey across the Niagara River to freedom. Also depicted in the monument is Josiah Tryon, the Lewiston man who assisted enslaved people along the Underground Railroad. The monument is between Center Street and the banks of the Niagara River, near the Silo Restaurant.

Fatima Shrine

The inspiring **Fatima Shrine** (1023 Swann Rd., Lewiston, 716/754-7489, www.fatimashrine.com, 9am-5pm daily Jan.-mid-Nov., 9am-9pm mid-Nov.-Dec., free) is formally known as the **National Shrine Basilica of Our Lady of Fatima.** Thousands of Roman Catholics make a pilgrimage to this site each year to see the glass-domed basilica, Avenue of the Saints, and the bell tower. This 16-acre site is for prayer and contemplation, but anyone can appreciate the beauty of the religious art and statuary. Also on the shrine's campus is the Pilgrim Center, which has a gift shop and a cafeteria. The shrine is especially popular at the holidays, when the Festival of Lights illuminates the property in nightly splendor.

TOP EXPERIENCE

★ Old Fort Niagara

Well worth the 25-minute drive north from Niagara Falls is **Old Fort Niagara** (Fort Niagara State Park, Youngstown, 716/745-7611, www.oldfortniagara.org, 9am-7pm daily July-Aug., 9am-5pm daily Sept.-June, $15 adults, $10 children 6-12). The fort dates back to 1679 when the French constructed an outpost that became Fort Niagara. During the French and Indian War, France and Britain grappled for control of North America. After the British won, they occupied the fort until 1796, more than a decade after the United States won the Revolutionary War.

1: Whirlpool State Park **2:** Earl W. Brydges Artpark
3: Whirlpool Jet Boat on the lower Niagara River
4: Old Fort Niagara

The First Railway Suspension Bridge

In 1855, John Roebling, who would later build the Brooklyn Bridge, completed the world's first railway suspension bridge across the Niagara Gorge. The 825-foot (251-m) Niagara Falls Suspension Bridge was an engineering marvel and featured two decks. Trains used the upper deck, while carriages and pedestrians used the lower deck. While the bridge, for a brief period of time, was a "must see" attraction for tourists visiting Niagara, it also served as an important pathway for Blacks who were escaping enslavement in the U.S. and going to Canada to find lasting freedom.

However, as trains became larger and heavier over time, they exceeded the safety specifications of the bridge's wooden structure. And after over four decades of use, the Niagara Falls Suspension Bridge was dismantled and replaced with the steel Whirlpool Rapids Bridge in 1897.

During the War of 1812, British troops again took control of the fort, finally leaving in 1815. The United States has since maintained control of Fort Niagara, which eventually served as a camp for German prisoners during World War II. Fort Niagara has the distinction of being the longest continually occupied military base in the United States.

Plan to spend at least two hours wandering the expansive grounds of the fort. A well-produced video at the visitors center is definitely worth viewing, as it gives context to the fort's long history. Costumed reenactors demonstrate how soldiers and civilians lived and died in the 18th and 19th centuries. There are live musket and cannon firings as well as blacksmithing and food preparation demonstrations.

The most impressive building within the fort is the French Castle. The French built this two-story structure in 1726, cleverly disguising a functional garrison as a trading post. The castle housed officers' quarters, soldiers' barracks, a chapel, and jail cells. Next to the French Castle is the Bake House, dating back to 1756, which is essentially two giant stone ovens. The cooks would build a fire inside the oven, then let it burn until a few embers remained. Then they swept the embers from the oven and placed bread inside to be cooked by the stored heat.

Make a stop at the Powder Magazine to see where the fort's ammunition was stored. Built in 1757, this thick masonry building was designed to withstand hits from cannon fire without exploding. Today it has been restored, so visitors can appreciate the lengths to which armies went to keep their powder safe and dry. As you walk the perimeter of the fort, imagine the strategic importance of this facility, guarding the mouth of the Niagara River and the gateway to the New World. The view of Lake Ontario is stunning—on clear days, you can see Toronto on the northern shore.

The fort is no longer a functioning military base, although the Coast Guard operates out of the dock on its grounds. The legions of reenactors seen here throughout the year—French, British, American, and Native American—are all volunteers. The largest annual event here is the commemoration of the 1759 siege of the fort, when Britain took control of it from France. Each year, during the weekend closest to July 9, more than 1,000 reenactors stage battles that recall the history-changing conflict. In addition to battle scenes, reenactors also create camps to show how people lived, ate, and amused themselves during the 1750s.

Surrounding the fort is **Fort Niagara State Park** (Rte. 18F, Youngstown, 716/745-7273, www.nysparks.com, 9am-5pm daily Sept.-June, 9am-7pm daily July-Aug., free), with picnic facilities, a swimming pool, and boat launches.

RECREATION

Hiking

The **Whirlpool Rapids Trail** (Whirlpool State Park, off Robert Moses Pkwy.,

716/284-5778, www.nysparks.com, dawn-dusk daily mid-May-Nov., free) is a difficult, 1.4-mile (2.25-km) trail with stairs, wooded paths, and some boulders to navigate. The hike is well worth the effort, as it takes you down to the water's level and up close to the Class VI rapids and the whirlpool. Use caution, as the whirlpool and rapids are unforgiving to people who accidentally fall in. The trail is open to hikers ages 8 and older. Alcoholic beverages, camping, and fires are prohibited. To find the trailhead, exit out the back of the stone shelter in Whirlpool State Park and follow the path to the rim of the gorge (with a beautiful view of the whirlpool). Continue in a clockwise direction on the path, and in less than 0.5 mile (0.8 km), you'll find stairs marking the start of the trail.

A little farther north along the gorge is the 2.5-mile (4-km) **Devil's Hole Trail** (716/284-5778, www.nysparks.com, dawn-dusk daily mid-May-Nov., free). This trail is a moderate one, with approximately 300 stone stairs to climb. Upon descending them, you'll see the Devil's Hole Cave, a natural feature shrouded in legend. The limestone cave is safe to enter, but watch for trash and broken bottles discarded here. Be careful: Native American legend says that any person who enters the cave is destined for tragedy. Then continue down the stairs to the stone picnic tables. This is a great spot for a rest or snack, but remember to pack out all your trash. The trail winds along the gorge floor and has excellent views of the lower rapids of the Niagara River, giant boulders, and lightly wooded areas. Heading south along the river path, you'll arrive at stairs that ascend to Whirlpool State Park. Once topside, head back (north) along the Gorge Rim Trail to arrive back at Devil's Hole Park and the end of the loop.

Parks

Joseph Davis State Park (4143 Lower River Rd., Lewiston, 716/754-4596, www.nysparks.com, dawn-dusk daily, free) has excellent largemouth bass fishing in old quarry pits filled with water. There are picnic facilities, a nature trail, and a 27-hole disc golf course.

Fishing and Boating

A boat launch is available at the **Village of Lewiston Marina** (145 N. 4th St., Lewiston, 716/754-8271, dawn-dusk daily, free Mon.-Wed., $14 Thurs.-Sun.), also known as the Sands Dock.

There are several areas for shore fishing, including from the fishing platform at the base of the Niagara Power Vista, along the hiking trails in Artpark, and on the waterfront at the Lewiston Marina.

Obtain a **fishing license** (one-day, week-long, or annual license) by phone or online (866/933-2257, www.dec.ny.gov/permits) or in person at most sporting goods stores. One-day nonresident licenses are $10. Fish are abundant in the Niagara River, and anglers can expect to encounter bass, perch, pike, salmon, sunfish, and trout. A complete list of fish species, licensing requirements, and angling tips are provided at the **New York State Department of Conservation** website (www.dec.ny.gov).

Winter Activities

All state parks in this area, including Whirlpool, Devil's Hole, Joseph Davis, and Fort Niagara, are accessible for **cross-country skiing** and **snowshoeing.** However, there are no local outfitters that rent this type of equipment, so visitors must bring their own. Niagara Falls State Park rents snowshoes for free at the Cave of the Winds (9am-3pm daily Jan.-Feb.).

ENTERTAINMENT AND EVENTS

Nightlife

The village of Lewiston has just 2,700 people, so some of the best nightlife consists of meandering along Center Street on a quiet evening, watching the sunset from a park bench along the riverbank, or eating an ice-cream cone near the water's edge. Nightlife here typically centers on a meal, with drinks from the bar. Few establishments focus on libations and music, which is ironic since many believe that the cocktail was invented here in the 1800s.

Local historians say Catherine Hustler, proprietor of Hustler's Tavern, invented the cocktail when she used the feather of a domestic bird (a cockerel) to stir a gin-based drink in the early 1800s. Although the Hustler Tavern is no more, it was the only building left undisturbed by the British when they burned the village in 1813. Legend has it that the redcoats couldn't bear to raze the tavern they had enjoyed so often before the war. Mrs. Hustler and her husband were quite the hosts, too: After they entertained author James Fenimore Cooper, he included them as fictional characters in one of his books.

One hub of activity after dark is **Brickyard Brewing Co.** (436 Center St., 716/754-7227, www.brickyardbrewingcompany.com, 4pm-10pm Mon.-Fri., 11am-11pm Sat., 10am-2pm and 4pm-9pm Sun.) The owners of the popular Brickyard Pub & BBQ in Lewiston decided to open a new brewpub, complete with a separate food menu, next door in 2017. The expansive two-floor brewery—Lewiston's first and only—draws a crowd most nights and features a dozen different beers made in-house on tap.

The Arts

The **Castellani Art Museum** (Niagara University, Lewiston, 716/286-8200, www.castellaniartmuseum.org, 11am-5pm Tues.-Sat., free) is on the Niagara University campus in Lewiston. It has more than 5,700 works of modern art by artists such as Picasso, Dalí, and Warhol.

Festivals and Events

SUMMER

In the summer, the **Lewiston Council on the Arts** (716/754-0166, www.artcouncil.org) sponsors free blues concerts in **Hennepin Park** at the gazebo (4th and Center Sts., Lewiston) at 7pm on Mondays. If you need to cheer up after the blues, come back on Wednesdays to hear the seven-piece Lewiston Jazz Project—also at 7pm and free.

In August, the **Lewiston Art Festival** (716/754-0166, www.artcouncil.org, free) draws more than 175 artists who display more than 20,000 pieces of art. The festival is so large that Center Street is closed to traffic from 4th to 8th Streets for the weekend. Look for a visitors booth at 5th and Center Streets for information on exhibitors.

The last weekend of August brings the **Lewiston Jazz Festival** (www.lewistonjazz.com) to Center Street. This is Western New York's largest outdoor jazz festival, a two-day event that draws 30,000 attendees to more than 30 performances, food and wine demonstrations and more.

FALL

Held in early September, the **Niagara County Peach Festival** (www.lewistonpeachfestival.org, free) is the largest festival in the county, with amusement rides, a parade, and cooking contests. During the three-day fest, various peach confections can be purchased, a Peach Queen is crowned, and judges inspect the chins of young men to find the best peach fuzz. There is also live music and a shuttle bus service.

Lewiston's **Marble Orchard Ghost Walks** (476 Center St., www.artcouncil.org., 7pm Sat. Sept.-Oct., $15) are a real scream! Local actors present the ghoulish past of Lewiston's former residents inside the Marble Orchard cemetery. A costumed guide leads you through this family-friendly walk recounting the burning of Lewiston, mysteries of the Underground Railroad, and other events, such as the disappearance of the man who threatened to reveal the secret rituals of the Freemasons.

FOOD

Lewiston

The **Silo Restaurant** (115 N. Water St., 716/754-9680, www.lewistonsilo.com, 10am-10pm daily May-Sept., $11) is a local institution and a place to take the family for hot dogs, hamburgers, and a view of the Niagara River. Set in a renovated coal silo, this family restaurant is famous for the "haystack," which is rib-eye steak with melted mozzarella and toasted hash browns served on a large roll.

Just down the waterfront from the Silo Restaurant is **Water Street Landing** (115 S. Water St., 716/754-9200, www.waterstreetlanding.com, 11:30am-9pm Mon.-Fri., 10am-11pm Sat.-Sun., $30), known for its waterfront view and ambience. The dining room is quiet and a bit formal, while the patio and pub are relaxed but busier. The food and service are generally better in the dining room. Try the crab cakes rémoulade appetizer for a tasty treat.

Carmelos (425 Center St., 716/754-2311, www.carmelos-restaurant.com, 5pm-9pm Tues.-Thurs., 5pm-9:30pm Fri.-Sat., $25) is regarded as the best restaurant in the village. This intimate neighborhood eatery serves excellent Italian and modern American fare. The menu changes frequently because the chef uses locally grown, seasonal ingredients. You'll enjoy world-class food at local prices here.

Hibbard's Custard (105 Portage Rd., 716/754-4218, www.hibbardscustard.com, 11am-8pm Sun.-Thurs., 11am-9pm Fri.-Sat., spring-fall) has been delighting Lewiston with frozen treats since 1939. This is some of the richest, creamiest custard in existence, served in a variety of flavors. Hibbard's uses considerably less air than average when producing its custard fresh on-site each day, resulting in a denser product that needs to be scooped instead of twisted out of a machine.

Youngstown

The Youngstown **Village Diner** (425 Main St., 716/745-9858, www.youngstownvillagediner.com, 6am-8pm Mon.-Thurs., 6am-2pm Fri.-Sat., 6am-1:30pm Sun.) has become an institution over its two decades of operation. The diner is known for its nightly specials—from liver and onions on Tuesday to fish fries on Wednesday, Thursday, and Friday—as well as hand-pressed burgers, a "kickin' chicken" corn chowder, and a menu of other items made in-house.

In the heart of Youngstown is one of the longest-running businesses in Western New York, **The Ontario House** (358 Main St., 716/219-4073, 11am-3am daily), also known as "The Stone Jug" because the roof of the stone building looks like a jug from its side. This tavern has been in continuous operation since 1842, back to when army officials visiting nearby Old Fort Niagara would stay in rooms over the bar, according to its owners. The current wooden bar and beer coolers date from the 1930s, and much of the village seems to congregate here on weeknights for $2 Labatt Blue Light drafts during happy hour. The tavern also features a limited food menu—the chicken fingers have gained a devoted following—and the owners restored the former inn upstairs into Airbnb rentals.

ACCOMMODATIONS

Lewiston

The **Niagara Crossing Hotel and Spa** (100 Center St., 716/754-9070, www.niagaracrossinghotelandspa.com, $200) has an unbeatable waterfront view. Built in 2005, the hotel has both the charm of a historic country inn and the amenities of a modern luxury boutique hotel. All 78 rooms feature fireplaces, and some include whirlpool tubs and balconies that overlook the Niagara River. River-view rooms cost more but are well worth the extra expense. Request one of the corner suites on the third and fourth floors. The spa service is exquisite; try the Queen or King for an Hour spa package for a treat. The main drag of Lewiston is just a few minutes' walk uphill.

Brickhaus Inn (860 Onondaga St., Lewiston, 716/754-7936, www.brickhausinn.com, $129) is a great getaway spot for those looking for privacy. The owner's pride is apparent in the furnishings and rooms; after all, her grandfather built the stately home in 1940. Enjoy a peaceful evening in the backyard while savoring some wine at the pond. Breakfast is not provided, but you have full run of a kitchenette should you want to prepare your own meals. The inn is located in a quiet residential area a few minutes' drive from the waterfront, Artpark, and Center Street.

Youngstown

Would you like a room, a cabin, or an entire cottage? You'll find all three at the **Lakeview Motel and Cottages** (2000 Lake Rd., 716/791-8668, www.lakeviewmotelandcottage.com, Mar.-Nov., $95-195). The motel room, cabin, and cottage rates are all reasonable, and the property is close to Lake Ontario.

INFORMATION AND SERVICES

A handy source of information is the **Niagara River Region Chamber of Commerce Welcome Center** (895 Center St., Lewiston, 716/754-9500, www.niagarariverregion.com, 8:30am-4:30pm Mon.-Fri.). The **post office** (150 S. 8th St., Lewiston, 716/754-8000) is one block south of Center Street.

There is a **Tops supermarket** (906 Center St., Lewiston, 716/215-1350, www.topsmarkets.com, 5am-1am daily) and a **CVS Pharmacy** (795 Center St., Lewiston, 716/754-2370, www.cvs.com, 9am-9pm daily) along the main street in the village.

In Youngstown, there is a **Rite Aid pharmacy** (214 Lockport Rd., 716/745-3313). **Key Bank** (493 Center St., 716/405-5089) has a 24-hour ATM.

GETTING THERE AND AROUND

Reaching Lewiston and Youngstown from Niagara Falls is easy on the free **Discover Niagara Shuttle** (www.discoverniagarashuttle.com). The service operates from May to October and connects more than a dozen attractions and points of interest in Niagara County, from the Niagara USA Visitor Center in downtown Niagara Falls to Old Fort Niagara. The shuttle buses run every 35-40 minutes 9am-6pm daily, with additional service every 45-60 minutes 6pm-midnight on Fridays and Saturdays. Visit the website to download the Discover Niagara Shuttle app, which provides real-time schedule information and a list of stops including eight locations in Lewiston and Youngstown.

Lewiston

The municipal **bus service** (www.metro.nfta.com) connects Lewiston to the city of Niagara Falls, via Route 50. The fare for the 50-minute ride is $2 each way. There are several bus stops along the main thoroughfare, Center Street.

Most visitors drive, accessing the village via I-190, exit 25B. Those traveling from Niagara Falls can take the more scenic Robert Moses Parkway that winds along the gorge rim, a trip of about 20 minutes.

Once in Lewiston, you'll find the main thoroughfare, Center Street, very walkable, with most attractions along a 0.5-mile (0.8-km) stretch. There is ample parking at both the east end (at the Tops supermarket) and west end (Water Street municipal parking lot) of Center Street. During winter (Dec.-Mar.), street parking is not allowed 3am-6am to facilitate snow removal.

Youngstown

There are no municipal or commercial buses that serve Youngstown, so most visitors arrive in the village by car. The 14-mile (22.5-km), 25-minute trip from Niagara Falls is scenic, especially if you take Robert Moses Parkway, exiting at Route 93 (Lockport Rd.), the last exit before entering the state park at Old Fort Niagara.

Street parking is always available in Youngstown. The fort is more than 1 mile (1.6 km) away from the village, so it's best to drive to the fort and park there. Old Fort Niagara includes a sprawling park, and you'll do a lot of walking within the complex.

Buffalo

Architectural restorations, entrepreneurial immigrants, millennial enthusiasm, and economic innovation have provided new wings to Buffalo, New York's second-largest city. Buffalo's redeveloped waterfront restored architectural gems, and reinvigorated neighborhoods—filled with new hotels, restaurants, breweries, and public art—have turned the city into one of America's most exciting examples of urban transformation.

The city's historic role as an economic powerhouse provided it with an outstanding collection of turn-of-the-20th-century architecture that weaves its way into every visitor's experience today. Buffalo is a living architectural museum, boasting buildings designed by great American architects including Frank Lloyd Wright, Louis Sullivan, Henry

Highlights

Look for ★ to find recommended sights, activities, dining, and lodging.

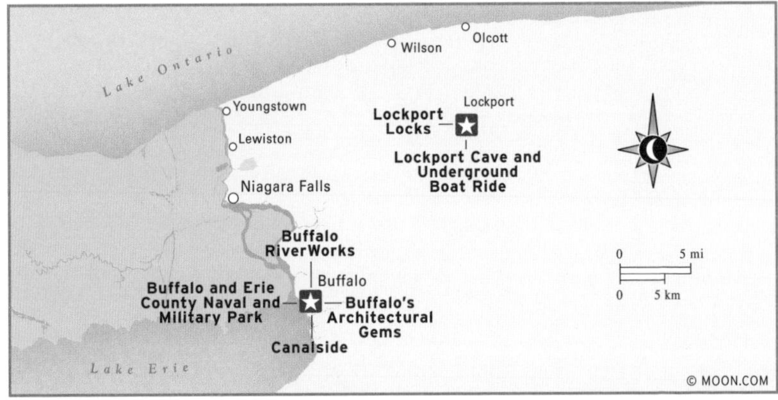

★ **See stunning architecture:** View the works of great American architects, such as Louis Sullivan, Robert Upjohn, Daniel Burnham, H. H. Richardson, and Frank Lloyd Wright (page 101).

★ **Wander Canalside:** This vibrant cultural space has emerged as the epicenter of Buffalo's renaissance (page 104).

★ **Tour Buffalo and Erie County Naval and Military Park:** Experience the dramatic stories of war veterans while touring decommissioned Navy vessels moored in the nation's largest inland naval park (page 106).

★ **Experience Buffalo RiverWorks:** This massive entertainment complex on the Buffalo River includes a brewery, water sports rentals, grain silo tours, boat docks, and a restaurant (page 107).

★ **See the Lockport Locks:** These ingenious gateways take you on a gentle journey back to the time when the Erie Canal was the country's first superhighway (page 128).

★ **Take an underground boat ride:** Explore subterranean industrial history in **Lockport Cave** while enjoying the longest underground boat ride in the United States (page 129).

Charlotte Community Library
Charlotte MI 48813

Hobson (H. H.) Richardson, and Edward Brodhead Green. Many of these buildings have been restored or adapted for new and creative uses, from a former asylum turned into a hotel, to grain silos that have become a rock climbing wall and zip-lining course.

Today the quickly developing waterfront, once a slumbering giant, is now awakening, offering year-round activities from historic boat tours and stand-up paddle-boarding in the summer to ice biking and curling each winter. While residents embrace the cold winter, they welcome the warmth of the spring, summer, and fall with festivals and events every weekend.

Residents call this area Buffalo-Niagara because Buffalo and Niagara County are perfect neighbors, offering a dual city and country experience. The fertile lands of Niagara County are ideal for growing many fruits and produce interesting and distinctive wines. The area's 20 wineries are known for the variety of their vintages, from fruit wines to an obscure favorite that tastes like a Tootsie Roll.

The glory days of the Erie Canal are still alive here, where you can voyage back in time with a canal boat ride. This area is also known for its role as the last stop on the Underground Railroad, the route for fugitive enslaved people who found permanent freedom across the water in Canada.

HISTORY

History buffs refer to the region's past in two distinct eras—Before Canal (BC) and After Digging (AD). The Erie Canal opened in 1825 and fundamentally changed every aspect of life for those living in this area.

At the start of the War of 1812, Buffalo was a village of approximately 500 people. During the war, it grew because of its proximity to Canada. The United States sent troops to the region to fight along the Niagara frontier. In December 1813, British troops and their Mohawk Indian allies burned Buffalo and Niagara Falls, New York, to the ground as the violence escalated to include attacks on civilians. Following the end of hostilities in 1814, Buffalo was rebuilt and enjoyed moderate growth.

Completed in 1825, the Erie Canal was merely 40 feet (12 m) wide and 4 feet (1.2 m) deep, with a speed limit of 4 miles per hour (6.4 kph). This was the country's first superhighway. As the terminus of this highway, Buffalo became the crossroads of the nation. Immigrants heading west and natural resources being sent east stopped in Buffalo. Some immigrants stayed, swelling the German, Irish, Polish, and Italian working-class communities that fed the city's insatiable demand for labor. Ships had to be loaded and grain elevators filled. Manufacturers needed people with strong backs and even stronger constitutions to meet the requirements of a growing country.

Burgeoning commerce yielded wealth and influence. By the turn of the 20th century, two of Buffalo's sons, Millard Fillmore and Grover Cleveland, had occupied the White House. By the 1930s, railroads were the norm in transportation and reduced the importance of the Erie Canal. The region kept growing, though, as manufacturers such as Ford, Chevrolet, Bethlehem Steel, Allied Chemical, Carborundum, DuPont, and Dunlop Tire expanded. However, forces outside of Buffalo's control conspired to strangle the region's manufacturing and transshipment fortunes. The opening of the St. Lawrence Seaway in 1959 and the ever-expanding Welland Canal allowed most shipping to bypass Buffalo. Thousands of jobs were lost as manufacturers throughout the Northeast ceased production or moved to areas with lower taxes and less regulation.

Today Buffalo's fortunes are beginning to reverse, as various sectors, including government, banking, and healthcare, are employing the region's capable and well-educated

Previous: skyline of Buffalo, New York; the Colored Musicians Club; the Erie Canal in Lockport.

Buffalo

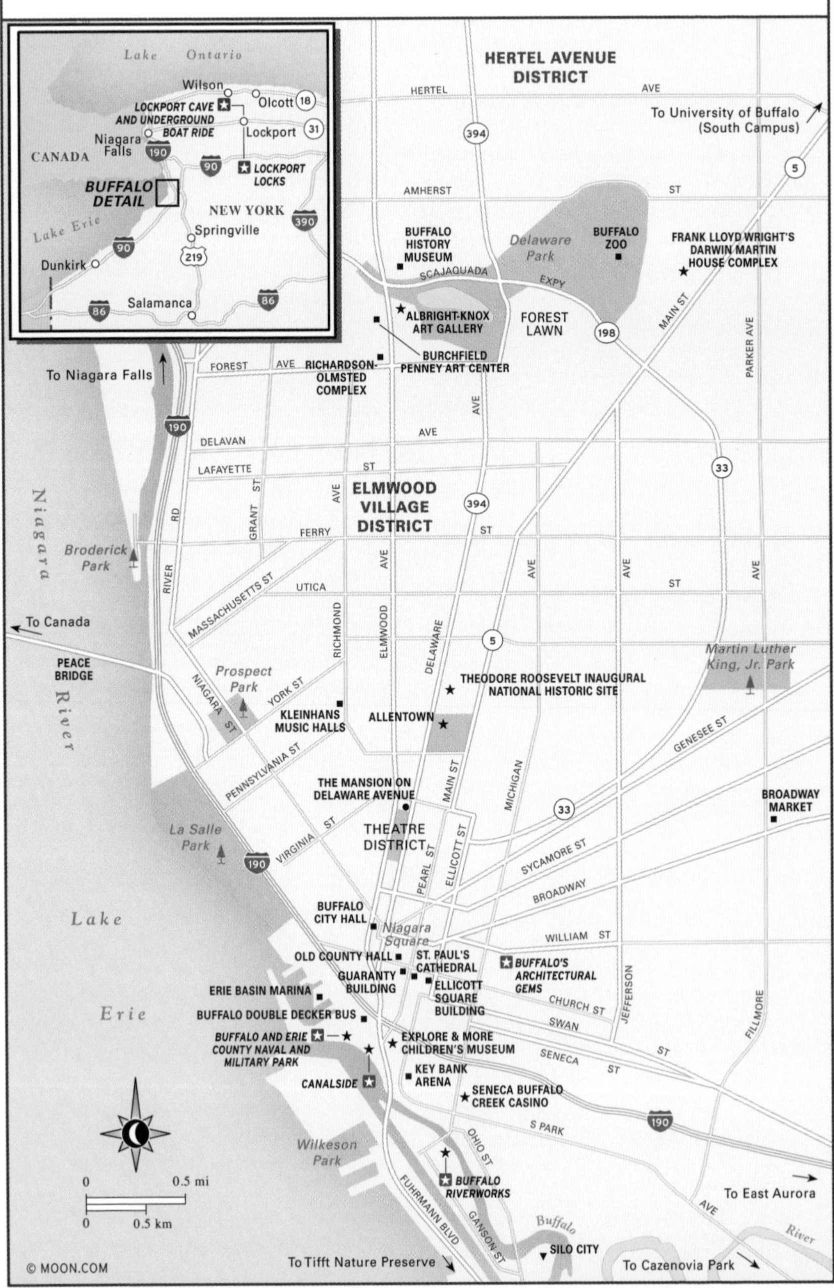

Lake Ontario
Wilson
Olcott
18
LOCKPORT CAVE AND UNDERGROUND BOAT RIDE
Lockport
31
Niagara Falls
CANADA
190
90
LOCKPORT LOCKS
BUFFALO DETAIL
NEW YORK
390
Lake Erie
Springville
90
219
Dunkirk
Salamanca
86
HERTEL AVENUE DISTRICT
HERTEL AVE
To University of Buffalo (South Campus)
394
5
AMHERST ST
BUFFALO HISTORY MUSEUM
Delaware Park
BUFFALO ZOO
FRANK LLOYD WRIGHT'S DARWIN MARTIN HOUSE COMPLEX
SCAJAQUADA EXPY
ALBRIGHT-KNOX ART GALLERY
FOREST LAWN
198
MAIN ST
PARKER AVE
BURCHFIELD PENNEY ART CENTER
FOREST AVE
RICHARDSON-OLMSTED COMPLEX
To Niagara Falls
DELAVAN AVE
LAFAYETTE ST
33
ELMWOOD VILLAGE DISTRICT
Niagara River
RD
GRANT ST
FERRY ST
Broderick Park
RIVER
MASSACHUSETTS ST
UTICA ST
RICHMOND
ELMWOOD AVE
DELAWARE AVE
To Canada
PEACE BRIDGE
Martin Luther King, Jr. Park
THEODORE ROOSEVELT INAUGURAL NATIONAL HISTORIC SITE
Prospect Park
YORK ST
NIAGARA ST
KLEINHANS MUSIC HALLS
ALLENTOWN
GENESEE ST
PENNSYLVANIA ST
THE MANSION ON DELAWARE AVENUE
MAIN ST
MICHIGAN
BROADWAY MARKET
La Salle Park
VIRGINIA ST
THEATRE DISTRICT
ELLICOTT ST
PEARL ST
SYCAMORE ST
BROADWAY
Lake Erie
BUFFALO CITY HALL
Niagara Square
WILLIAM ST
OLD COUNTY HALL
ST. PAUL'S CATHEDRAL
BUFFALO'S ARCHITECTURAL GEMS
GUARANTY BUILDING
ELLICOTT SQUARE BUILDING
ERIE BASIN MARINA
CHURCH ST
JEFFERSON
BUFFALO DOUBLE DECKER BUS
SWAN
FILLMORE
BUFFALO AND ERIE COUNTY NAVAL AND MILITARY PARK
EXPLORE & MORE CHILDREN'S MUSEUM
SENECA ST
KEY BANK ARENA
CANALSIDE
SENECA BUFFALO CREEK CASINO
S PARK
Wilkeson Park
OHIO ST
BUFFALO RIVERWORKS
0 0.5 mi
0 0.5 km
To East Aurora
AVE
FUHRMANN BLVD
GANSON ST
Buffalo River
SILO CITY
© MOON.COM
To Tifft Nature Preserve
To Cazenovia Park

workforce. Following years of inactivity, Buffalo's waterfront, Canalside, has emerged as a new entertainment center for the region. Entrepreneurs and preservationists have joined forces to save and renovate landmarks, creating new spaces for living and entertaining. The region is capitalizing on its organic strengths—world-class architecture, a beautiful waterfront, and proximity to Canada—to reclaim its place as Queen City of the Great Lakes.

PLANNING YOUR TIME

Buffalo and Niagara County, its northern neighbor, can be explored in two days by focusing one day on Buffalo and another day on Niagara County's attractions. Make Buffalo your base for travel. It has the greatest concentration of lodgings in the downtown area, including hostels, boutique hotels, and well-known chain establishments. There is a concentration of attractions on the waterfront that you can easily walk to from downtown Buffalo, while Allentown and the Elmwood Village, two walkable neighborhoods filled with dining and shopping options, are also in close proximity.

From Lockport in Niagara County, you can access the winery region by going west or east. Part of your route should include the shore of Lake Ontario, the northern edge of Niagara County.

Sights

TOP EXPERIENCE

★ ARCHITECTURAL GEMS

Buffalo has been called a living architectural museum. The city's grand buildings represent many of the masters of American architecture, including Louis Sullivan, Frank Lloyd Wright, H. H. Richardson, and Daniel Burnham. Many of these landmarks were built during Buffalo's meteoric rise in wealth following the completion of the Erie Canal. The city's extraordinary built environment serves as part of most visitors' experience, whether they stay overnight in a building converted to a boutique hotel or see a show, grab a bite to eat, or even play on the waterfront, in the shadow of Buffalo's repurposed concrete grain silos.

Guaranty Building

Louis Sullivan's **Guaranty Building** (140 Pearl St., 716/854-0003, www.hodgsonruss.com/Louis-Sullivans-Guaranty-Building.html, 8:30am-5pm Mon.-Fri.) may be the most prominent jewel in Buffalo's architectural crown. Completed in 1896, it was officially registered as a national landmark in 1975 and is now an office for a law firm. Sullivan is considered the creator of the skyscraper. The 13-story building was an aggressive use of technology and design for its day.

The Guaranty Building is all about verticality and features beautiful lines and a terra-cotta tile exterior. Situated on the corner of Church and Pearl Streets, the building is best appreciated from a distance before examining it up close. Prepare to stretch your neck as you gaze upward to behold this monument. Notice the intricate designs covering the exterior—Sullivan utilized the ornamental beauty of terra-cotta to decorate the building with designs of flowers and trees. If you visit during the week, enter the atrium to see the interior at the reception area, then learn about the history and design of the building through a free interpretive center on the first floor. The friendly guards at the reception desk are happy to answer questions about the building. Preservation Buffalo Niagara offers regular tours of the Guaranty Building; visit preservationbuffaloniagara.org for dates and times.

Downtown Buffalo

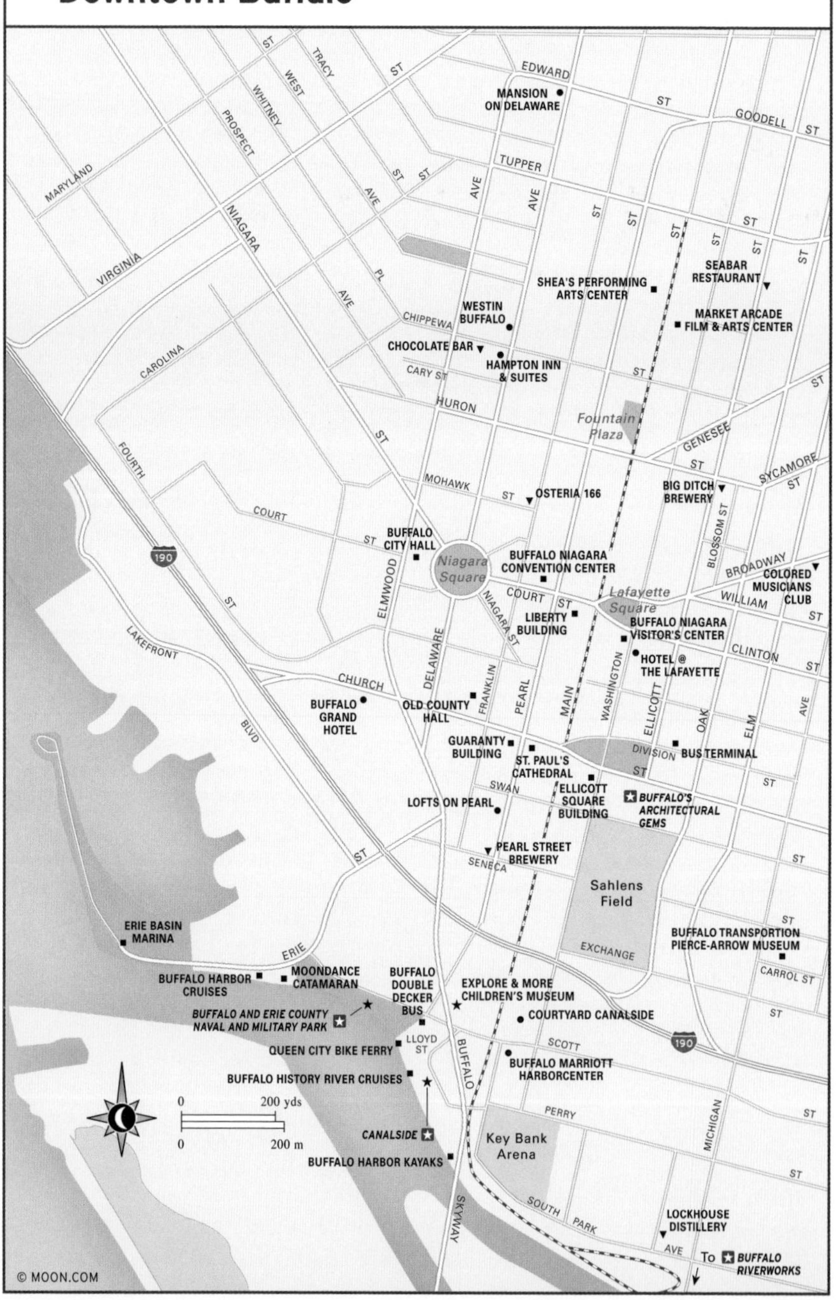
MANSION ON DELAWARE
SHEA'S PERFORMING ARTS CENTER
SEABAR RESTAURANT
MARKET ARCADE FILM & ARTS CENTER
WESTIN BUFFALO
CHOCOLATE BAR
HAMPTON INN & SUITES
Fountain Plaza
OSTERIA 166
BIG DITCH BREWERY
BUFFALO CITY HALL
Niagara Square
BUFFALO NIAGARA CONVENTION CENTER
Lafayette Square
COLORED MUSICIANS CLUB
LIBERTY BUILDING
BUFFALO NIAGARA VISITOR'S CENTER
HOTEL @ THE LAFAYETTE
BUFFALO GRAND HOTEL
OLD COUNTY HALL
GUARANTY BUILDING
ST. PAUL'S CATHEDRAL
BUS TERMINAL
ELLICOTT SQUARE BUILDING
BUFFALO'S ARCHITECTURAL GEMS
LOFTS ON PEARL
PEARL STREET BREWERY
Sahlens Field
ERIE BASIN MARINA
BUFFALO TRANSPORTION PIERCE-ARROW MUSEUM
BUFFALO HARBOR CRUISES
MOONDANCE CATAMARAN
BUFFALO DOUBLE DECKER BUS
EXPLORE & MORE CHILDREN'S MUSEUM
BUFFALO AND ERIE COUNTY NAVAL AND MILITARY PARK
COURTYARD CANALSIDE
QUEEN CITY BIKE FERRY
BUFFALO MARRIOTT HARBORCENTER
BUFFALO HISTORY RIVER CRUISES
CANALSIDE
Key Bank Arena
BUFFALO HARBOR KAYAKS
LOCKHOUSE DISTILLERY
To BUFFALO RIVERWORKS
EDWARD ST
GOODELL ST
TUPPER
MARYLAND
VIRGINIA
NIAGARA ST
PROSPECT AVE
WHITNEY PL
WEST AVE
TRACY ST
CHIPPEWA
CARY ST
HURON
CAROLINA
FOURTH
GENESEE
SYCAMORE ST
MOHAWK ST
COURT ST
BROADWAY
WILLIAM ST
CLINTON ST
CHURCH
ELMWOOD
DELAWARE
FRANKLIN
PEARL
MAIN
WASHINGTON
ELLICOTT
OAK
ELM
BLOSSOM ST
DIVISION ST
SWAN
SENECA
LAKEFRONT BLVD
ERIE
EXCHANGE
CARROL ST
LLOYD ST
SCOTT
BUFFALO SKYWAY
PERRY
MICHIGAN
SOUTH PARK AVE
190
0 200 yds
0 200 m
© MOON.COM

St. Paul's Episcopal Cathedral

Directly across from the Guaranty Building, **St. Paul's Episcopal Cathedral** (128 Pearl St., 716/855-0900, www.stpaulscathedral.org) occupies an unusual triangular plot of land. This Gothic revival cathedral was consecrated in 1851. It's the work of renowned architect Richard Upjohn, considered America's foremost builder of Gothic-style churches. Due to its triangular lot, St. Paul's could not be built in the traditional cruciform style, in which the main aisles of the church form a cross. The magnificent church houses three pipe organs and a Tiffany stained-glass window on the northeast side of the structure.

Old County Hall

One block away from St. Paul's stands the impressive structure known as **Old County Hall** (92 Franklin St., 8am-5pm Mon.-Fri.). Built atop one of the city's first cemeteries, this Romanesque-style building was completed in 1876 and is guarded by an imposing statue of George Washington, adorned in a Freemason's smock. This was Buffalo's city hall until the current City Hall was completed in the early 1930s. High atop the clock tower stand four statues representing Mechanical Arts, Justice, Agriculture, and Commerce. It is rumored that Buffalo's mayor at the time requested that his wife's face be used as a model for the visage of each statue.

Inside you'll find signage commemorating this building as the place where President McKinley lay in state as thousands paid their respects following the president's assassination in Buffalo in 1901. There's also a plaque on the first-floor courtroom where McKinley's assassin was tried and found guilty. The structure is an office building that houses state courts, so you'll need to pass through metal detectors to enjoy the interior spaces.

City Hall

Buffalo's **City Hall** (65 Niagara Sq., 8:30am-4:30pm Mon.-Fri.) is the centerpiece of the downtown skyline. Designed by architect John Wade, and constructed between 1929 and 1931 to coincide with Buffalo's centennial, this art deco masterpiece filled with intricate detail and ornamentation offers a couple of can't-miss visitor experiences. Preservation Buffalo Niagara leads a free tour of the building from its expansive lobby every weekday at noon, including stops at the elaborate Common Council chambers and inside the mayor's office. The tour concludes at the building's 28th-floor free observation deck, which is open on weekdays and has sweeping views of the city, Lake Erie, and, on a clear day, Niagara Falls.

Frank Lloyd Wright Architecture

DARWIN MARTIN HOUSE COMPLEX

The **Darwin Martin House Complex** (125 Jewett Pkwy., 716/856-3858, www.martinhouse.org) is considered by many scholars to be Frank Lloyd Wright's best work in the Prairie style. The Martin House design features long, horizontal exterior lines, cantilevered roofs, wide eaves, and flowing interior spaces free of walls. Wright referred to this structure as his "opus" and wrote that the Martin House was "a well-nigh perfect composition." In 2019, the Martin House completed a 25-year, $52 million restoration project, one of the most ambitious of its kind in the United States, allowing visitors to experience Wright's genius just as its first occupants did in 1907.

The estate comprises several structures, including three residences, a 100-foot-long (30.5-m-long) pergola, a conservatory, and a stable, as well as a visitors welcome center and a small café. The only way to explore the interior of the house is by joining a **docent-led tour** (Wed.-Mon., $22-45). Purchase your tickets in advance, as tours frequently sell out, especially in the summer.

The Martin House Complex is in a residential neighborhood; free street parking is available on Jewett Parkway as well as nearby Woodward and Summit Avenues, but pay attention to alternate parking rules.

Photography is strictly prohibited inside complex buildings except on designated photography tours offered each month ($55).

OTHER FRANK LLOYD WRIGHT DESIGNS

Buffalo has several other examples of Wright's genius, including the posthumously designed **Fontana Boat House** (1 Rotary Row, 716/362-3140, www.wrightsboathouse.org, tours by appointment), **Blue Sky Mausoleum** (Forest Lawn Cemetery, 1411 Delaware Ave., 716/885-1600, www.blueskymausoleum.com, daily, free), and a **filling station** (Pierce Arrow Museum, 263 Michigan Ave., 716/853-0084, www.pierce-arrow.com, $10 adults, $5 children) that have been constructed to the architect's specifications. There is also the lakeside **Graycliff Estate** (6472 Old Lake Shore Rd, Derby, 716/947-9217, https://experiencegraycliff.org, tours by appointment), a summer home on the Lake Erie shoreline, 30 minutes south of Buffalo in Derby. See them all on the **All Wright All Day Tour** (offered seasonally 8:30am-5:15pm Fri.-Sat. and Mon., $160).

Richardson Olmsted Campus

The **Richardson Olmsted Campus** (444 Forest Ave., 716/601-1150, www.richardson-olmsted.com, daily, free), a former state asylum built in stunning Romanesque revival style, was the largest commission for architect H. H. Richardson. The park-like grounds and farmland surrounding the hospital were designed by Frederick Law Olmsted, who also designed Buffalo's park system and Niagara Falls State Park. The building's recent reinvention into an 88-room hotel and restaurant make it one of the most inspiring examples of Buffalo's transformation.

When development of the Buffalo State Asylum for the Insane began in 1870, the complex was a state-of-the-art facility that reflected a new doctrine in treating mental illness. The buildings became the embodiment of Dr. Thomas Kirkbride's therapy methods, which favored a holistic approach to rehabilitation. Richardson designed a hospital that divided patients by severity of illness, while allowing them access to sunlight, ventilation, and outdoor recreation.

Over 20 years, 11 imposing buildings sprang up on the complex's 200 acres. The iconic main building features Gothic towers. Over the years that followed, the campus was divided and developed. Some buildings were knocked down, and others were abandoned.

Today the focus is on preserving and restoring the campus. The opening of the 88-room Hotel Henry Urban Resort and Conference Center in 2017 within the campus's central three buildings marked the first phase of its transformation. The hotel's spacious rooms, flooded with natural light, and its restaurant, 100 Acres: The Kitchens at Hotel Henry, honor much of the National Historic Landmark's original design while also incorporating a host of modern amenities.

Undeveloped portions of the former asylum are only accessible to visitors via seasonal **guided tours** (www.richardson-olmsted.com, May-Sept., $10 and up). Twilight tours accentuate the ambience of the complex, with its distinctive architecture. Indoor photography is not allowed unless you are on a special tour designated for photographers. The tour of the undeveloped buildings provides a stark contrast to the hotel, underscoring the amazing work that went into phase one of the campus's redevelopment. The campus's parking lot and main entrance are on its north side, reachable via the intersection of Rockwell Road and Cleveland Circle.

TOP EXPERIENCE

★ CANALSIDE

After languishing for many years, Buffalo's waterfront is now the hub of the city's transformation, and nowhere is that redevelopment more apparent than the public space known as **Canalside** (716/574-1537, www.

1: Louis Sullivan's Guaranty Building **2:** USS *Little Rock* at Buffalo and Erie County Naval and Military Park

1

2

Last Stop on the Underground Railroad

Prior to the Civil War, Buffalo was a hotbed for abolitionist sentiment, and the city's proximity to Canada made it an important stop on the Underground Railroad. Historians have noted that Buffalo differed from other locales that helped enslaved people find freedom. Buffalo's tolerance and support of abolition fostered an environment where those fleeing slavery could move about relatively freely.

When bounty hunters would arrive in Buffalo, people escaping enslavement found shelter inside the **Michigan Street Baptist Church** (511 Michigan Ave., 716/837-3226, call ahead to arrange an informal tour), hiding in secret spaces. Visitors can view these secret spots in the loft of the church, above the choir, as well as in a recess hidden underneath what appears to be a stairwell. In the basement of the church, a modest interpretive center has artifacts and general information on the Underground Railroad. Tours are free, but donations are welcome.

The last stop on U.S. soil for enslaved people escaping through Buffalo was **Broderick Park** (west end of Ferry St.), along the Niagara River in the shadow of the Peace Bridge. Enslaved people traveled in secrecy on foot for months to reach this spot—a short boat ride to Canada, then freedom. This island park includes an amphitheater and signage that tell the compelling story of these freedom-seeking people.

buffalowaterfront.com, 24 hours daily, free). Canalside includes the Central Wharf, a boardwalk lining the Buffalo River, and the unearthed and restored **Commercial Slip,** the original terminus of the Erie Canal. Throughout the area's 21 waterfront acres, interpretive signs explain the history of the area, shedding light on the canal's role in commerce, technology, labor, and the Underground Railroad.

Open year-round, Canalside is most active June-August, when there are daily entertainment events, most of which are free. Entertainment includes music acts, historical tours, family games, group exercise classes, and street performances. Kayak rentals, historic boat tours, and other opportunities to get out on the water can be found at kiosks lining the boardwalk. Near the original Erie Canal terminus is a historic replica of the Canal, which freezes over each winter and becomes the **Ice at Canalside** (Nov.-Mar.), a 32,000-square-foot skating rink that's one of the largest in the Northeast. Curling, skating, ice bumper cars, and ice bowling are all available, but the Ice at Canalside's highlight may be the **Ice Bikes of Buffalo** (www.waterbikesofbuffalo.com/ice-bikes). This made-in-Buffalo creation features a stainless steel frame with blades, allowing customers to glide and pedal seamlessly along the ice, regardless of skill and experience.

★ Buffalo and Erie County Naval and Military Park

Just north of the Central Wharf at Canalside is the **Buffalo and Erie County Naval and Military Park** (1 Naval Park Cove, 716/847-1773, www.buffalonavalpark.org, 10am-5pm daily Apr.-Sept., 10am-4 pm daily Oct., 10am-4 pm weekends in Nov., $15 adults, $12 seniors, $9 children 5-12). This impressive waterfront campus is a living museum dedicated to all branches of the U.S. military. Three decommissioned U.S. naval ships dominate the park: a guided missile cruiser, USS *Little Rock;* a destroyer, USS *The Sullivans;* and a submarine, USS *Croaker.* All are open for tours. Use caution when navigating inside these great ships—stairwells are steep, bulkhead openings are shin-knockers, and there are low clearances.

Dockside, there is a museum and an outdoor collection of decommissioned tanks, jets, and helicopters that saw action in conflicts from World War II to Vietnam. Also on the park grounds, a peaceful area for reflection has monuments to soldiers who saw action in Korea, Iraq, Afghanistan, and other conflicts.

Plan on at least two hours to tour the ships, museum, and grounds. Chat up some of the volunteer military veteran tour guides stationed throughout the naval park. Their stories bring to life the sacrifices, hardships, and camaraderie of the men and women who join the armed services.

EXPLORE & MORE: THE RALPH C. WILSON JR. CHILDREN'S MUSEUM

In 2019, **Explore & More: The Ralph C. Wilson Jr. Children's Museum** (130 Main St., 716/655-5131, www.exploreandmore.org, 10am-4pm Mon. and Wed.-Fri., 9am-5pm Sat., 11am-5pm Sun., $11, free for babies under 1) found a new state-of-the-art, 43,000-square-foot home in Canalside. The museum's interactive exhibits, designed for children up to 12 years old, center around the region's history, geography, sports scene, architecture, and agriculture. Marvel at the museum's two-story waterfall, which cascades into an exhibit about canals and waterways, or inspire your child to become the next Frank Lloyd Wright or Louis Sullivan at the Building Buffalo architecture exhibit. Imagination knows no bounds at this waterfront gem. Inexpensive parking can be found nearby inside the garage at HarborCenter, 100 Washington Street.

GRAIN ELEVATORS

The **grain elevators** of Buffalo's waterfront, located along the Buffalo River upstream from Canalside, are often referred to as a concrete Atlantis. These sturdy commercial cathedrals were a part of this nation's breadbasket, with Buffalo transshipping more grain than any other U.S. port. Prior to the grain elevators, loading and unloading grain was a labor-intensive task, that relied on thousands of mostly immigrant workers, many of them Irish. Buffalo merchant Joseph Dart is credited with pioneering the world's first grain elevator in 1842, a steam-powered device that employed a giant belt with metal buckets to transfer grain from a ship's cargo hold to the top of a grain silo. In one hour, the elevator was able to transfer as much grain as laborers could transfer in an entire day.

By 1900, more than 52 grain elevators abutted Buffalo's waterfront. Many of these wooden silos burned down due to the combustible nature of grain dust. Today more than a dozen concrete-reinforced elevators remain, one of the largest such collections in the world. A few remain commercially active, including those at the city's waterfront General Mills plant, which since 1941 has produced the signature aroma of Cheerios that often wafts through downtown. Many are cavernous, quiet giants: sentinels from a time when Buffalo was the sixth-busiest port in the world.

In recent years, some grain elevator owners along "Elevator Alley"—the section of the Buffalo River lined with these structures—have taken the bold step of reimagining some of them into an outdoor recreation destination, brewery, beer garden, and hub for artistic performances. The reinvention of these distinctive structures has been one of the most exciting developments in Buffalo's transformation, an opportunity to take once-blighted properties that were a reminder of Buffalo's faded industrial past and turn them into an extraordinary experience for locals and visitors. Check them out at two properties along the Buffalo River: Buffalo RiverWorks and Silo City.

★ BUFFALO RIVERWORKS

At **Buffalo RiverWorks** (359 Ganson St., 716/342-2292, www.buffaloriverworks.com, 4pm-10pm Mon.-Wed., 11am-10pm Thurs. and Sun., 11am-midnight Fri.-Sat.), developers transformed a former grain silo and warehouse brownfield into a massive entertainment complex that has emerged since 2015 as the place to be on the waterfront. On any day in the summer, you'll find hundreds of guests who've arrived via car, bike, boat, or

The Fighting Sullivans

One of the most poignant stories told at the Buffalo and Erie County Naval and Military Park is the sad but inspiring story of the Sullivan brothers. In World War II, five brothers from a working-class Irish family in Waterloo, Iowa, joined the Navy to avenge the death of a friend who was killed during the attacks on Pearl Harbor.

The five Sullivan brothers—George, Francis, Joseph, Madison, and Albert— insisted that the Navy allow all of them to serve aboard the same ship and fight together. The Navy reluctantly agreed and stationed the brothers aboard the USS *Juneau*. In November 1942, the *Juneau* was sunk near the island of Guadalcanal in the South Pacific, and 687 sailors, including all the Sullivan brothers, perished.

Americans were outraged when the tragedy of the *Juneau*'s sinking and the deaths of the Sullivans were made public. The Navy named a new destroyer after the brothers, USS *The Sullivans*, with the motto "We Stick Together." The brother's mother christened it in 1943. Today, USS *The Sullivans* is one of three decommissioned Navy vessels docked at the **Buffalo and Erie County Naval and Military Park.**

on foot to enjoy food and drink indoors or outdoors along the waterfront.

Pull up an Adirondack chair and gather around a firepit after renting a kayak, paddleboard, or water bike. Scream your way across the world's first grain silo zip line, which launches from the top of one of the 100-foot-tall structures, or scale your way up RiverWorks' grain silo rock-climbing walls. Then kick back with a craft beer brewed onsite inside the silos. In the winter, ice-skating and curling are offered; in the summer, the ice rinks are home to backyard games, pickleball, and roller hockey. An on-site bar, restaurant, concert stage, and the home rink for the Queen City Roller Derby league round out Riverworks' offerings. The complex offers ample parking that's free except during occasional summer concerts and events.

SILO CITY

Just down the street from RiverWorks—but a world apart in other ways—is **Silo City** (85 Silo City Row, www.silo.city). Where RiverWorks has actively redeveloped the grain silos, Silo City has intentionally left the several structures on its property much as they have been for the last several decades: gritty and raw. These silos have become the canvas for a host of seasonal creative events, from monthly summer poetry readings by Just Buffalo Literary Center to an annual performance by Torn Space Theater Company to other concerts and art installations that make use of the incredible acoustics in the cavernous, hollow, 100-foot-tall structures.

Visitors can explore Silo City on a guided tour offered seasonally by **Explore Buffalo** (www.explorebuffalo.org), which offers a Silo City: Vertical tour for those looking to climb the structures' interiors, or a Silo City: Grounded tour for those who would prefer to remain on the silos' ground floor. **Buffalo River History Tours** (www.buffaloriverhistorytours.com) also offers a boat tour originating at Canalside that stops at Silo City. While access to the silos is otherwise restricted, visitors can enjoy the surrounding property year-round thanks to **Duende** (www.duendesilo.city, 3pm-10pm Wed.-Thurs., 3pm-midnight Fri.-Sat., noon-7pm Sun.), a bar and restaurant inside a former administration building that incorporated materials from the surrounding silos into its interior. The restaurant serves up cold pints, a host of small plates, and a steady schedule of live music.

Future plans for Silo City include artist lofts in some of the structures, the next step in the reinvention of one of the most extraordinary spaces to explore in all of Buffalo—and beyond.

ERIE BASIN MARINA

The **Erie Basin Marina** (329 Erie St., 716/851-6501, www.eriebasinmarina.org, 24 hours daily May-mid-Oct., free) is a wonderful place for a relaxing walk or romantic sunset. Downtown workers often dash out for a quick lunch or snack along the break wall. The marina's beautiful sunsets and cityscapes are best enjoyed by foot or bike. The road to the marina can become congested with vehicles, so park outside the marina; it's free.

Stroll through the gardens, where different flowers and plants are tested each year for their ability to survive Buffalo's climate. Walk to the end of the marina for a bird's-eye view of the waterfront from the lookout tower. From here it is easy to see where Lake Erie ends and the Niagara River begins its journey north eventually tumbling over the world-famous falls.

ALLENTOWN

Head north from downtown Buffalo, and you'll enter the bohemian district known as **Allentown** (www.allentown.org). The epicenter for the arts, live music, and gay culture, Allentown is bordered by Plymouth Avenue and North, Edward, and Main Streets.

The heart of Allentown is Allen Street. On weekends, the area is perfect for people-watching as hipsters, live-music lovers, bar-hoppers, and college students flow in and out of the numerous bars, restaurants, and cafés.

Allentown was one of the first and largest communities in the United States to earn recognition as a residential historic district, thanks to the well-preserved architectural gems on nearly every street. Within its modest borders are landscapes crafted by Frederick Law Olmsted and Calvert Vaux; a mansion designed by H. H. Richardson; a National Historic Landmark; and a National Historic Site. This small community has more architectural history than many cities. The district takes its name from Lewis Allen, who originally owned much of the land now known as Allentown. Mr. Allen was the uncle of President Grover Cleveland and was responsible for getting him his first job in a law firm.

Historic Architecture

Delaware Avenue is well worth a walk. Of the many notable mansions, highlights include **438 Delaware,** which was designed by H. H. Richardson for William Dorsheimer, a former lieutenant governor of New York.

Although the house where Samuel Clemmons (aka Mark Twain) lived at **472 Delaware** is gone, the carriage house remains. **The Midway** is a stretch of stunning row-style houses that comprise 471-499 Delaware Avenue. Among the jewels here is **477 Delaware,** a Georgian revival-style building donated to the Daughters of the American Revolution by wealthy socialite Katherine Pratt Horton.

Just as grand are the structures that line Symphony Circle, Porter and Richmond Avenues, and North and Pennsylvania Streets. Sprawling Victorian houses and impressive mansions ring Symphony Circle, which takes its name from the **Kleinhans Music Hall** (3 Symphony Circle, 716/883-3560, www.kleinhansbuffalo.org). The hall, completed in 1940 and considered acoustically perfect, was designed by the father-and-son architectural team of Eliel and Eero Saarinen.

Also here is the **First Presbyterian Church** (1 Symphony Circle, 716/884-7250, www.firstchurchbuffalo.org, 10am-3pm Tues.-Fri.), which houses the city's oldest congregation. The church's Romanesque style and towering 163-foot (50-m) steeple are reminiscent of the Richardson Olmsted Campus. Call for times that religious services are offered.

Theodore Roosevelt Inaugural Site

On the southern edge of Allentown is the **Theodore Roosevelt Inaugural Site** (641 Delaware Ave., 716/884-0095, www.trsite.org, 9am-5pm Mon.-Fri., noon-5pm Sat.-Sun., \$12 adults, \$9 seniors and students, \$7 children 6-18). In this house, the former Wilcox Mansion, Roosevelt took the presidential oath

2
3

4
Buffalo Double Decker
Bus Tours
Buffalo Double Decker Bus Tours
Sightseeing Tours • Murder Mysteries • Tavern Tours
www.BuffaloDoubleDeckerBus.com

in September 1901, following the assassination of President William McKinley at the Pan-American Exposition in Buffalo. The hasty inaugural event is used as a springboard to explore America at the turn of the 20th century, the optimism of the Pan-American Exposition (which McKinley was attending when he was shot), and the complicated issues facing the first modern-day president. It's all impeccably retold and made relevant to today through the site's interactive exhibits.

Guided tours run about an hour, but budget at least two hours to fully appreciate this place. Check the website for special events such as historical fashion shows, dinners, and Victorian teas during the holidays. The site is fully accessible. The best parking is accessed from behind the building via Franklin Street.

ELMWOOD VILLAGE

The vibrant **Elmwood Village** (www.elmwoodvillage.org) overlaps with Allentown and provides visitors with cultural entertainment, shops, and relaxing park spaces. The neighborhood is loosely defined as the area bordered by Richmond and Delaware Avenues, North Street, and Delaware Park. Elmwood Village is more bustling than Allentown but still maintains a unique identity, blending museums, retail shops, parks, and a college campus. The village has been named "one of the 10 Great Neighborhoods in America" by the American Planning Association.

The village also boasts green spaces designed by Frederick Olmsted. Olmsted and landscape designer Calvert Vaux created Bidwell, Chapin, and Lincoln Parkways to connect with Delaware Park.

The Buffalo History Museum

The Buffalo History Museum (1 Museum Ct., 716/873-9644, www.buffalohistory.org, 10am-5pm Tues. and Thurs.-Sat., 10am-8pm Wed., noon-5pm Sun., $10 adults, $5 seniors and students, $2.50 children 7-12) tells the story of Western New York via artifacts and displays of historic materials inside the only structure that remains from Buffalo's famed 1901 Pan American Exposition. Frequently changing exhibits keep the narrative relevant and engaging. It is worth a visit just to see the grounds, including the south portico's statue of Abraham Lincoln and the Japanese garden.

1: Buffalo RiverWorks 2: The Buffalo History Museum 3: grain elevators 4: Buffalo Double Decker Bus

HERTEL AVENUE

Just a few blocks north of Delaware Park and Frank Lloyd Wright's Darwin Martin House Complex is a business district that has experienced more change in recent years than perhaps any other in Buffalo. A host of new restaurants, bars, public art murals, and stores line Hertel Avenue in North Buffalo, a neighborhood anchored by the glowing neon marquee of the **North Park Theatre** (1428 Hertel Ave., 716/836-7411, www.northparktheatre.org). The 1920 movie theater's extensive restoration of its stunning interiors coincided with a renewed interest in this once-fading commercial strip, which now has as much foot traffic on a Friday or Saturday evening as any thoroughfare in Buffalo.

TOURS

Hop aboard **Buffalo Double Decker Bus** (One Naval Park Cove, 716/246-9080, www.buffalodoubledeckerbus.com, several times daily May-Oct., $23 and up) for an engaging mix of humor and history. Costumed guides take you throughout the city and back in time aboard an authentic 65-passenger British double-decker bus. The focus is on entertainment rather than education, but you'll learn a little while you laugh. In town over the weekend? Check out the company's interactive Murder Mysteries ($35 pp) on Friday and Saturday evenings in season.

Explore Buffalo (One Symphony Circle, 716/245-3032, www.explorebuffalo.org, $5-45) has evolved into Buffalo's largest touring company, offering hundreds of tours throughout the year on foot, by bike, and by bus of the city's architecture, neighborhoods, waterfront, and food scene.

Open Air Autobus (716/854-3749, www.openairbuffalo.org, $25) gives whirlwind tours of Buffalo's notable architecture in a school bus that has had its roof removed.

Haunted History Ghost Walks (21 S. Grove St., East Aurora, 716/655-6663, www.hauntedhistoryghostwalks.com, $15) explore the paranormal haunts of Buffalo and its surrounding suburbs. Based on more than 10 books about local spirits by Mason Winfield, these walks blend history, folklore, and firsthand ghost stories. Tours are available in summer and autumn.

Preservation Buffalo Niagara (617 Main St., 716/852-3300, www.preservationbuffaloniagara.org, 9am-5pm Mon.-Fri.) offers more than 50 tours of Buffalo throughout the year. Most tours are $10 per person. It provides free tours of Buffalo City Hall at noon Monday-Friday.

Recreation

TOP EXPERIENCE

BOATING

Buffalo is situated where Lake Erie ends and the Niagara River begins, positioning it for great water access. If you are traveling by boat, there are several public and private marinas that rent dock space and provide maintenance and fuel services, including **Erie Basin Marina** (329 Erie St., 716/851-5238, www.eriebasinmarina.org), **Safe Harbor Marina** (1111 Fuhrman Blvd., 716/828-0027, www.safeharbormarina.com), and **Rich Marine Sales** (5 Austin St., 716/873-4060, www.richmarinesales.us).

Just outside of the marina, along Erie Street, two boats offer excursions. **Buffalo Harbor Cruises** (716/856-6696, www.buffaloharborcruises.com, July-Labor Day, $16 adults, $11 children 4-11) provides narrated cruises aboard the venerable *Miss Buffalo II*. If one hull isn't enough for you, try the ***moondanceCat*** (716/854-7245, www.moondancecat.com, $24 adults, $11.50 children 17 and under) for a ride on a catamaran.

many recreation opportunities are available near and around Buffalo.

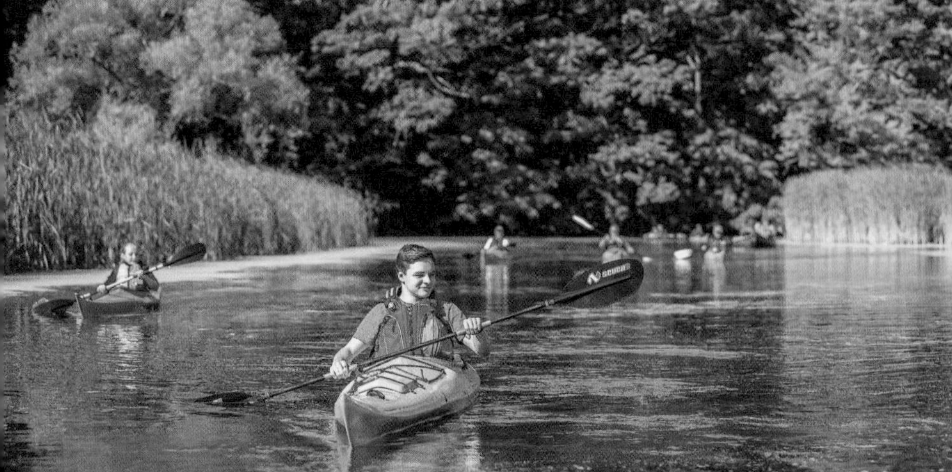

Canalside

Boaters can access the Central Wharf at **Canalside** (www.buffalowaterfront.com) from the Buffalo River. Docking space is available along the Buffalo River through **First Buffalo Marina** (32 Fuhrman Blvd., 716/867-9271, www.firstbuffalomarina.com). Docking fees are based on vessel size. Spaces are on a first-come, first-served basis and cannot be reserved. Overnight docking is permitted. Daily launch fees are $10.

If you don't own a boat, there are several ways to enjoy the water from Canalside. Housed at the far end of the wharf is **Buffalo Harbor Kayaks** (1 Naval Park Cove, 716/228-9153, www.bfloharborkayak.com, 9am-6pm daily). Stand-up paddleboard (SUP) and kayak (single or tandem) rentals start at $25 an hour, with half-day packages available. One-hour SUP rentals are offered for $30, and guided river tours ($35) are available.

Canalside is the home port for the **Queen City Bike Ferry** (Central Wharf, 716/796-4556, www.queencityferry.com, noon-8pm daily mid-May-Sept., $1). The ferry service connects the inner and outer harbors of Buffalo. This is a perfect way to hop from the inner harbor (Canalside) to the Outer Harbor as a pedestrian or cyclist. Pay at the kiosk at the front of the Liberty Hound Restaurant in the naval park area.

The bike ferry is operated in conjunction with **Buffalo River History Tours** (Central Wharf, 716/796-4556, www.buffaloriverhistorytours.com, cruises depart several times daily, $23 and up). Various tours are offered including a land and sea adventure that takes you up the Buffalo River and on land for a tour inside an abandoned grain silo. Not interested in narration but just want a relaxing time on the water? Try the Caribbean Cruise ($28) for live Caribbean music and a cash bar.

The magnificent ***Spirit of Buffalo*** (Central Wharf, 716/796-7210, www.spiritofbuffalo.com, daily May 15-Oct. 1, $32 adults, $18 children), a 73-foot (22-m) sailboat, has the best of both worlds: the look and feel of a schooner, but the safety and amenities of a modern boat. These two-hour scenic cruises are a relaxing way to see the inner and outer harbors of Buffalo. Crew members of this family-operated enterprise share information on landmarks and let passengers help raise the sails. Although the *Spirit of Buffalo* has daily service, you must call for reservations and times. The boat does not sail if there are fewer than 10 reservations for a particular time slot. Families with young children could consider the Saturday morning **pirate cruise** ($25 and up), hosted by costumed pirates who will ensure young landlubbers have a good time.

FISHING

If you plan on fishing in the Niagara River, Lake Erie, or Lake Ontario, a license is needed. **One-day licenses** for nonresidents are $15 (www.dec.ny.gov). Anglers will find plentiful bass, trout, northern pike, walleye, and salmon in the local waters. Excellent spots for shore fishing abound, including **Broderick Park** (foot of W. Ferry St.), along the **Riverwalk** (accessed from Niagara St. near Ontario St.), and the **Safe Harbor Marina** (1111 Fuhrman Blvd.).

PARKS

Frederick Law Olmsted described Buffalo as "the best planned city, as to its streets, public places, and grounds, in the United States, if not in the world." Olmsted and his partner Calvert Vaux planned an ideal cityscape with large parks and beautiful, broad, tree-lined parkways. Most of that envisioned park system remains today.

Delaware Park (199 Lincoln Pkwy., 716/886-0088, www.bfloparks.org, dawn-dusk daily) is the crown jewel of Buffalo's park system. Like New York City's Central Park, it was designed by Frederick Law Olmsted, and it serves as a cultural and recreational meeting place. Delaware Park has 350 acres of meadows, woods, and water. It is bordered by the Museum District, Forest Lawn Cemetery, and the Buffalo Zoo. The park includes an 18-hole public golf course,

Frederick Law Olmsted's Legacy

Regarded as a pioneer of American landscape design, Frederick Law Olmsted (1822-1903) left an indelible mark on the city of Buffalo and its people. Olmsted is widely remembered for his conservation efforts and his designs of Central Park in Manhattan and Prospect Park in Brooklyn. Buffalo, some argue, is Olmsted's masterpiece: a system of parks that realized his philosophy about the essential role of recreational space within the fabric of urban communities.

Olmsted believed that parks were needed to temper the alienation, pollution, and fast pace of emerging U.S. industrial cities. He saw green spaces as having a positive social and political impact on citizens, who could use a common area to share their common humanity. Buffalo would be his proving ground.

Olmsted's ambitious plans for Buffalo began in 1868 and were implemented primarily over the next 30 years. The heart of his design was three major parks that were connected by broad streets. The parks were dispersed through the city so that all citizens could have equal access. The 200-foot-wide (67-m-wide) parkways that joined the parks featured large, grassy medians and were lined by trees, providing a green oasis for a city heated by coal and shrouded in smog.

The three original parks are now known as Delaware, Front, and Martin Luther King, Jr. Parks. Cazenovia, Riverside, and South Park were added to the design over the years. Olmsted's legacy is a vibrant system of green spaces that plays an important role in the lives of everybody in the region. In these places, people relax, play sports, exercise, congregate, fish, cross-country ski, see Shakespeare productions, and snap wedding photos. In short, Mr. Olmsted has created spaces for everyone in Buffalo to commune.

Locals and visitors alike can enjoy these interconnected parks for free. The **Buffalo Olmsted Parks Conservancy**'s website (www.bfloparks.org) is the best resource to help you find the parks and learn what is going on at each of them. Olmsted's contributions have made Buffalo a much better city in which to live.

17 tennis courts, three playgrounds, six soccer fields, and two lawn-bowling courts. Ring Road encircles the golf course and playing fields, providing an excellent paved route for jogging, biking, and rollerblading. The beautifully restored Marcy Casino building overlooks Hoyt Lake, where people gather to relax and watch kids practice catch-and-release fishing for sunfish. Behind the Marcy Casino is the Rose Garden, a popular place for wedding vows and pictures.

Cazenovia Park (25 Cazenovia St., 716/826-7820, www.bfloparks.org, dawn-dusk daily) is a 186-acre park named after the creek that runs through it. Known as "Caz" to locals, this pastoral strip of green is the heart of South Buffalo's working-class neighborhood. Originally built in 1893 by Olmsted, the park has been expanded over the years and has some of the most mature stands of trees in the entire city. Cazenovia Creek meanders through the park, eventually joining up with the Buffalo River and Lake Erie. The park also has a nine-hole public golf course, swimming pool, playground, jogging trail, three soccer fields, four baseball diamonds, and a public ice-skating rink (Sept.-Apr. 7).

SPECTATOR SPORTS

Buffalo is a sports town, home to the NFL's **Buffalo Bills** (www.buffalobills.com) and the NHL's **Buffalo Sabres** (www.sabres.nhl.com).

The Buffalo Bills play football at **New Era Field** (1 Bills Dr., Orchard Park, 716/648-1800), about 15 miles (24 km) south of the city in Orchard Park. No matter what the weather, the tailgating begins as soon as the parking lots open. On game day, it may take an hour to get to the stadium from Buffalo.

The Buffalo Sabres are equally beloved, selling out many of their home ice-hockey games in the **Key Bank Center** (1 Seymour H. Knox III Plaza, 716/855-4444). Fans jam downtown bars and restaurants before games. The arena is also home to the **Buffalo Bandits** (www.bandits.com) of the National Lacrosse League.

The **Buffalo Bisons** (www.milb.com) are a AAA minor league baseball team that plays at **Sahlen's Field** (275 Washington St., 716/846-2000) in the heart of downtown Buffalo. In stark contrast to the excitement and action of Bills and Sabres games, watching the Bisons play is a relaxing experience, best enjoyed with a hot dog and a brew. The Bisons are a farm team for the MLB Toronto Blue Jays.

Entertainment and Events

NIGHTLIFE

Buffalo is a city that works hard and plays hard; many bars here stay open until 4am. There are four primary districts with clusters of bars and clubs—downtown/Chippewa Street, Allentown, Elmwood Avenue, and Hertel Avenue.

Sportsmens Tavern (326 Amherst St., 716/874-7734, www.sportsmenstavern.com, 11am-midnight Tues., 11am-3pm and 5pm-midnight Wed. and Thurs., 4pm-2am Fri., 2pm-2am Sat., 2pm-9pm Sun., cover $5-40) is not in any of the entertainment districts, but it is the best live music venue in the city. Nestled in the aging working-class neighborhood known as Black Rock (10 minutes north of downtown), Sportsmens is owned and operated by musicians. Owner Dwane Hall has created a space where local musicians can play and also listen to some of the best traveling acts in country, blues, folk, and indie rock. It's easy to believe you are in Austin or Memphis at an authentic honky-tonk. There is no bohemian or dive bar pretension here—just honest music in a perfectly comfortable venue. The kitchen is surprisingly good, serving more than just pub grub. This is truly one of the city's best-kept secrets.

Downtown

For many years, Chippewa Street was *the* entertainment district for Buffalo. Some of its luster has faded, but the Chip Strip still draws the college-age crowd, especially on Friday and Saturday evenings. A number of other bars and clubs have begun to populate the blocks surrounding Chippewa Street. Business types emerge on Friday after work but generally clear out by 7pm. Most venues are open until 4am, and this district can get somewhat rowdy after 2am.

Soho (64 W. Chippewa St., 716/856-7646, www.sohobarbuffalo.com, 11am-close Tues.-Sun.) is one of the mainstays of the Chip Strip. Head upstairs and grab a spot at this bar's second-floor patio, which features great views of the city skyline and of the hubbub below on Chippewa Street. Hungry patrons shouldn't miss the burgers, which were once so popular that the business rebranded as Soho Burger Bar for a time. This is a fine starting point to get an overview of the surrounding area and plot out your next stops downtown.

Although the **Chocolate Bar** (114 W. Chippewa St., 716/332-0484, www.thechocolatebar.com, 4pm-11pm Mon.-Thurs., 4pm-1am Fri., noon-1am Sat., 3pm-11pm Sun.) is both a restaurant and a bar, forget about the entrées. Focus on the desserts and the exotic chocolate drinks. Drinks are expensive, but worth it. The Dirty Girl ($12.95) is a liquor milkshake that tastes like a Girl Scout Thin Mint. Martinis start at $10.95 and include flavors such as Swedish fish, peanut butter cup, and banana cream pie.

One of the most storied watering holes in Buffalo can be found a couple blocks north of Chippewa Street, at **Founding Fathers Pub** (75 Edward St., 716/855-8944, 11:30am-1am Mon.-Thurs., 11:30am-2am Fri., noon-4am Sat., 5pm-10pm Sun.). Owner Mike Driscoll was a former social studies teacher who decided to switch careers in the 1980s and create a presidential-themed bar. Campaign posters, portraits, and other memorabilia line nearly every square inch of this pub, which has gained the attention of media outlets like Buzzfeed and Esquire. Driscoll can still be found tending bar most nights, and he loves to quiz patrons with trivia on Buffalo and a variety of other subjects (his trivia night on the first Tuesday of every month is usually standing room only). Free popcorn and nachos round out one of the most unique bar experiences in Western New York.

On the fringe of the entertainment district, inside an 1863 building, is an Irish tavern, **Eddie Brady's** (97 Genesee St., 716/854-7017, 11am-1am Mon.-Thurs., 11am-4am Fri.-Sat.). Check out the 1950s Iroquois Beer signs, vintage cash register, and picture of owner Eddie's grandfather above the bar. The eclectic jukebox features songs by Tony Bennett, Louis Armstrong, and the Talking Heads. This charming tavern serves a working-class clientele with moderately priced drinks and stick-to-your-ribs food, all cooked on a grill just behind the bar. If your diet permits, try the fried bologna sandwich.

Choose from more than 300 varieties of whiskey and scotch at **Lucky Day Whiskey Bar** (320 Pearl St., 716/322-0547, www.luckydaywhiskeybar.com, 4pm-midnight Tues.-Thurs., 4pm-2am Fri.-Sat.). The bartender has to use a ladder to reach all the bottles of spirits lining the high, wide shelving units behind the bar. Brick walls and hardwood floors give the bar a classy vibe, and live music is a staple on Friday and Saturday nights. Lucky Day also has one of the most delicious late-night menus in the city, with options like gouda mac and cheese and a rotating selection of savory hand pies.

Skee-Ball, Pac-Man, and pinball are all on the menu alongside drinks and food at **Misuta Chow's** (521 Main St., 716/259-8228, www.misutachows.com, 11:30am-midnight Mon.-Wed., 11:30am-2am Thurs.-Fri., 3pm-2am Sat., 3pm-midnight Sun.). This two-story, Japanese-themed bar, restaurant, and arcade has a wide selection of cocktails, beers, whiskeys, and sake cups to make the wide variety of games on its second floor even more entertaining. While the whole family can enjoy the games and dining options like ramen, bao buns, and miso soup earlier in the evening, Misuta Chow's becomes a 21 and older bar after 10pm.

Almost anything goes at **Club Marcella** (439 Pearl St., 716/847-6850, www.clubmarcella.com, 10pm-4am Thurs.-Sat.), Buffalo's most exciting LGBTQ nightclub. The club hosts drag shows and audience-participation beauty pageants (where contestants strip down to their undies). The club is welcoming to all and is known for its excellent techno music. If you are looking for a good place to dance, Club Marcella is it. Admission varies based on the acts or events each night.

Allentown

The Old Pink (223 Allen St., 716/884-4338, 11am-4am Mon.-Sat., noon-4am Sun.) is the most venerated dive bar in Buffalo. Unforgettable nights always seem to end at The Pink, affectionately called The Stink. The closer it is to 4am, the more varied the clientele. You'll find college students, urban hipsters, bikers, punks, and cool middle-age folks gathered over strong, cheap drinks and surprisingly good grilled food. The steak sandwiches are legendary. They're cooked right before your eyes by the bartender. The Pink is a must for last call.

A stumble away from The Pink, you'll find **Mulligan's Brick Bar** (229 Allen St., 716/881-0545, noon-4am daily). Here you will find inexpensive drinks (but no draft beer). The extroverted barkeeps are entertaining and will even share a shot with you. The front patio is a makeshift porch, usually tightly packed with smokers and those watching the parade of partyers pass by. The atmosphere is playful and skews to the 30-plus crowd, although the clientele is diverse.

Nietzsche's (248 Allen St., 716/886-8539, www.nietzsches.com, noon-2am Sun.-Wed., noon-4am Thurs.-Sat., cover $5 and up), which hosts live music every night of the week, is the place to see bands in Allentown. Music acts are eclectic (blues, indie, rock, world, funk, jazz, Celtic), as is the crowd. The bohemian ambience and good acoustics are perfect for enjoying the bands. However, the layout is not conducive to dancing, since a bottleneck in the floor design leads to some congestion. But the crowd is cool, and if you are patient, you'll make your way to the cash-only bar. The bathrooms here are grungy.

Elmwood

One of the two anchors for nightlife along the Elmwood Strip is **Mr. Goodbar** (1110 Elmwood Ave., 716/882-4000, www.mrgoodbarbuffalo.com, noon-4am daily). Once a college bar (it's one block from Buffalo State College), it has kept its comfortable vibe while appealing to a wider age range. You'll find 30 brews on tap at all times, served by bartenders who are happy to chat knowledgeably about the qualities of the beers and ciders they pour. There is live music multiple nights a week; check the calendar on the website.

Coles (1104 Elmwood Ave., 716/886-1449, www.colesbuffalo.com, 11am-11pm Mon.-Thurs., 11am-midnight Fri.- Sat., 11am-10pm Sun.) is right next door to Mr. Goodbar. It has embraced the craft beer craze and has 36 beers on tap. You'll pay a bit more here for a pint ($6 and up), but selections are consistently diverse and interesting, including local craft beers. Those looking to drink in the storied atmosphere of a classic neighborhood pub can't do much better in Buffalo than Cole's, which has been open since the 1930s . It attracts a healthy mix of adults 25 and older. If you are barhopping, Coles is a good place to start, when your wallet is a bit thicker and your taste for alcohol is more discerning.

One of the neighborhood's best hidden gems is **The Place** (229 Lexington Ave., 716/882-7522, www.theplacebuffalo.com, 4pm-2am Mon., 11am-2am Tues.-Sun.). Tucked away on a mostly residential street one block from Elmwood, The Place's roots as a neighborhood tavern and restaurant date back to the late 1870s. Dark mahogany walls, a copper-top bar, and dark plaid wallpaper evoke another era. This bar is steeped in tradition, particularly around the holidays, when it serves Buffalo's most popular version of the warm, boozy Tom and Jerry drink (rum, brandy, meringue, nutmeg, and hot water), complete with a mug customers can take home.

Hertel Avenue

Buffalo's first food truck, which launched in 2010, has since evolved into its own brick-and-mortar restaurant—and one of the city's most popular cocktail bars. **Lloyd Taco Factory** (1503 Hertel Ave., www.whereslloyd.com, 11 am-midnight Mon.-Thurs., 11 am-2am Fri.-Sat.) serves up standards like margaritas alongside their own unique creations such as the Snozzberry Mule (vodka, blueberry shrub, lemon, and ginger beer) and the Last of the Mojitos (gin, green Chartreuse, lime, Thai basil, lemongrass). The drinks are the perfect accompaniment for Lloyd's popular burritos and tacos, and can be chased with some of the richest, creamiest soft serve in Buffalo, served next door at Lloyd's other company, Churn.

Buffalo's premier soccer bar is **Més Que** (1420 Hertel Ave., 716/836-8600, http://mesque.com, 4pm-midnight Mon., 4pm-1am Tues.-Thurs, 2pm-2am Fri., 8am-2am Sat., 10am-midnight Sun.). Legions of fans can be seen on a Saturday morning, sporting jerseys of their favorite European teams, shouting at the television screen, and sharing a pint together. Més Que's draft selections include a half-dozen beers from across the pond, from Poland's Okocim pilsner to Fuller's extra special bitters from England, that pair perfectly with the match.

Wine aficionados need to find their way to **The Little Club** (1197 Hertel Ave, 716/427-6700, www.thelittleclub.bar, 5pm-midnight Tues.-Thurs., 5pm-1am Fri.-Sat., 5pm-10pm Sun.), which has one of the widest selections in the city. Some two dozen or more options are always available. Generations of the Lombardo family have left their imprint on this section of Hertel: Thomas J. Lombardo has owned Ristorante Lombardo, one of the most renowned and elegant Italian restaurants in the city, since the 1970s, and his son Tommy opened The Little Club right across the street in 2018. The polished, stylish interior makes The Little Club perfect for drinks before dinner or a night out on the town—or it can be the main event of the evening.

TOP EXPERIENCE

CRAFT BREWERIES AND DISTILLERIES

Buffalo has always been a blue-collar town with a thirst for beer. At one time, it was home to more than 30 breweries, thanks to excellent German brewmasters and its proximity to good, clean water and grain. Today an explosion of craft brewing and distilling has swept the region and reinvigorated formerly fraying warehouse districts and industrial neighborhoods; there are nearly as many breweries in the region as there were pre-Prohibition.

The **Pearl Street Grill and Brewery** (76 Pearl St., 716/856-2337, www.pearlstreetgrill.com, 11am-11pm Mon.-Sat., noon-11pm Sun.) was the first to produce beer in the city of Buffalo in more than 25 years when it opened in 1997. The best place to catch a summer sunset is on the New Orleans-style patio here, where you can relax with a pint from the 16 original craft brews on tap, including the signature Trainwreck German ale and the Blue-Eyed Blueberry Blonde. The vibe is casual, and the walls feature enormous murals of life along the Erie Canal in the 1800s. Brewery tasting tours ($10) are offered daily at 11am, 1pm, and 3pm.

Big Ditch Brewing (55 E. Huron St., 716/854-5050, www.bigditchbrewing.com, 11am-10pm Mon.-Thurs., 11am-midnight Fri., noon-midnight Sat., noon-8pm Sun.) won the TAP NY Award for best craft brewery in the state. The popular downtown brewery also offers good food, including the breuben (a massive Reuben with corned beef braised in their beer) and hand-cut fries with a choice of six different dipping sauces. Their beers—including the Hayburner IPA and Excavator Brown ale—are some of the most popular in Buffalo and often found at other establishments. Started by two scientists who were bored and looking for an interesting new endeavor, Big Ditch has taken a once-forgotten corner of downtown formerly occupied by a phone warehouse and turned it into a spacious two-floor taproom that is one of the city's hot spots.

The first legal distillery opened in Buffalo since Prohibition is the **Lockhouse Distillery** (41 Columbia St., 716/768-4898, www.lockhousedistillery.com, 4pm-midnight Tues.-Fri., noon-midnight Sat.). The distillery is conveniently located in the Cobblestone District close to Canalside, the hockey arena, and the Buffalo River. Try one of their signature vodka or gin spirits in the tasting area or on the sidewalk patio. Lockhouse is licensed to dispense drinks or sell bottles of their fine products over the bar. Tours of the production facilities are offered 4pm-10pm Tuesday-Saturday. Everything they create is distilled from locally grown grapes.

On the cusp of downtown is the **Flying Bison Brewing Company** (840 Seneca St., 716/873-1557, www.flyingbisonbrewing.com, 4pm-9pm Wed.-Thurs., noon-9pm Fri.-Sat.). The company has roots that stretch back more than two decades, well before the current explosion in local brewing. Enjoy a tour of the production facility Thursday and Friday at 6pm or at 1pm and 4pm on Saturday. Among the most popular beers is Rusty Chain, which goes great with chicken wings.

One of Buffalo's most unusual breweries is nestled in the shadow of the city's waterfront grain silos. **Gene McCarthy's/Old First Ward Brewing Co.** (73 Hamburg St., 716/855-8948, www.genemccarthys.com, 11am-midnight Sun.-Fri., 11am-1am Sat.) is a neighborhood pub that dates back to the 1960s, when grain scoopers used to wet their whistles at the bar after a long day at the silos. Gene McCarthy's didn't add the brewery until 2014. The brewery's offerings, including a smooth hefeweizen and the Red Clover Irish Red Ale, pair perfectly with one of the best pub grub menus in Buffalo, including Buffalo wings served McCarthy's style (with a tangy sauce comprised of barbecue sauce, hot sauce, and blue cheese).

Buffalo's largest distillery is also its most beautiful. **Lakeward Spirts at the Barrel Factory** (65 Vandalia St., 716/541-1454, www.lakewardspirits.com, noon-11pm Mon.-Thurs., noon-midnight Fri.-Sat., noon-6 pm Sun.) captures the true "spirit" of Buffalo's renaissance by resurrecting an abandoned barrel factory (circa 1904) and transforming it into a distillery, craft brewery, winery, restaurant, and event space. Lakeward pioneered the area's first craft vodka made from three grains (barley, wheat, rye) to produce a bold spirit with a true nose to it. All spirits are created with ingredients sourced in New York State, except for the rum, as sugarcane is not grown this far north. Guests may purchase a bottle over the bar or enjoy one of a dozen handcrafted cocktails in the tasting room.

Resurgence Brewing Co. (55 Chicago St., 716/381-9868, www.resurgencebrewing.com, 4pm-10pm Tues.-Thurs., 3pm-11pm Fri., noon-11pm Sat., noon-5pm Sun.) specializes in beers found only in Buffalo. Their offerings include a sponge candy stout that is a modern take on a Buffalo confectionery classic, and loganberry wit, a sweet beer that has its origins in the loganberry soft drink that's also found only in Western New York. Resurgence's taproom in a century-old machinery factory on Chicago Street is a scene-stealer, and it's close to most of the city's waterfront attractions.

In 2012, Buffalo's craft beer scene began to take off, and **Community Beer Works** (520 7th St., 716/759-4677, www.communitybeerworks.com, 3pm-10pm Wed., 3pm-midnight Fri., 11am-midnight Sat., noon-4pm Sun.) helped lead the charge. What began as a small warehouse with a 1.5-barrel system grew into a 20-barrel production facility churning out favorites like The Whale brown ale (a TAP NY winner for best craft beer in New York State), That IPA (a bronze medalist at the Great American Beer Festival), and Let's Go Pils lager. CBW's expansive brewery and taproom includes two patios and a game room.

THE ARTS

The arts scene in Buffalo is thriving, thanks to a deeply rooted creative community and anchor institutions that are completing significant investments in the city. The **Albright-Knox Art Gallery** is embarking on a 30,000-square-foot expansion that will more than double the number of works the museum can show from its world-renowned collection of modern and contemporary art. This expansion necessitated the closure of the Elmwood Avenue campus until 2022. During the closure, people can view traveling exhibits and installations at **Albright-Knox Northland** (612 Northland Ave., 716/882-8700, www.albrightknox.org, noon-7pm Fri., 10am-5pm Sat.-Sun., pay-what-you-wish admission), a 15,000-square-foot refurbished warehouse on the city's east side. The Albright-Knox also sponsors an extensive public art program (www.albrightknox.org/community/ak-public-art) with dozens of murals like the *Freedom Wall,* which honors local and national African American leaders, woven throughout the city's neighborhoods.

Just across the street from the Albright-Knox's Elmwood Avenue campus, on the Buffalo State College campus, is the **Burchfield Penney Art Center** (Buffalo State College, 1300 Elmwood Ave., 716/878-6011, www.burchfieldpenney.org, 10am-5pm Tues.-Wed. and Fri.-Sat., 10am-8pm Thurs., 11am-4pm Sun., $10 adults, $8 seniors, $5 students). The art center's mission is to showcase works of local artists, notably the watercolors of Charles Burchfield, an artist known for townscapes and nature paintings. The center is an incubator for local artists and displays eclectic artwork, including sculpture, drawings, and photography. Active members of the U.S. military and their families are admitted for free.

Kleinhans Music Hall (3 Symphony Circle, 716/885-5000, www.kleinhansbuffalo.org) is a treat for the eyes and the ears. The rounded building is a beautiful 1940s collaboration of famed Finnish architects Eliel and Eero Saarinen. The acoustics are world renowned, providing an excellent environment for enjoying the **Buffalo Philharmonic Orchestra** (www.bpo.org) or contemporary music acts. Parking is a challenge, so arrive early to find a spot in the adjacent lot.

Step back into the regal 1920s by catching a show at **Shea's Performing Arts Center** (646 Main St., 716/847-1410, www.sheas.org) in the heart of Buffalo's theater district. A National Historic Site, Shea's hosts Broadway musicals, dramatic productions, ballets, live music performances, and top-notch comedy acts. The theater's design is reminiscent of the grand European opera houses of the 17th century. The interior design by Louis Comfort Tiffany includes massive crystal chandeliers, a huge marble lobby, and beautiful, grand staircases.

The likes of Dizzy Gillespie, Miles Davis, John Coltrane, and other legends of jazz once jammed at the **Colored Musicians Club** (145 Broadway, 716/855-9383, www.cmctheclub.com), one of the oldest clubs of its kind in the United States. The CMC has hosted a Sunday-night jam session (6 pm, $5 cover charge) almost every week since it first opened in 1935, and has big bands perform for free every Monday (7 pm) and Thursday (8 pm) in its upstairs club, which still has its original wooden bar. Grabbing a cold beer and listening to music in the club where some of the greatest names in American jazz once performed is an extraordinary experience. An interactive museum downstairs tells the story of jazz in Buffalo and the African American musicians union that founded the club; it's open 11am-4pm Thursday-Saturday ($10).

FESTIVALS AND EVENTS

Cold winters teach Buffalonians to fully appreciate the warmer months. In the summer, there's a festival nearly every weekend in the city. A complete list of festivals is on the calendar page of **Visit Buffalo** (www.visitbuffaloniagara.com).

Spring

Everybody is Polish on **Dyngus Day** (www.dyngusdaybuffalo.com), the traditional spring festival held on the Monday following Easter Sunday. Now that the solemnity of Lent is over, it's time to get your polka on. Celebratory events, parades, and parties are held throughout the city.

Summer

During the **Allentown Art Festival** (www.allentownartfestival.com) in June, the city shuts down Delaware Avenue for a weekend to display the works of more than 400 artists.

Celebrate the culture and contributions of local African Americans at the **Juneteenth Festival** (www.juneteenthofbuffalo.com) in Martin Luther King, Jr. Park. The festival runs on the Saturday and Sunday closest to June 15.

Occurring the second weekend of July, the **Taste of Buffalo** (www.tasteofbuffalo.com) is one of the largest two-day food festivals in the nation. Bring your appetite to Niagara Square to enjoy samples from more than 200 vendors.

Buffalo hosts the largest free, self-guided garden tour in the United States during the last weekend of July. During **Garden Walk Buffalo** (www.gardensbuffaloniagara.com), thousands of visitors descend upon several city neighborhoods and wander block to block to see how creative Buffalo homeowners can be within the scope of an urban garden. Nearly 400 Garden Walk homeowners, in turn, welcome visitors to their backyards (often whipping up a pitcher of iced tea or lemonade for their guests) and explain the process behind their creativity. It's not just for aspiring green thumbs; Garden Walk is a wonderful opportunity to see Buffalo's urban fabric up close—its tree-lined streets and charming homes—and to experience the city's wonderful hospitality. If the last weekend of

July doesn't work for you, a series of smaller garden tours take place on Thursdays and Fridays in July called Open Gardens (www.gardensbuffaloniagara.com), which offer some of Garden Walk's greatest hits in a more relaxed environment.

Some like it hot, others medium or mild. No matter how you like your wings, the **National Buffalo Wing Festival** (www.buffalowing.com) fills Sahlen Field (275 Washington St.) in downtown Buffalo with the best wings in the world during Labor Day weekend. To sound like a local, though, be sure to call them chicken wings, not Buffalo wings.

At the **Italian Heritage Festival** (www.buffaloitalianfestival.com) in July, you can *mangi* (eat) to your heart's content along Niagara Square. During the two-day festival, you can try your hand at boccie and grape stomping, and meet the winner of the Miss Italian Festival contest.

From April to October, **Food Truck Tuesdays** (www.larkinsquare.com) have become a weekly staple of the Buffalo festival schedule in the revitalized warehouse district known as Larkinville. Dozens of food trucks from as far away as Rochester gather in Larkin Square, a public space in the heart of the district that also features a bandstand with live music.

Shopping

The **Buffalo Niagara Visitor Center** (403 Main St., 716/852-2356, www.visitbuffaloniagara.com/businesses/buffalo-niagara-visitor-center, 10am-4pm Mon.-Fri.), on the first floor of the historic Brisbane building along Lafayette Square, sells authentic, made-in-Buffalo foodstuffs, poster art, apparel, mugs, calendars, stationery, and even chicken wing bottler-opener refrigerator magnets. The store also provides free information on events and attractions in the region.

Everything Elmwood (740 Elmwood Ave., 716/883-0607, www.eegiftshop.com, 10am-7pm Mon.-Sat., 11am-5pm Sun.) is the largest boutique gift store in the Elmwood Avenue shopping district. Because of its size, the store is not as intimate as other boutiques—but it is completely filled (almost cluttered) with gifts from around the world. The large jewelry counter has gifts in the $20-40 range. Whether you're shopping for a baby shower or a 70th birthday, you'll find a unique gift here. The shop offers free gift wrapping.

The unique thing about **Thin Ice** (719 Elmwood Ave., 716/881-4321, www.thiniceonline.com, 10:30am-7pm Tues.-Sat., 11am-6pm Sun.-Mon.) is that all the merchandise is locally sourced. You can find jewelry, clothing, pottery, candles, and soap, all created by artists from the region. Gifts range from the creative and practical (soap made with beer and lime) to the medieval (a chain-mail bikini top). The store is open and airy, with three main display areas, hundreds of handcrafted items, and a friendly cat named Atticus.

ShopCraft (773 Elmwood Ave., 716/882-0306, www.buffaloshopcraft.com, 11am-6pm Sun. and Tues.-Wed., 11am-7pm Thurs.-Sat.) began as a pop-up within Thin Ice, then moved into its own space down the street in 2019. Like Thin Ice, the store focuses on locally sourced goods; some of the 3,000 items packed into the 820-square-foot space came from as close as a few blocks away. From candles and soaps to Buffalo-themed magnets and ornaments, from historical Pan-American Exposition prints to chicken wing earrings, the store has a host of options for a lasting gift from Buffalo.

Walking into **Talking Leaves Books** (951 Elmwood Ave., 716/884-9524, www.tleavesbooks.com, 10am-9pm Mon.-Fri., 10am-6pm Sat.-Sun.) is like putting on an old, well-worn sweater on a crisp autumn day. The store has a familiar warmth that you won't

1

2

find at a chain bookstore. The resident cat is aloof, the floor is worn, and the secondhand book shelves come from parochial schools and libraries. You'll likely hear the hushed tones of like-minded readers discussing literature. The eclectic selection of new and used books emphasizes local authors and subject matter.

Oxford Pennant (731 Main St., 716/500-6669, www.oxfordpennant.com, noon-7pm Tues.-Fri., 11-5pm Sat.) designs wool felt pennants inspired by American sports traditions and ships them across the continent to clients that have included Google, Adidas, and Facebook. The manufacturer opened a retail store downtown in 2018 that also sells apparel emblazoned with its custom designs, including the now-iconic "Keep Buffalo a Secret" slogan that has even appeared on a wall-size mural nearby.

Stitch Buffalo (1215 Niagara St., 716/495-9642, www.stitchbuffalo.org, 9am-4pm Tues. and Thurs.-Fri., 10am-2pm Sat.) is unlike any other store in the city. Stitch's staff have trained more than 50 immigrant women in sewing skills through weekly classes. The women come from around the world and now live in the surrounding neighborhood. They produce handcrafted goods sold in the store and receive a portion of the sale. From "BuffaLove" heart pins to scarves to small stuffed elephants, a gift from Stitch celebrates Buffalo's growing diversity and supports recent immigrants as they adjust to life in the United States.

Food

TOP EXPERIENCE

WINGS

No stop in the city is complete without sampling some Buffalo wings (or "wings," as locals simply say). These fried treats are typically served with sides of celery, carrot sticks, and blue cheese (it is considered poor form to dip your wings in Ranch dressing). Make certain to have an abundance of napkins and wet-naps and dig in!

Local lore tells us wings were invented at **Anchor Bar** (1047 Main St., 716/886-8920, www.anchorbar.com, 11am-11pm Mon.-Sat., noon-10pm Sun., $12) after bar matron Teressa Bellissimo improvised a late night snack for her son. Of course, the wings are legendary, but so is the restaurant atmosphere—numerous world class European racing motorcycles hang from the ceiling and more than 500 license plates adorn the walls. Take a look at the celebrity photos to find that John Lennon, Elvis Presley and many other luminaries chose to try the Anchor Bar's wings. If you arrive at a busy time of the day (4 pm-8 pm) you'll find faster service at the bar instead of waiting for a table to open.

In a town famous for chicken wings, **Duff's Famous Wings** (3651 Sheridan Dr., 716/834-6234, www.duffswings.com, 11am-11pm Mon.-Thurs., 11am-midnight Fri.-Sat., noon-10pm Sun., $10) has the best. For the adventurous, "suicidal" and "death" sauces are available; a safe strategy is to order your wings medium or hot, then get a side order of the suicidal or death sauce for dipping.

For old school style wings served in an amazing atmosphere it is hard to beat **Gabriel's Gate** (145 Allen St., 716/886-0602, 11:30am-1am Mon.-Thurs., 1:30 am-midnight Fri.-Sat., noon-10pm Sun., $12.95). The building dates back to 1864 and exudes Allentown charm. Enjoy the wooden booths and wood burning fireplaces. The wings are served without any frills (crispy, hot sauce and butter) but that's the way most people like them!

FINE DINING

Hutch's Restaurant (1375 Delaware Ave., 716/885-0074, www.hutchsrestaurant.com,

1: Dyngus Day Parade **2:** Anchor Bar

5pm-10pm Mon.-Thurs., 5pm-11pm Fri.-Sat., 4:30pm-9pm Sun., $32) is a reliable favorite with excellent food and service. Expect American cuisine with an emphasis on seafood. The tables are very close together and the noise level very high, making it good for a family or group gathering, but not for a quiet, romantic dinner.

Buffalo's best chef, Mike A., dishes out the best seafood in town at the ★ **Seabar Restaurant** (475 Ellicott St., 716/332-2928, www.seabarsushi.com, 5pm-10pm Mon.-Thurs., 5pm-midnight Fri.-Sat., 4pm-9pm Sun., market-priced fish entrées). Most hospitality staffers recommend this restaurant to visitors because Seabar consistently delivers creative and contemporary fish delights. Choose from more than 10 market-priced fish selections, sushi, or fish tacos—it's all good.

AMERICAN

Enjoy tasty New American cuisine at **The Left Bank** (511 Rhode Island St., 716/882-3509, www.leftbankrestaurant.com, 5pm-11pm Mon.-Thurs., 5pm-midnight Fri.-Sat., 11am-2:30pm and 4pm-10pm Sun., $19). This restaurant finds the perfect balance with an atmosphere that is lively, but the space isn't crowded or loud. Try any of the world-class appetizers and the amazing house ravioli stuffed with pork and zucchini.

The **Lafayette Brewing Company** (391 Washington St., 716/856-0062, www.lafbrewco.com, 10am-11pm daily, $18) satisfies your hunger for food and heritage in downtown Buffalo. The restaurant is part of the magnificently restored 1904 Hotel Lafayette and is themed to reflect the world's fair that was hosted by the city in 1901. Entrées are simple and satisfying, especially the roast beef Lafayette Dip. After lunch or dinner, consider taking a walk through the restaurant to explore the Murals Room, Theodore Roosevelt Room, or the ornate marble bar. Choose from seven craft beers brewed on-site to round out the experience.

ITALIAN

Siena (4516 Main St., 716/839-3108, www.siena-restaurant.com, 11:30am-2pm and 5pm-10pm Mon.-Fri., 5pm-10pm Sat., 4:30pm-9pm Sun., $28) serves contemporary Italian fare in an upscale but casual atmosphere. Among the excellent appetizers, check out the "three ways" fried calamari or the stuffed hot peppers. While the restaurant is famous for its traditional entrées, you won't be disappointed if you try the wood-oven pizzas.

Don't be in a hurry when you come to **Osteria 166** (166 Franklin St., 716/858-3118, www.osteriabuffalo.com, 11am-10pm Mon.-Thurs., 11am-11pm Fri., 5pm-11pm Sat., $25). Loosely translated, "osteria" means an Italian pub—and the restaurant welcomes you to enjoy a leisurely dining experience. Start off with the four-cheese appetizer and ease into an entrée featuring homemade sausage or some of the largest meatballs in the city. Flat-iron pizzas are a treat, but don't be surprised when your pie arrives—the chef uses white sauce, not red, on the pizzas.

BARBECUE

Suzy Q's Bar-B-Que Shack (2829 River Rd., 716/873-0757, 11am-8:30pm Tues.-Thurs., 11am-9pm Fri., noon-9pm Sat., $10) does look like a shack, but inside are treats fit for a king. The barbecue served here is authentic, fresh, and inexpensive. If you close your eyes when you're eating the pulled pork, you could easily believe you're in Dixie. Balance your entrée with a side of sweet potato sticks or macaroni and cheese. If you arrive after 7pm, some of the main dishes will be gone, but don't worry: Your second and third choices will still be outstanding.

Accommodations

In the heart of it all is the **Buffalo Marriott HARBORCENTER** (95 Main St., 716/852-0049, www.marriott.com, $256), with 205 rooms, a pool, and two ice hockey rinks, just a few steps from the aboveground trolley. Some rooms enjoy amazing lake views. It's the perfect place to be in the epicenter of Buffalo's bustling waterfront renaissance.

Across the street is another newer Marriott property, the **Courtyard Buffalo Canalside** (125 Main St., 716/840-9566, www.marriott.com, $313), which offers more than 100 rooms, an indoor pool, and a fitness center, all overlooking the Canalside entertainment district. Convenience is the key here—it's an easy walk to the waterfront, sports arenas, and entertainment.

The Lofts on Pearl (92 Pearl St., 716/856-0098, www.loftsonpearl.com, $220) give you extra room to relax in a convenient location. Previously loft apartments, these one- and two-bedroom suites (32 in total) feature hardwood floors, fireplaces, full kitchens, and high ceilings. You can't beat the location in the heart of the Brewery District, close to Canalside, First Niagara Arena, and Sahlen Field.

Hotel @ The Lafayette (391 Washington St., 716/853-1505, www.thehotellafayette.com, $169) offers style, comfort, and convenience in a renovated 1904 French Renaissance-style building. Its 57 rooms blend historic and contemporary design, including grand murals of Buffalo's 1901 World's Fair (the Pan-American Exposition) and modern, European-style bathrooms. Explore the lobby and ballrooms for a sense of life at the turn of the 20th century. Former presidents Woodrow Wilson and Franklin Roosevelt stayed here.

The ★ **Westin Buffalo's** (250 Delaware Ave., 716/858-5900, www.westinbuffalo.com, $455) modern, all-glass exterior is balanced by super comfortable, down-blanketed beds. This property is a few blocks from downtown but just on the edge of the nightlife district known as the Chippewa Strip. Check out the airy atrium, which somehow successfully merges the feeling of contemporary art with a cozy lodge.

Escape the bustle of downtown at **The Parkside House** (462 Woodward Ave., 716/480-9507, www.theparksidehouse.com, $180) bed-and-breakfast. Snuggled in a residential neighborhood close to Delaware Park, this place has three comfy rooms, excellent food, and many spaces for relaxing or reading a book. The hosts are gracious and knowledgeable about the area; ask them about Frank Lloyd Wright's nearby Darwin Martin House on Jewett Avenue, just a few minutes' walk from the hotel. Some dates require a two-night stay.

The **Inn Buffalo** (619 Lafayette Ave., 716/432-1030, www.innbuffalo.com, $259) allows you to relive the splendor of Buffalo's Gilded Age. This nine-suite boutique hotel was once the home of a wealthy industrialist, whose houseguests included President Grover Cleveland. Today this restored mansion is truly one of Buffalo's hidden gems, located in the desirable Elmwood Village. There's no better place to stay while exploring Buffalo's museums, colleges, and architecture.

Buffalo's most lavish boutique hotel is a treat for the weary traveler and a trip back in time. Built in 1867 and completely restored in 2001, the ★ **Mansion on Delaware** (414 Delaware Ave., 716/886-3300, www.mansionondelaware.com, $300) gives you a taste of how the wealthy lived during the Gilded Age. The 24-hour service by your personal butler includes cocktails in the Fireside Salon, clothes pressing, and shoeshines—all complimentary. If you need to head downtown for dinner, a butler will drive you in a Land Rover. The 28 rooms are comfortable yet not too large, with plenty of authentic detail and historic charm. In an area of moderately priced attractions, why not splurge a little?

Transportation and Services

Emergency help is available by calling **911.** Non-emergency information requests are fielded by city hall during business hours by calling **311.**

The best tourism information and event calendar is found at **Visit Buffalo Niagara** (403 Main St., 716/852-2356, www.visitbuffaloniagara.com, 10am-4pm Mon.-Sat. Memorial Day-Labor Day, 10am-4pm Mon.-Fri. Labor Day-Memorial Day).

Being a midsize city has its advantages. One is the **Buffalo Niagara International Airport** (BUF, 4200 Genesee St., Cheektowaga, 716/630-6000, www.buffaloairport.com), which is easy to navigate because of its smaller size. Many air travelers from Toronto come here to enjoy significantly reduced fares, easy parking, and faster boarding times. Several air carriers serve the airport, including Southwest, United, American, Delta, and JetBlue. Buffalo is a very car friendly city, and from the airport, it's a 15-minute drive to downtown Buffalo and a 25-minute drive to Niagara Falls.

Buffalo's main bus terminal, the **METRO Transportation Station** (181 Ellicott St.) is downtown. All local transit bus routes have stops within a three-block radius of this station. The local transit service, **Niagara Frontier Transit Authority** (716/855-7300, www.nfta.com) operates buses and trains in Erie and Niagara Counties. Bus route 24 ($2) connects the METRO Transportation Station with Buffalo Niagara International Airport. Bus route 40 ($2) will take you to Niagara Falls, New York. Check the online schedules, as route coverage changes on weekends and holidays.

Intercity motor coach service providers that stop at the METRO Transportation Station include **Greyhound** (716/855-7531, www.greyhound.com), **Coach USA** (800/352-0979, www.coachusa.com), **MegaBus** (877/462-6342, www.us.megabus.com), **Neon** (800/231-2222, www.neonbus.com), **New York Trailways** (800/776-7548, www.trailwaysny.com), and **Coach Canada** (800/461-7661, www.coachcanada.com).

East Aurora

Western New York's own version of Mayberry is only a 25-minute drive southeast of downtown Buffalo. The idyllic village of East Aurora—with a family-owned five-and-dime store, tree-lined streets filled with charming homes, and a Main Street lined with cafes, restaurants, and boutiques—is creative to its core, thanks to a rich history as a leading community in America's Arts and Crafts movement.

Relive East Aurora's Arts and Crafts legacy at **The Roycroft Campus** (31 S. Grove St., 716/655-0261, www.roycroftcampuscorporation.com, 10am-5pm daily, free). At the turn of the 20th century, the campus's buildings hosted a community of makers who produced jewelry, books, wooden furniture, and more. The Roycroft has been lovingly restored and features a museum, guided tours, and weekly classes offering everything from jewelry making to letterpress printing. The Copper Shop on campus sells a wide variety of items, including work from guild-certified artisans.

Across the street from the campus, the **Roycroft Inn** (40 S. Grove St., 716/652-5552, www.roycroftinn.com, $165) is the perfect spot for a meal or overnight stay in the village. This National Historic Landmark, which accommodated visiting artisans during the campus's heyday, features intricate woodwork in its rooms and common spaces, and an open-air peristyle that's an ideal spot on a summer Sunday morning for enjoying one of the most popular brunches in Western New York.

Vidler's 5 and 10 (676 Main St., 716/652-0481, www.vidlers5and10.com, 9am-6pm Mon.-Thurs. and Sat., 9am-9pm Fri., 11am-5pm Sun.) is one of the last merchants of its kind in the United States. In business since 1930, the family-owned general store sells more than 75,000 items spread over two floors and four interconnected buildings. This is a place to find everything you need and some things you didn't know you needed, from treats from an extensive, old-fashioned candy counter and retro toys to household wares and novelty items like a collapsible back scratcher.

Knox Farm State Park (437 Buffalo Rd., 716/652-0786, www.friendsofknoxfarm.org, dawn-dusk, free), just outside the village, provides more than 600 acres for hiking across rolling meadows and forests on the former estate of the region's prestigious Knox family. Walking through the Western New York countryside at Knox Farm is a serene experience.

North Tonawanda

To the north of Buffalo is a vibrant canal community known as "the Tonawandas." This region can be confusing because it encompasses three communities: the City Of Tonawanda, the Town of Tonawanda, and North Tonawanda. In the summer, the region bustles with activities, many of them focused on celebrating the heritage of the Erie Canal.

The Herschell Carrousel Factory Museum (180 Thompson St., 716/693-1885, www.carrouselmuseum.org, noon-4pm Wed.-Sun. Apr.-June and Sept.-Dec., 10am-4pm Wed.-Sat., noon-4pm Sun. July-Aug., $7 adults, $5 seniors, $3.50 children 2-6) retraces North Tonawanda's proud legacy as one of the nation's leading producers of merry-go-rounds a century ago. The museum, in one of the former factory buildings of the Alan Herschell Carrousel Company, shows visitors the process of making these amusement park fixtures. Admission includes one ride token; a visit here isn't complete without taking a spin on the museum's large 1916 carousel, which includes 36 hand-carved horses. Other children's rides operate seasonally.

The Riviera Theatre (67 Webster St., 716/692-2413, www.rivieratheatre.org) has operated in North Tonawanda since 1926 as one of the region's leading entertainment venues. The Riviera stands apart with its meticulously restored 1926 Mighty Wurlitzer organ, a type of organ which North Tonawanda produced for decades. The organ has 3,000 different pipes and often serenades guests prior to a concert or movie screening.

Gateway Harbor (1 Young St., www.tonawandasgatewayharbor.net, dawn to dusk) is the place to be on summer evenings. This park straddling the Erie Canal hosts a variety of events in the summer, from a Wednesday evening concert series to the 8-day Canal Fest of the Tonawandas each July (www.canalfest.org). Even a simple walk along the water at dusk on quieter evenings is worth the trip.

In August, **Canal Fest** (www.canalfest.org) is a fun community celebration where Tonawanda and Ellicott Creeks meet in downtown Tonawanda. It runs for one week in mid-July and has a parade, fireworks, live music, and numerous food vendors. Highlights include an arts-and-crafts show, a classic car night, and a charity toy duck race in the creek.

The Remington Tavern and Seafood Exchange (184 Sweeney St., 716/362-2802, www.remingtontavern.com, 4:30pm-10pm Mon.-Thurs., 4:30pm-11pm Fri.-Sat., 4:30pm-9pm Sun., $30) offers a wide selection of beef, seafood, and pasta dishes in a restored 1895 trolley barn along North Tonawanda's waterfront. The Remington's outdoor patio facing the canal is especially popular on summer evenings.

Lockport and the Niagara Wine Trail

Northeast of Tonawanda, fertile land stretches outward, encompassing the historic city of Lockport and eventually reaching Lake Ontario. The Niagara Escarpment cuts through on an east-west axis, creating a perfect microclimate for growing fruit between the ridge and the lake. Wine country spreads northward from the escarpment to Lake Ontario like a green blanket, nurturing nearly 20 wineries. The imposing dolostone of the escarpment yielded to ingenuity and hard labor in Lockport, where the Erie Canal manages to flow uphill.

SIGHTS

Erie Canal Discovery Center

Despite its speed limit of 4 miles (6.4 km) per hour, the Erie Canal was the first U.S. superhighway, fundamentally changing both the region and the country. The **Erie Canal Discovery Center** (24 Church St., Lockport, 716/439-0431, www.niagarahistory.org, 9am-5pm daily May-Oct., 10am-3pm Thurs.-Sat. Nov.-Apr., $6 adults, $5 seniors, children free when accompanied by a parent or guardian) is the best way to understand the canal, its legacy, and its importance to Lockport. This is no musty museum! The highly educational and entertaining center has contemporary interactive exhibits. Try your hands at piloting a model boat through the locks or take a virtual nighttime ride aboard a packet boat along the canal.

Other displays tell the compelling stories of "canawlers," the men, women, and children whose lives depended on the Erie Canal. The City of Lockport Visitor Center is in the lower level of the complex. The volunteers here can provide excellent information about local attractions and festivals.

★ Lockport Locks

Diggers of the Erie Canal faced a monumental problem as they excavated the 363-mile (584-km) waterway in the early 1800s. Engineers needed to find a way to allow boats to climb the 60-foot (18-m) increase in elevation at Lockport's escarpment. An ingenious series of five twin locks permitted canal boats to safely make the journey up and down the escarpment, the geological ridge over which Niagara Falls originally flowed.

Today the Erie Canal has transitioned from an essential economic artery for a burgeoning country to a pastoral waterway enjoyed by recreational boaters and curious travelers. Thanks to advances in technology, the original five locks have been replaced by two. The work involved in elevating the boats 60 feet (18 m) is just as fascinating as it was in 1825 when the Erie Canal opened.

Locks 34 and 35, built in 1913, are the main attractions. They are in the heart of Lockport, where Pine Street crosses over the canal. You can observe the locks in action from either side of the canal. The west side features a bike path accessible from Canal Street. This path affords a great view of these two locks, as well as the original locks from 1825 that are no longer operational and act as a spillway. Observing from the east side of the canal is the best way to experience the new locks up close as they gently raise and lower the boats. As you walk over the canal on Main Street (heading southwest), you will travel over the widest bridge in North America (399 ft/121 m wide, but only 129 ft/39 m long).

Lockport Locks and Erie Canal Cruises (210 Market St., Lockport, 716/378-0352, www.lockportlocks.com, May-mid-Oct., $17.50 adults, $9 children 4-10) offers a slow-paced, two-hour cruise along the canal and back in time. This ride is an excellent antidote for an otherwise busy vacation, as it forces you to relax and appreciate life at the pace of the canal. The boat's captain provides excellent narration and is eager to answer any questions. If you enjoy America's industrial history, this is a real winner.

Lockport

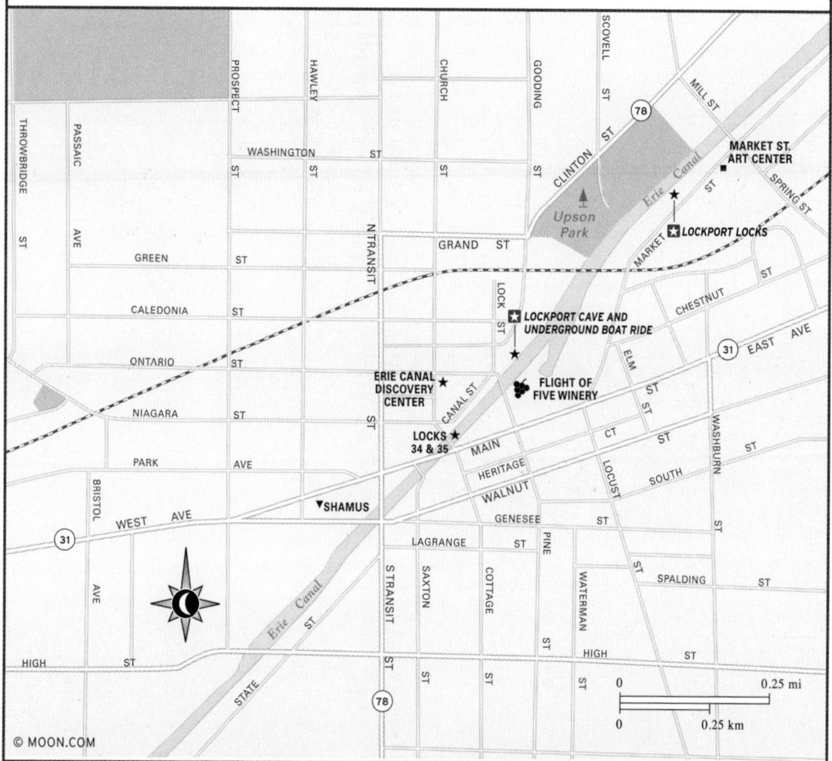

★ Lockport Cave and Underground Boat Ride

Both literally and figuratively, the coolest thing to do in Lockport is to experience the **Lockport Cave and Underground Boat Ride** (5 Gooding St., 716/438-0174, www.lockportcave.com, tour times vary May-mid-Oct., $15 adults, $10 children 5-12). During the hour-long guided tour, you'll explore a large tunnel blasted out of solid rock in the 1850s. The tunnel provided flowing water to various factories, which used it for hydraulic power. Today the tunnel is an eerie portal to the industrial history of the United States.

The tour also includes what is purported to be "America's longest underground boat ride." While the boat trip is relaxing, be prepared to do some uphill walking and stair climbing—the attraction is not wheelchair-accessible. Your tour guide will talk about the locks and the history of Lockport as you walk along the canal and before you enter the cave.

WINERIES

For many years, the farmers of this area grew peaches, apples, and table grapes. It wasn't until the 1990s that winegrowers began to seriously cultivate grapes for wine. The **Niagara Wine Trail** (www.niagarawinetrail.org) has blossomed into a region supporting more than 20 wineries. After the Wisconsin

1

2

3

glacial era ended some 11,000 years ago, it left behind soil perfect for growing temperamental wine grapes.

The wineries are as diverse as the vintages they create, with some focusing on handcrafted traditional wines, while others experiment with wines made from apples, apricots, and cherries.

The Winery at Marjim Manor (7171 E. Lake Rd., Appleton, 716/778-7001, www.marjimmanor.com, 10am-6pm Mon.-Sat., noon-6pm Sun., $5 tasting fee) serves fruit-based wines with a side helping of ghost stories. Owners Margo and Jim Bittner began farming in the early 2000s. Today they make wines using apples, plums, pears, apricots, blueberries, and many other fresh fruits, along with locally grown grapes. There are tastings at Marjim Manor, a beautiful, historical building from the 1850s that boasts a spooky history. Although there are no on-site winemaking facilities, it is nonetheless one of the best stops on the Niagara Wine Trail.

A Gust of Sun Winery (4515 Baer Rd., Ransomville, 716/731-4878, www.agustofsun.com, noon-6pm Fri. and Sun., 10am-6pm Sat. Jan.-Mar., 10am-6pm Sat., noon-6pm Sun.-Fri. Apr.-Dec., $4 tasting fee) is a true family-owned and -operated enterprise. Erik and Shane Gustafson moved here to try their hand at winemaking shortly after they were married. The couple planted vines and renovated an old Amish barn into a tasting room and lounge in the loft. Their hard work has paid off, with their sweet and dry white wines winning medals at competitions regionally and in the Midwest. A partnership with a local chocolate maker has led to a novel tasting where five wine samples are paired with five chocolates custom made to complement the Gustafsons' wine.

Vizcarra Vineyards at Becker Farms (3724 Quaker Rd., Gasport, 716/772-2211, www.beckerfarms.com, 11am-6pm daily May-Nov., noon-5pm Wed.-Mon. Dec.-Apr., $5 tasting fee) believes in growing the best fruit on its 340-acre farm, then making it into wine for people to enjoy. In addition to traditional grape wines, Vizcarra offers apple, plum, strawberry-rhubarb, cherry, and raspberry wines. The most recent addition is the "sinful series"—heavily fortified, port-style wines fermented to 17 percent alcohol by volume. Vizcarra is part of the Becker Farms estate, which includes a microbrewery, farmers market selling fresh fruits and vegetables, and a small bakery and snack shop.

For the founders of **Freedom Run Winery** (5138 Lower Mountain Rd., Lockport, 716/433-4136, www.freedomrunwinery.com, noon-6pm Sun.-Wed., 10am-6pm Thurs.-Sat., tasting fees vary), wine is art. The sweeping elegance of their winery was designed to enhance the wines. The contemporary, airy tasting rooms display works from local artisans, with an emphasis on stunning handcrafted glass. The wines crafted here are works of art as well—they've won several medals from regional tasting competitions. Among Freedom Run's successful vintages are pinot noirs that thrive in the heavy clay soils of their vineyards.

It's a story of "gravel to grapes" at the **Spring Lake Winery** (7373 Rochester Rd., Lockport, 716/439-5253, www.springlakewinery.com, noon-5pm daily, $3 tasting fee). Before it was a winery, Spring Lake was a gravel pit. The Varallo family saw the potential of the pit and purchased 78 acres of land surrounding the excavation. The pit filled with natural spring water and is now a small lake with a beautiful vista for wine tastings, picnics, and weddings. The land's unique sandy soil is best suited to growing Riesling grapes. Spring Lake's Rieslings have won medals at tasting competitions nationally and internationally. Visitors can walk among the vines, see the processing machinery, and explore the pastoral area around the lake. The lakeside gazebo is a picturesque place to sip wine or to host a wedding. The winery hosts

1: Erie Canal Discovery Center **2:** Erie Canal in Lockport **3:** Lockport Cave and Underground Boat Ride

The Niagara Wine Trail

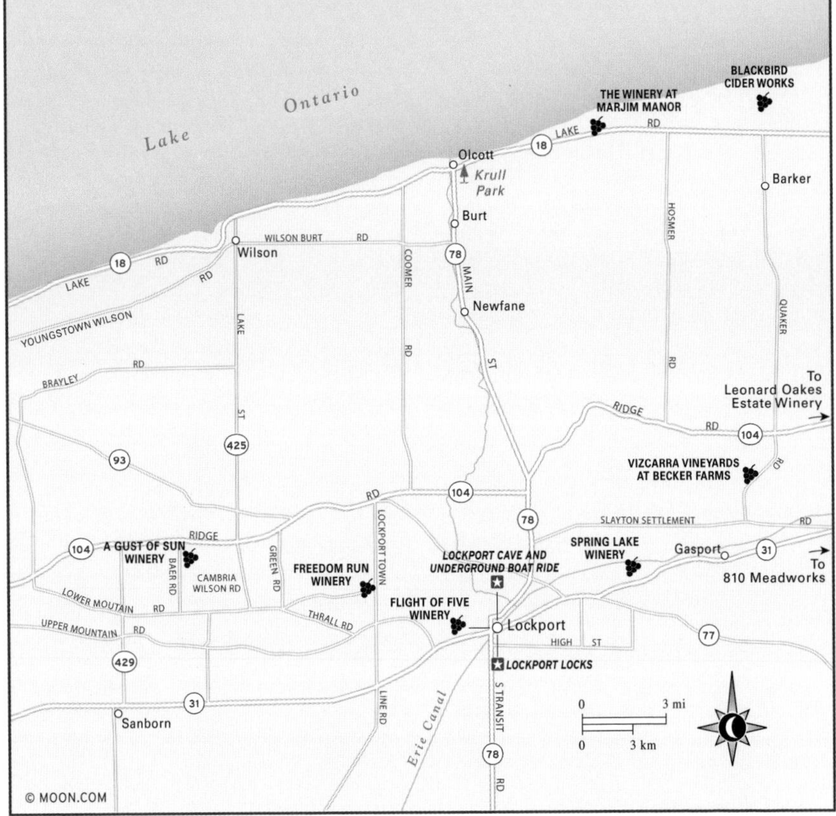

paint nights and popular murder mysteries, which include a train ride on the railway that abuts the property.

You can practically taste the history in the wines served at the **Flight of Five Winery** (2 Pine St., Lockport, 716/433-3360, www.flightoffivewinery.com, noon-7pm Thurs.-Sun. Jan.-Apr., noon-7pm daily May-Dec., $14 tasting fee includes food pairing). The winery is in the historic and beautiful building that once housed Lockport's City Hall. The winery draws its name from the original flight of five locks built here to allow boats to ascend and descend the escarpment through which the Erie Canal flows.

Farther down the canal but well worth the trip is **810 Meadworks** (113 W. Center St., Medina, 585/542-9810, www.810meadworks.com, noon-6pm Wed. and Sun., noon-10pm Thurs., noon-midnight Fri.-Sat., $5 tasting fee). Meadworks focuses on creating wines and other beverages from honey, which some believe predates the grape as the first substance fermented by humans. Although you might guess that all wines using honey are sweet, that is not the case. The mead produced here runs the gamut from sweet to bone dry. Ingredients such as cucumbers, coffee beans, tea leaves, currants, and lavender are incorporated into the wines to create a diverse and satisfying tasting experience. This winery is more urban than most on the trail. It occupies a famous Medina landmark, a former shirt factory that tailored custom dress wear for the likes of the Astors, Winston Churchill, and Bob Hope.

Also in Medina, you'll find the **Leonard Oakes Estate Winery** (10609 Ridge Rd., Medina, 585/318-4418, www.oakeswinery.com, noon-6pm Sun.-Fri., 10am-6pm Sat. Jan.-Apr., 11am-6pm Mon.-Fri., 10am-6pm Sat., noon-6pm Sun. May-Dec., $4 tasting fee). Ninety years of family farming tradition go into every bottle of wine produced. The winery creates vintages with numerous accents including plum, vanilla, peach, and gooseberry. It's also a relaxing venue to enjoy craft beer and cider.

Another unique property on the trail that is well worth the trip is the **Blackbird Cider Works** (8503 Lower Lake Rd., Barker, 716/795-3580, www.blackbirdciders.com, 11am-6pm Mon.-Sat., noon-6pm Sun. May-Nov., call for availability Dec.-Apr., $3 tasting fee). This facility is the only craft hard cider producer in the region, using only apples grown on a family farm overlooking Lake Ontario. Try one of the more than 10 ciders including Buffalo Bluegrass Kentucky Barrel Aged Hard Cider, which is aged in Kentucky bourbon barrels. You're likely to find something here for every palate, as the ciders range from sweet to dry and bottled to draft.

RECREATION

Parks

In Wilson, **Wilson Tuscarora State Park** (3371 Lake Rd., Wilson, 716/751-6361, www.nysparks.com, dawn-dusk daily, free) has more than 450 acres of woods and meadows to explore, along with a 4-mile (6.4-km) nature path, picnic facilities, and a boat launch ($7). Located on Lake Ontario, the park allows for swimming, fishing, and hiking.

Krull Park (6108 Lake Rd., Olcott, 716/778-7711, www.niagaracounty.com/parks, dawn-dusk daily Memorial Day-Labor Day) is a 325-acre community park on the shore of Lake Ontario, with a splash pool, beach, playground, and picnic shelters.

Fishing

The lower Niagara River and Lake Ontario afford numerous opportunities for fishing from

along the winery trail in Niagara County

shore or a chartered vessel. Careful stewardship of area waterways has allowed for sustainable populations of bass, trout, pike, catfish, sunfish, salmon, and many other freshwater species. Adult anglers need to obtain a **fishing license** from the state (www.dec.ny.gov).

Wilson Tuscarora State Park (3371 Lake Rd., Wilson, 716/751-6361, www.nysparks.com) and **Golden Hill State Park** (9691 Lower Lake Rd., Barker, 716/795-3885, www.nysparks.com) provide boat launches ($7) and good spots for shore fishing. A good resource listing all public places to fish, as well as guidelines and regulations, is found on the website of the **Department of Conservation** (www.dec.ny.gov).

ENTERTAINMENT AND EVENTS

The Arts

The **Market Street Art Center** (247 Market St., Lockport, 716/478-0239, www.marketstreetstudios.com, 10am-5pm Tues.-Sat., 11am-4pm Sun., free) features the multimedia works of local artists and offers art classes, too. The building that houses the artists is an old factory built in the 1880s, which provides the perfect industrial backdrop for the labors of local artists. The art center has large interior spaces with brick walls, I-beams, and large steel pipes. Artists who rent the spaces produce watercolor paintings, photography, pottery, jewelry, chainsaw sculptures, embroidery, quilting, leatherwork, and finely crafted furniture.

Fine art pieces by local artists are found at the **Kenan Center House Gallery** (433 Locust St., Lockport, 716/433-2617, www.kenancenter.org, noon-5pm Mon.-Fri., 2pm-5pm Sun. June-Labor Day, noon-5pm Mon.-Fri., 2pm-5pm Sat.-Sun. Labor Day-May, free) in Lockport. The gallery hosts an eclectic array of works, including paintings, sculptures, graphic designs, metal work, pottery, and prints. The Kenan Center is a 25-acre campus that includes the gallery and a sports arena, theater, and educational building. The gallery dates back to 1858 and was the home of businessperson William Rand Kenan. A portion of this sprawling, Victorian-style building houses the gallery, while the rest is used for administrative offices.

Festivals and Events

Niagara's longest-running juried art show, the **100 American Craftsmen Art Show** (www.kenancraftshow.com, $6) displays the works of local artists. It is hosted at the beautiful **Kenan Center Arena** (195 Beattie Ave., Lockport) for three days in late May each year.

Olcott's **Niagara Celtic Heritage Festival and Highland Games** (www.niagaraceltic.com) in Krull Park (6108 Lake Rd., Olcott) celebrates all things Celtic for a weekend in mid-September. The festival provides seminars on Celtic customs and genealogy, with costumed reenactors. Traditional Scottish Highland games are played, such as the caber toss, in which men wearing kilts throw 19-foot (6-m) wooden poles in an attempt to land them upright. During the festival, you can enjoy contemporary Celtic music, falconry, and a demonstration of kilt folding. If you enjoy the music, foods, and traditions of Ireland, Scotland, and Wales, you'll enjoy this festival.

FOOD

Lockport's **Shamus Restaurant** (98 West Ave., Lockport, 716/433-9809, www.theshamus.com, 11am-9pm Mon.-Thurs., 11am-10pm Fri.-Sat., $23) is where the locals enjoy good food at reasonable prices. A few steps away from the canal locks, Shamus serves generous portions, as well as craft beer.

In Lockport, **Kalamata Family Restaurant** (5690 S. Transit Rd., 716/433-2626, www.kalamatafamilyrestaurant.com, 7am-9pm Sun.-Wed., 7am-10pm Thurs.-Sat., $11) has a wide selection of Greek food that comes in huge portions.

ACCOMMODATIONS

Brookins Inn & Suites (2697 Maple Ave., Newfane, 716/870-6244, www.brookinsinn.com, $130) has three suites and two guest rooms, all with private baths. It's a convenient location for people on the Niagara Wine Trail. Home-baked chocolate chip cookies are a nice plus.

Lockport Inn & Suites (315 S. Transit Rd., Lockport, 716/434-5595, www.lockportinnandsuites.com, $150) is a good value, especially the suites, which have fireplaces and whirlpool tubs. The rooms to the rear (farther from the road) are newer and quieter.

GETTING THERE AND AROUND

Lockport is approximately 20 miles (32 km) north of Buffalo (40 min.) and 19 miles (30 km) northeast of Niagara Falls (35 min.). Driving from Buffalo, use Route 78 (Transit Rd.) to reach Lockport; Route 31 joins Lockport with Niagara Falls.

Public transit is provided by **Niagara Frontier Transit Authority** (716/855-7300, www.nfta.com). Bus route 44 ($2 one-way) joins Buffalo and Lockport. The trip takes about 90 minutes. The main bus stop in Lockport is at Locust and Main Streets.

Niagara-on-the-Lake and Wine Country

When war-weary Winston Churchill came to Niagara Falls, Ontario, in August 1943, he found relaxation and beauty during the 13-mile (21-km) drive from the falls to Niagara-on-the-Lake. The prime minister remarked that the trip is "the prettiest Sunday afternoon drive in the world." Those words ring true as you wind your way along the Niagara River Gorge, stopping to visit any of the dozens of wineries in the area.

The Canadian vineyards literally have their roots in Europe. Local vintners imported European grapevines to this region for grafting experiments. Grafting allowed wine-quality grapes to be grown in this climate, yielding sophisticated vintages. Ice wine events, which celebrate this type of dessert wine that is made from grapes that were

Highlights

Look for ★ to find recommended sights, activities, dining, and lodging.

★ **Experience Fort George:** Learn about the dangerous and difficult life of soldiers and civilians who called Fort George home during the War of 1812 (page 143).

★ **Stroll Queen Street:** Explore the heart of the "Prettiest Town in Canada." Stroll, shop, and sip along this street that appears frozen in Victorian times (page 145).

★ **Ride the rapids:** Experience the rapids of the Niagara River on a **Whirlpool Jet Boat Tour** (page 145).

★ **Visit the Lock 7 Viewing Complex:** Enjoy the spectacle of massive freighters gently gliding by as they navigate the locks of the Welland Canal (page 162).

★ **Go back in time at Old Fort Erie:** Guarding the mouth of the Niagara River, Fort Erie survived Canada's bloodiest battle. Historical reenactments bring the drama to life (page 163).

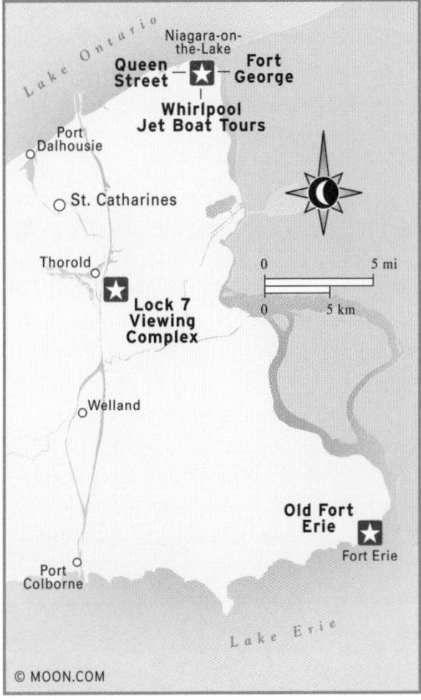

frozen on the vine, are held throughout the year. February, in particular, is a popular time for these events and often feature outdoor tasting bars carved from ice. People gather around fires and toast marshmallows made from wine sugar.

During the War of 1812, American soldiers burned the village of Niagara-on-the-Lake, known in those days as Newark. The entire village was rebuilt and today stands preserved in Victorian time, with many homes and buildings dating to 1814-1820. This is a most romantic place to window-shop and enjoy a perfectly paired wine with dinner.

Lake freighters circumvent the Niagara River via the Welland Canal. This 26-mile (42-km) waterway joins Lake Erie with Lake Ontario, allowing enormous ships safe passage. The canal is used in equal measure for commerce and leisure, coming alive in the summer with numerous festivals in the major towns dotting its edges. The region hosts a tall-ship regatta, Canada's largest single-day music festival (S.C.E.N.E.), Shakespeare in the Vineyard, and many other events year-round.

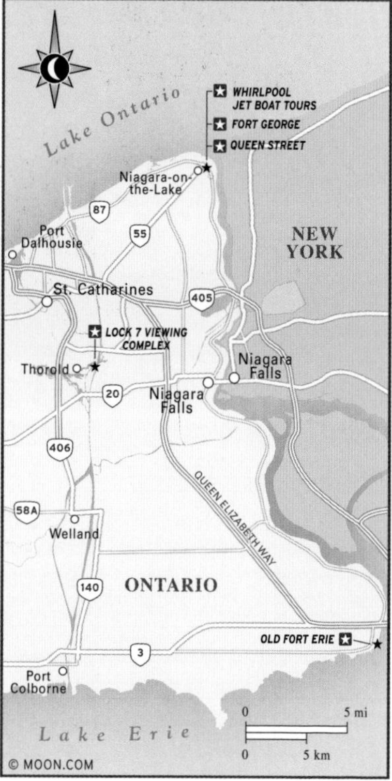

HISTORY

The two indigenous groups that dominated Ontario prior to European exploration were the Algonquins and Iroquois. At times, these groups struggled against each other, and they each eventually sided with one of the two main European powers that explored the region.

By 1615, both the French and the English were exploring Ontario with an eye on trade and colonization. The Algonquins primarily allied themselves with the French, while the Iroquois sided with the English. Following much bloodshed, the English defeated the French during the Seven Years' War, also known as the French and Indian War. By 1780, more than 9,000 English loyalists settled in Ontario, along with many Iroquois who fled New York State following the American Revolution. For a time, Niagara-on-the-Lake was the regional capital, but eventually Toronto was given that designation.

Ontario was in the breach during the War of 1812, witnessing the bloodiest engagements of that conflict. In the end, no land was lost or gained, but the region began moving toward a unified country of Canada. By 1867, Ontario was declared a province and Canada was established as an autonomous dominion, eventually becoming an independent nation with historic and symbolic ties to Britain.

Southern Ontario is culturally diverse. Immigrants from Europe and elsewhere settled here to seek opportunities in agriculture

Previous: Morningstar Mill; Whirlpool Jet Boat Tours on the lower Niagara River; re-enactors at Old Fort Erie

and industry. The region has successfully balanced the challenges and benefits of its three major industries—tourism, farming, and light manufacturing. Transportation is another important economic driver, due to the region's international border and proximity to Toronto.

PLANNING YOUR TIME

This region forms a crescent that surrounds Niagara Falls. It is largely rural, with excellent roadways for easy driving and cycling. Though the regional highlights can be seen during a long (and hectic) day trip, it's better to take two days at a relaxed pace. Some travelers use Niagara Falls as their base, but you may prefer staying overnight in Niagara-on-the-Lake at an inn or bed-and-breakfast.

Visit the towns along the Welland Canal on a single day's adventure. Niagara-on-the-Lake and the wine country are a perfect escape for a separate one-day jaunt.

Niagara-on-the-Lake

Niagara-on-the-Lake (NOTL), a small town of 17,500 residents, has emerged as the center of a region unrivaled in beauty, charm, and historic significance. Located on the shore of Lake Ontario, it is surrounded by thousands of acres of vineyards. In the 1970s, NOTL was at the vanguard of the movement to bring wine-quality grapes from Europe to Canada. Over the years, this area has attracted internationally acclaimed winemakers and chefs. High-end wineries and restaurants thrive because of NOTL's unique proximity to Toronto and Niagara Falls.

SIGHTS

Queenston Heights Park

Queenston Heights Park (14184 Niagara Pkwy., 877/642-7275, www.niagaraparks.com, 24 hours daily, free) is a memorial park with a magnificent view of the Niagara River and lands stretching from the escarpment ridge to Lake Ontario. The strategic value of this perch along the Niagara Gorge was not lost on the combatants in the War of 1812. The British occupied it, and the Americans needed to take it. Thus came the Battle of Queenston Heights, fought on October 13, 1812. The park serves as a memorial of that battle.

This park is all about the view. The Niagara Parkway runs through Queenston Heights, and along it, there's a small paved parking lot (just after a hairpin turn) with a panorama of the green glacial plain that stretches from the escarpment (where you're standing) to Lake Ontario 7 miles (11 km) away. From here, you can see white dots in the water that are not rapids, but sailboats. The river slows and widens, cutting an irregular line that separates Canada from the United States. In summer, the vista is verdant; in fall, it is a festive palette of orange, red, and brown.

Within the park, at the top of **Brock's Monument** (Queenston Heights Park, 905/468-6621, www.friendsoffortgeorge.ca, 10am-5pm daily May-Aug., 11am-4pm Wed.-Sun. Sept.-Oct. 13, $4.50 adults, $3.50 children 6-16) is another magnificent vista. Reaching the top of the 185-foot (56-m) monument involves climbing a seemingly endless circular staircase (235 stairs), which requires some maneuvering to accommodate visitors who are descending (there is no elevator). The view is worth it, but be advised that it is equal to climbing 18 stories' worth of stairs.

Brock's Monument is dedicated to Isaac Brock, the audacious general who died while rallying his troops to repel the invading American forces during the Battle of Queenston Heights. Just outside the monument, there are interpretive plaques that tell the story of the Battle of Queenston Heights, as well as a memorial to Laura Secord, another hero of the War of 1812. Laura Secord is a Canadian folk hero who braved a 20-mile

Niagara-on-the-Lake

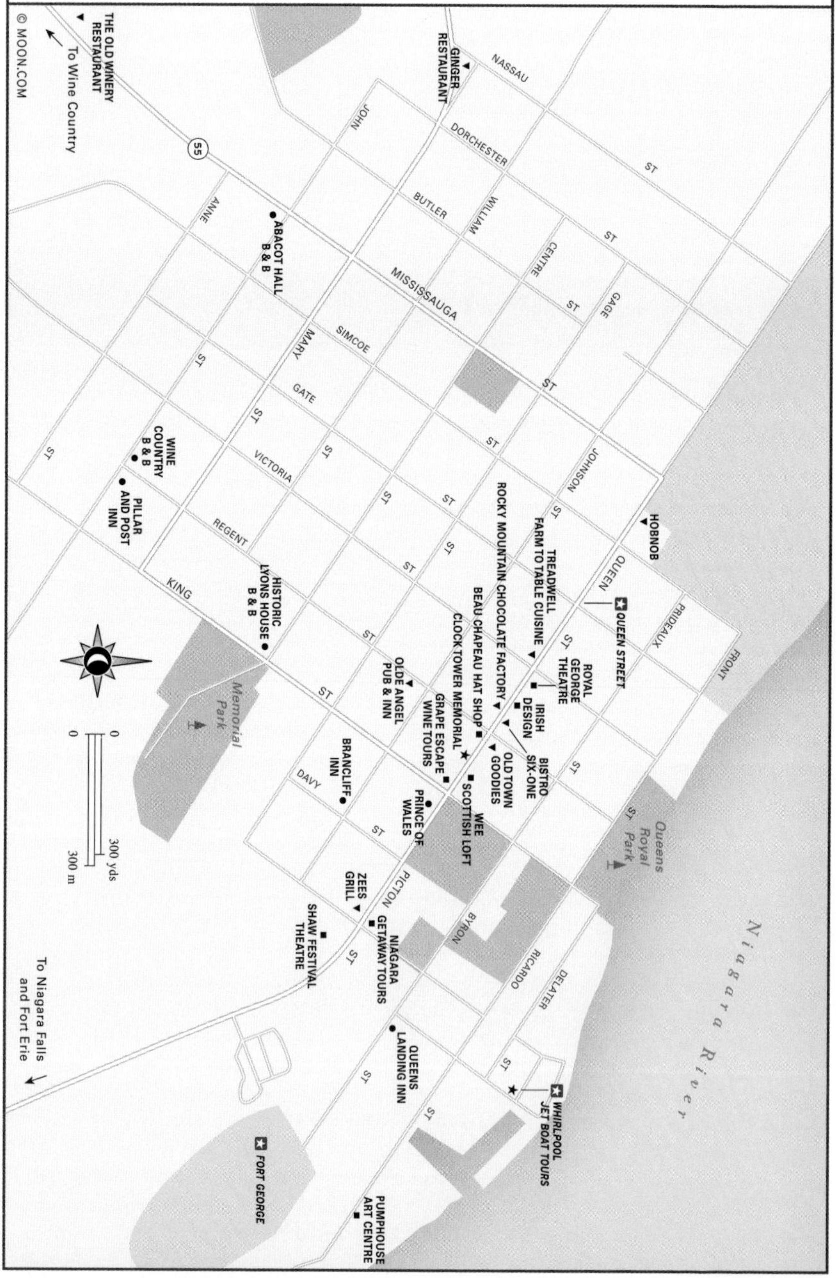

THE OLD WINERY RESTAURANT
To Wine Country
GINGER RESTAURANT
NASSAU
JOHN
DORCHESTER
ST
BUTLER
WILLIAM
ST
CENTRE
ST
GAGE
ANNE
ABACOT HALL B & B
MISSISSAUGA
ST
SIMCOE
MARY
GATE
ST
ST
ST
VICTORIA
WINE COUNTRY B & B
PILLAR AND POST INN
REGENT
KING
ST
ST
ST
ST
ST
JOHNSON
ST
HOBNOB
QUEEN
QUEEN STREET
PRIDEAUX
FRONT
TREADWELL FARM TO TABLE CUISINE
ROCKY MOUNTAIN CHOCOLATE FACTORY
ROYAL GEORGE THEATRE
IRISH DESIGN
BEAU CHAPEAU HAT SHOP
CLOCK TOWER MEMORIAL
BISTRO SIX-ONE
OLD TOWN GOODIES
GRAPE ESCAPE WINE TOURS
WEE SCOTTISH LOFT
HISTORIC LYONS HOUSE B & B
OLDE ANGEL PUB & INN
ST
Memorial Park
BRANCLIFF INN
PRINCE OF WALES
DAVY
ST
ST
Queens Royal Park
0
300 yds
0
300 m
ZEES GRILL
PICTON
BYRON
NIAGARA GETAWAY TOURS
SHAW FESTIVAL THEATRE
ST
RICARDO
DELATER
Niagara River
To Niagara Falls and Fort Erie
QUEENS LANDING INN
ST
ST
WHIRLPOOL JET BOAT TOURS
ST
FORT GEORGE
PUMPHOUSE ART CENTRE

© MOON.COM

(32-km) walk through enemy lines to alert British forces of an impending American attack. The Secord monument was the first Canadian monument built in honor of a woman.

The grounds at Queenston Heights are everything you'd expect from Niagara Parks, including meticulously groomed greenery, acres of open space, well-maintained picnic facilities, clean restrooms, and plenty of parking. It is the best location in the region for family picnics.

The entrance to the park is at the traffic circle on Niagara Parkway. Bear right to park near Brock's Monument; turn left to park next to the picnic areas.

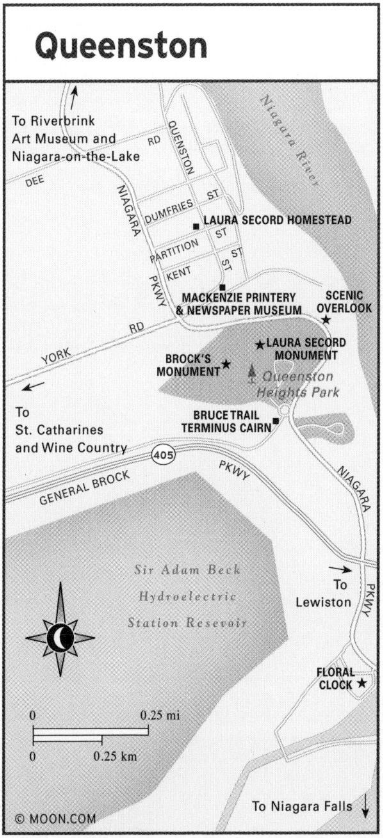

Mackenzie Printery and Newspaper Museum

The power of the press in determining Ontario's fate is on display at the **Mackenzie Printery and Newspaper Museum** (1 Queenston St., 905/262-5676, www.niagaraparksheritage.com, 10am-5pm daily May-Aug., 10am-5pm Sat.-Sun. Sept.-Oct., \$6.42 adults, \$4.42 children 6-16). The printery is a restoration of the home of William Lyon Mackenzie, a 19th-century publisher and advocate for government reform. The museum is a stately limestone, Federal-style home built using the original plans of Mackenzie's 1850s home. It's small but allows for hands-on learning on a historical printing press.

Mackenzie was a businessperson who wanted to change the existing political framework that favored British-born subjects at the expense of those who had emigrated from the United States. Mackenzie was elected to office, led an ill-fated and ineffective revolt, spent time in jail, and helped create reform in Canada's government. Docents bring to life Mackenzie's firebrand advocacy and his principled resistance to government cronyism.

Docents also discuss 500 years of printing press history. The museum's collection of eight working presses includes the Louis Roy Press, which dates back to 1770 and is the oldest printing press in Canada. Docents supervise as visitors create documents using vintage linotype technology and a hand-operated wooden heritage press. The printery is a hidden gem that will take about an hour to explore.

Laura Secord Homestead

The **Laura Secord Homestead** (29 Queenston St., 905/262-4851, www.niagaraparksheritage.com, 10am-5pm daily May-Aug., 10am-4pm Wed.-Fri., 10am-5pm Sat.-Sun. Sept.-mid-Oct. \$9.73 adults, \$6.42 children 6-12) is the home of Canada's most famous heroine. Restored to its original condition, the homestead affords a glimpse into

1
2

the life of settlers who lived in this area in the early 1800s.

Laura Secord is remembered for her heroism during the War of 1812. Upon overhearing a remark from American soldiers about an impending attack against British troops, she set out on a 20-mile (32-km) trip to relay the information to the British Military Command. Visitors are led through the homestead by a costumed guide who relates the compelling story of the settlers who came to southern Ontario. The homestead itself becomes a character in the narrative as your guide uses furniture, kitchenware, and other artifacts to explain the experience of 19th-century settlers.

History fans will like this attraction; fans of Canadian history will love it. Plan to spend 30-60 minutes here.

McFarland House

Drink in the history and some wonderful tea at the **McFarland House** (15927 Niagara Pkwy., 905/468-3322, www.niagaraparksheritage.com, noon-5pm daily mid-May-Aug., noon-5pm Sat.-Sun. Sept.-Oct., $6.64 adults, $4.42 children 6-12). This restored home welcomes visitors into the well-mannered world of the early 1800s.

Built and occupied by shipbuilder John McFarland, this structure is unique because it survived the burning of Niagara-on-the-Lake in 1813, likely because it was used during the war as a hospital for wounded U.S. and British soldiers. The McFarland House is also the oldest structure owned and maintained by the Niagara Parks Commission; it was built in 1800. The house is surrounded by parkland with ample parking, picnic shelters, and a baseball diamond.

Guides dressed in period costumes provide tours of the home and share stories about 19th-century life in southern Ontario. They describe the civility and customs of the Georgian era against an authentic backdrop. Look for the antique rope bed that demonstrates the origin of the term "sleep tight."

For a relaxing break, try the afternoon tea, with freshly baked scones and light sandwiches (if you order scones, ask for the ice wine jelly). Choose among many teas, including the vividly named Delirium Blossom Flowering Tea. Grab a table at the conservatory, overlooking the river.

Allot 30 minutes to visit this house, and 45 minutes more if you stay for tea or a meal.

★ Fort George

The fortifications, buildings, and grounds of **Fort George** (51 Queen's Parade, 905/468-6621, www.friendsoffortgeorge.ca, noon-4pm Sat.-Sun. Dec.-Mar., 10am-5pm Sat.-Sun. Apr. and Nov., 10am-5pm daily May-Oct., $11.90 adults, $10.20 seniors, free for children 16 and under) are wonderful, but the staff here make it a must-see.

Costumed docents really get into character here as they depict life during the War of 1812. From your first interaction with the guardhouse sentry (who may play a tune on his pennywhistle for you) to the cannon-firing demonstration, there is an emphasis on authenticity. These lively docents know their history; they can easily answer questions and entertain with improvised interactions.

The fort is not just for history buffs. Children can try on uniforms and participate in some demonstrations. The Fife and Drum Corps fills the air with music while marching across the parade grounds with pageantry. Take a walk to the southern portion of the fort to find the powder magazine, the only original structure remaining from when the fort was first constructed in 1796. The thick stone walls of this single-story rectangular building were designed to withstand cannon fire. Inside the magazine are dozens of barrels representing the black powder that was stored here during the War of 1812, as well as interpretive signs describing the safety measures taken by soldiers who worked here. Do not miss the barracks, officers' quarters, and blacksmith—each reveals an engaging story

1: view from Queenston Heights Park
2: Brock's Monument in Queenston

1

2

about the simple but hard and dangerous life in the fort.

The fort hosts many special events throughout the year, such as battle reenactments and holiday festivals. Check the website's events calendar for more information. Budget at least 2-4 hours to fully appreciate Fort George.

★ Queen Street

Queen Street is the main thoroughfare of Niagara-on-the-Lake, and the heart of the charming village, which appears to have been frozen in Victorian times. The village was destroyed in 1813 by U.S. soldiers fleeing across the river and was then rebuilt, so many structures date back to the early 1800s.

Queen Street is quaint, picturesque, and romantic. The street is lined with shops, restaurants, hotels, and theaters. Flowers are everywhere in summer, bursting with color from planters and hanging baskets. Most visitors spend their time leisurely strolling the street, checking out the wares in one-of-a-kind shops like the Scottish Loft, Irish Design, and Beau Chapeau Hat Shop. NOTL draws visitors from around the world, so you're likely to overhear conversations in four or five different languages.

The village's identity is intertwined with the world-famous Shaw Festival, which features new productions of George Bernard Shaw's plays each year. Two of the four theaters participating in the festival are located on Queen Street.

A list of Queen Street shops and restaurants is on the official Niagara-on-the-Lake website (www.niagaraonthelake.com).

★ Whirlpool Jet Boat Tours

The number-one white-knuckle, death-defying attraction on this side of the Niagara River is the **Whirlpool Jet Boat Tours** (61 Melville St., 888/438-4444, www.whirlpooljet.com, 60 min., $72.95 adults, $44.95 children 12 and under). Jet boats are uniquely designed vessels capable of surviving the severe white-water conditions of the lower Niagara River.

Tours are in covered boats (Jet Domes) and open-air boats (Wet Jets). If your courage permits, choose the Wet Jet. The experience is exhilarating, frightening, and saturating. Each tour begins with a safety discussion and an explanation of what gear you need to wear. If you choose the Wet Jet, you and all your personal effects will be drenched. Do not take cameras or other electronic devices aboard unless they are specifically designed for underwater use.

The ride begins quietly as the boat glides through the relatively smooth waters of the river near the entrance to Lake Ontario. Heading south on the river, the boat can increase speed and perform a few stunts like 360-degree spins. A crew member narrates the trip, discussing the nature of the river's white water.

The jet boats take you through stretches of challenging Class V rapids in the narrow parts of the lower Niagara River. (Class VI waves are considered the most dangerous.) Here the boat manages to navigate waves 15-20 feet (4-6 m) high. At times, there will be a foot or more of water inside the boat, but don't worry: The boat's design allows it to safely conquer white water. Certain maneuvers result in a wall of water slamming over the boat, and though you are warned in advance, nothing can quite prepare you for this experience.

The exhilarating ride is scary, but safe. There is another location to board the Whirlpool Jet Boat Tours on the Canadian side at the **Queenston Dock** (55 River Frontage Rd., 888/438-4444, www.whirlpooljet.com), and there is a location for this tour on the U.S. side in **Lewiston** (115 S. Water St., Lewiston, 888/438-4444, www.whirlpooljet.com). All three tours are operated by the same company. However, the tour that leaves from the location at Melville Street in Niagara-on-the-Lake is 60 minutes round trip, and the tours from the Queenston Dock and Lewiston are 45 minutes round trip.

1: Mackenzie Printery and Newspaper Museum
2: Laura Secord Homestead

RECREATION

Hiking

The granddaddy of Ontario hiking trails is the **Bruce Trail** (http://brucetrail.org), which stretches 550 miles (885 km) north of Queenston to Tobermory along Georgian Bay. The Bruce Trail generally follows the Niagara Escarpment and is Canada's oldest and longest footpath. It's also a UNESCO World Biosphere Reserve that traverses public and private lands.

The Niagara section of the Bruce Trail covers an 11.5-mile (18.5-km) route from Queenston to St. Catharines through forested, rural, and urban areas. Hiking this portion of the trail will take you past the Niagara River, along vineyards, and through mature forests as you ascend 40 feet (12 m) in elevation. The Bruce is an out-and-back trail, so consider turning around where the Bruce Trail intersects the Upper Canada Heritage Trail (at 2.6 mi/4 km on the Bruce Trail).

The Queenston to St. Catharines section of the Bruce Trail is well maintained and accessible for hikers of all levels. The southern terminus for the Bruce Trail is in Queenston Heights Park (14184 Niagara Pkwy.). Look for a cairn in the main parking lot of Queenston Heights, near the entrance roundabout, and follow the white blaze markers.

Bicycling

The **Vineyards & Blossoms Trail** is a 25-mile (40-km) bike route that gives an excellent overview of Niagara-on-the-Lake. The route begins in the heart of NOTL, looping along the Niagara River Recreational Trail, the Lake Ontario Waterfront Trail, and through miles of vineyards. Should you desire a rest stop, there are eight wineries to investigate on this trail.

ENTERTAINMENT AND EVENTS

The Arts

NIAGARA PUMPHOUSE VISUAL ART CENTRE

The **Niagara Pumphouse Visual Art Centre** (247 Ricardo St., 905/468-5455, www.niagarapumphouse.ca, noon-4pm Mon.-Fri., 1pm-4pm Sat.-Sun. May-Nov., free) reminds us not to judge a book by its cover. The outside of this brick building is Victorian and blocky, but the interior explodes with creativity. This building once housed the pumps that brought water to the village of Niagara-on-the-Lake. Today it is home to the work of local artists and provides a space for new artists to learn their craft. Exhibitions change frequently, so check the website for updated information.

RIVERBRINK ART MUSEUM

The benefactor of the **Riverbrink Art Museum** (116 Queenston St., 905/262-4510, www.riverbrink.org, 10am-5pm daily late May-Oct., 10am-5pm Wed.-Sat. Nov.-late May, $5 adults, $4 seniors and students, free for children 12 and under), Samuel Weir, liked the facility so much that he is buried in the yard. Weir, an eccentric art collector and successful lawyer, found beauty in many things, especially art. His passion for collecting works is manifest in this museum, which was also his home.

The museum focuses on the works of Canadian fine artists, as well as other works of local interest. Many pieces depict life in southern Ontario, including a collection of paintings from the War of 1812 era. The museum is also well known for its Inuit sculpture. In all, there are more than 1,000 works in its collection, plus a robust exhibition schedule.

1: this cairn marks the terminus of the 560 mile long Bruce Trail **2:** a theater where Shaw Festival performances take place **3:** Beau Chapeau Hat Shop

THIS CAIRN MARKS THE
SOUTHERN
TERMINUS
OF
THE BRUCE TRAIL
A CROSS-COUNTRY FOOT TRAIL ESTABLISHED ALONG OR ADJACENT TO THE NIAGARA ESCARPMENT EXTENDING FROM TOBERMORY ON GEORGIAN BAY IN THE NORTH TO THIS SOUTHERN TERMINUS AT QUEENSTON HEIGHTS
1
SHAW
WHEN WE ARE MARRIED
PERFORMANCES BEGIN MAY 7
SHAW
ARMS AND THE MAN
THE ROYAL GEORGE
2
3
BeauChapeau
HAT SHOP
BOXING WEEK SALE
OPEN

Festivals and Events

Start the New Year properly by attending the **Niagara Icewine Festival** (www.niagarawinefestival.com), hosted by wineries throughout the Niagara region in the latter three weeks of January. Imagine drinking wine from a glass made of freshly carved ice or roasting ice wine marshmallows over a fire as you sip a perfectly paired vintage. Or enjoy dinner and wine with five friends inside a giant heated glass snow globe (just $999!). This festival marries two things for which southern Ontario is famous: good wine and freezing cold weather. It's a great reason to be outside. Tasting fees vary by winery, and events are open to people of all ages; sparkling grape juice is substituted for wine for underage participants or those who avoid alcohol. A **Discover Pass** (www.niagarawinefestival.com, $45) allows you eight wine-tasting experiences throughout the duration of the festival.

April-September, the stage is set in Niagara-on-the-Lake for the **Shaw Festival** (www.shawfest.com, $27 and up). The Shaw Festival started in 1962 and has grown to become a major Canadian event, drawing 250,000 people to performances annually. Each year, at least 10 new productions are brought to the stages of four theaters in NOTL. The festival is known for encouraging ingenious twists on existing plays. One production of *Joan,* the story of Joan of Arc, portrayed the story as occurring during the Balkan conflicts of the 1990s. The Shaw Festival has attracted dignitaries like Queen Elizabeth II, Indira Gandhi, and Canadian Prime Minister Pierre Trudeau.

SHOPPING

Queen Street has an eclectic group of shops selling wine, clothing, and Canadian-themed gifts. Shops here tend to skew to the high end, but given the unique nature of many of them, including ones that specialize in authentic Irish and Scottish wares, it's worth the splurge. Look for a list of Queen Street shops on the official Niagara-on-the-Lake website (www.niagaraonthelake.com).

The **Beau Chapeau Hat Shop** (42 Queen St., 905/468-8011, www.beauchapeau.com, 9:30am-6pm Mon.-Thurs., 9:30am-8pm Fri. and Sun., 9am-8pm Sat.) is a gorgeous, 1920s-themed store (think The Great Gatsby era). It has more than 10,000 hats for well-dressed ladies and gentlemen. The shop also sells gloves, scarves, umbrellas, and accessories.

Irish Design (75 Queen St., 905/468-7233, www.irishdesign.com, 9:30am-5:30pm Mon.-Fri., 9:30am-6pm Sat., 10am-6pm Sun.) is as quaint as Ireland is green. The selection of women's and men's sweaters, jackets, and coats is truly grand. In addition to clothing, you'll find accessories and official Guinness merchandise. Relax in the shop's Irish Tea Room and try a slice of Bushmills whiskey cake.

For the wee bit of Scot in all of us, try the **Wee Scottish Loft** (13 Queen St., 905/468-0965, www.scottishloft.com, 10am-5pm daily). This small shop caters to those interested in gifts, foods, and media from England, Wales, and Scotland. If you're in the market for a kilt, a Union Jack pillow, authentic sticky toffee pudding, or Benny Hill DVDs, you've found your place! If you are of Scottish descent, there are numerous gifts reflecting your clan's tartan pattern or crest.

Find hundreds of reasons to ignore your diet at the **Rocky Mountain Chocolate Factory** (70 Queen St., 905/468-0800, www.rockychoc.com, 10am-7pm daily May-Oct., 10am-5pm daily Nov.-Apr.). Most of the confections are handmade on-site, including caramels, candy apples, nut clusters, and toffees. For calorie-counters, there are sugar-free sweets and frozen yogurt. The shop also sells pet treats that are cocoa bean-free and safe for your pooch to eat.

FOOD

Pub fare, history, and a ghost are on the menu at the ★ **Olde Angel Inn** (224 Regent St., 905/468-3411, www.angel-inn.com, 11am-1am daily, $20). This authentic British pub serves pub grub such as ploughman's lunch (traditional English midday meal of bread, cheese, eggs, and beer) and shepherd's pie. The food is reasonably priced and served promptly. The hand-hewn wooden beams of the low ceiling and wood-burning fireplace may make you feel as if you're stepping into a pub in the misty English countryside. Olde Angel is reportedly haunted by the ghost of Colonel Colin Swayze, a British officer who was killed by American soldiers while visiting his beloved, a woman who worked at the former pub here. Legend has it that an apparition appears in the mirror of the ladies' room and that the taps of American draft beers mysteriously open, causing the American beer to flow into the drain.

If you're on Queen Street and you need good food fast, head to **Old Town Goodies** (29 Queen St., 289/868-9603, www.oldtowngoodies.ca, 10am-9pm daily, $8.50). The shop is set up for take-out orders only. The food is fresh and prepared quickly while you wait. The menu is a good selection of paninis and salads, with all items under $9. The Butler's Beef BBQ Panini ($8.95) is wonderfully satisfying and takes its name from a local soldier who was famous for raiding the United States during the American Revolution. Old Town Goodies is also great for a quick espresso or an ice-cream cone. In a town of high-end eateries, this ma-and-pa joint (operated by generations of the Pullman family) is short on pretense and big on value.

The **HOBNOB** (209 Queen St., 905/468-4588, www.niagarasfinest.com, 5pm-8pm Mon.-Fri., 11am-3pm and 5pm-8pm Sat.-Sun., $40) offers fine dining in a distinguished atmosphere. Meals are served in the exquisite dining room of a restored 1832 mansion in the northern end of Niagara-on-the-Lake. The dinner menu is not extensive, but it emphasizes a farm-to-table ethic where local foods are tastefully employed whenever possible. If you're not exactly hungry for dinner, try the lounge menu for smaller portions with a superior taste.

For great Asian food at reasonable prices, go to the **Ginger Restaurant** (390 Mary St., 905/468-3871, www.gingerrestaurant.ca, 5pm-9pm Wed.-Sun., $26). The dining room is small, with a capacity of only 40 people, but it's warm and inviting. Ginger's menu is a fusion of Japanese, Chinese, and Thai cuisine. Reservations are recommended, especially if you are planning to eat before or after a performance at one of the Shaw Festival theaters, all within walking distance.

Bistro Six-One (61 Queen St., 905/468-2532, www.bistrosixone.com, 11am-9pm Sun.-Thurs., 11am-10pm Fri.-Sat., $25) offers an alternative to high-priced restaurants along Queen Street. The ambience is casual and the menu is contemporary Canadian, as evidenced by the wonderful maple salmon dish. Another highlight is the pizza cooked in wood-burning brick ovens—try the potato and bacon pizza for a warm and filling meal. The bistro provides tastings of local wines at the bar.

Find contemporary Mediterranean food at the **Old Winery Restaurant** (2228 Niagara Stone Rd., 905/468-8900, www.theoldwineryrestaurant.com, 11:30am-9pm Sun.-Wed., 11:30am-10pm Thurs., 11:30am-midnight Fri.-Sat., $20). As the name suggests, the building is a renovated winery that is now a casual restaurant and wine bar with some Tuscan flair. As soon as you walk in the door, you can see and smell the brick pizza oven. If you enjoy dining to live music, take a table in the Wine Lounge, which has music acts on Friday and Saturday evenings.

You'll never be late for a show at the Shaw Festival if you dine at ★ **Zees Grill** (92 Picton St., 905/468-5715, www.zees.ca, 8am-10am, 11:30am-2:30pm, and 5pm-9pm daily May-Nov., $32). Zees is across the street from the Shaw Festival Theatre. Weather permitting, reserve a table on the front patio and experience one of the most beautiful dining venues in Niagara-on-the-Lake. Several popular dishes also have vegan versions, and there is a wide variety of local wines. Appetizers are a bit pricey ($14 average); desserts are wonderful, especially the local honey and ginger crème brûlée.

Chef Stephen Treadwell has a simple food philosophy: prepare dishes with as few ingredients as possible, and be sure they're locally sourced. This has been a recipe for success at **Treadwell Farm-to-Table Cuisine** (114 Queen St., 905/934-9797, www.

treadwellcuisine.com, 11:30am-3pm and 5pm-10pm Wed.-Mon., $30). Treadwell's restaurant has the feel of a modern bistro, with small tables tightly packed together and a serving counter where patrons can watch food being prepared as they eat. Most, if not all, of the meat is sourced from Cumbrae's farms, a consortium of local farmers in Ontario.

The **Kitchen 76** (240 John St., 905/468-0592, www.twosistersvineyards.com, 11:30am-3pm and 5pm-9pm daily, $35) delivers an authentic taste of Italy in a restaurant surrounded by one of the most beautiful wineries in NOTL. If possible, reserve a table on the patio overlooking the vineyards; you may feel as if you are dining in Italy. If it pairs well with your entrée, try the unoaked chardonnay for a unique experience.

ACCOMMODATIONS

One of the finest hotels in Niagara-on-the-Lake is the ★ **Queen's Landing** (155 Byron St., 888/669-5566, www.vintage-hotels.com, $350). Styled as a Georgian mansion, the hotel is close to all the main attractions in NOTL and just a few steps from the waterfront. Standard rooms are not overly large but have nice amenities, including a Keurig coffeemaker and turndown service with a rose left on the pillow. Queen's Landing is one of three luxury properties operated by Vintage Hotels in NOTL. The other two, **Prince of Wales** (6 Picton St., 905/468-3246, www.vintage-hotels.com, $370) and **Pillar and Post** (48 John St. W., 905/468-2123, www.vintage-hotels.com, $400), offer similar excellent accommodations.

Niagara-on-the-Lake is home to more than 150 bed-and-breakfasts. The **BranCliff Inn** (40 Platoff St., 905/468-8800, www.brancliffinn.com, $259) is among the top choices. Located one block away from Queen Street and the Shaw Festival Theatre, BranCliff exudes charm and comfort. All six rooms have bathrooms en suite, and five have gas fireplaces. The inn dates back to 1859 and has been tastefully renovated to maintain the historic sense of the structure, while providing modern comforts such as Wi-Fi and refrigerators stocked with complimentary drinks.

Enjoy English elegance at the **Historic Lyons House B&B** (8 Centre St., 905/468-2297, www.lyonshouse.ca, $269). Inside this 1835 home are three spacious guest rooms with a Georgian period theme and paintings by local Canadian artist Linda Hankin. Outside, enjoy the half-acre traditional English garden with its lush green lawn, fountain, shade trees, and friendly cat.

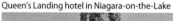

Queen's Landing hotel in Niagara-on-the-Lake

Abacot Hall B&B (508 Mississauga St., 905/468-8383, www.abacothall.com, May-Dec., $175) is a short walk away from NOTL's shopping, dining, and theater district. The B&B's three suites are decorated in a Victorian theme and include en suite bathrooms. Free Wi-Fi, a full breakfast, and the use of bicycles are provided, compliments of the owners, Irene and Ed. If you arrive on a Friday, a two-night minimum stay is required.

After visiting the **Wine Country B&B** (75 John St. W., 905/468-8701, www.winecountrybb.com, $189) for 12 years, the Mitchell family decided to buy and operate it. The property's three guest rooms have private baths, comfortable queen-size beds, and warm color schemes. The largest room, the Queenston Suite, has rich redwood furniture and a private balcony. Your hosts, Sharon and Mike, will make recommendations for visiting wineries and attractions. The front veranda is excellent for enjoying a glass of wine while you watch the sunset and unwind after a long day of touring, or you can relax in front of the fireplace if the evening is chilly.

GETTING THERE AND AROUND

There are three primary ways to get to Niagara-on-the-Lake from the main tourist area of Niagara Falls, Ontario. If you have transportation, the best way to arrive at NOTL is via the beautiful Niagara Parkway. This meandering scenic route takes you along the rim of the gorge. Much of the road is two lanes, with a speed limit of less than 40 miles per hour (64 kph). Most visitors embrace the slow pace of the journey and enjoy the view.

Highways can speed your drive to Niagara-on-the-Lake. From the Fallsview hotel area, take Route 420 to the Queen Elizabeth Way (QEW). From the QEW, you'll take the exit for Route 55, also known as Niagara Stone Road. This drive takes you to the back of NOTL village. You'll want to make your way to Queen Street to appreciate the major sites. One advantage of this route is that you'll pass several good wineries along the way, including Joseph Estates, Stratus, Pillitteri, and Jackson Triggs. All of these are worth a visit.

The third way to explore Niagara-on-the-Lake is via the convenient **WEGO** bus system (www.wegoniagarafalls.com). If you're using WEGO already, you'll find the $9 24-hour pass an exceptional value. Use the Green Line route to take you from Fallsview to the Floral Clock. Once there, you can purchase a round-trip ticket ($14 adults, $10 children 6-12) for the NOTL Shuttle, also known as the Orange Line route. This service is available April 30-October 30 only, and it operates 10:30am-6pm. Using WEGO allows you the opportunity to make stops along the way at several attractions, including Queenston Heights, Mackenzie Printery, Laura Secord Homestead, and the McFarland House. The last stop is Fort George, a pleasant, brief walk to the main village of Niagara-on-the-Lake.

Street parking in the main tourist area is metered, as are the five nearby public parking lots. Rates are reasonable and start from $1.75 per hour. Machines accept credit cards or Canadian coins, but not U.S. currency. A complete map of **street parking and public parking lots** is online (www.niagaraonthelake.com).

This area is easily navigated on foot. The main drag is Queen Street, with its many restaurants, shops, and theaters. The area of interest to visitors is roughly a seven-by-seven-block area bisected by Queen Street. There is a small public transit system in Niagara-on-the-Lake, but it is geared toward transporting residents into central NOTL for work. There is one portion of the NOTL Transit System (www.notl.org) that may be of use to travelers. May-October, daily **shuttle buses** connecting the Old Court House and Fort George run every 10 minutes. One-way fare is $3; you'll need exact change in Canadian currency. Hours of operation vary by day and month, so check the website for the most accurate information. The Old Court House faces Queen Street, but the bus stop is behind the building on a service road connecting two public parking lots.

Southern Ontario Wine Country

You may think Canada is all cold weather and maple syrup. Think again! The Niagara-on-the-Lake region contains more than 30 wineries and is the center for the crafting of world-class wines in Canada. Whether you tour by car, bus, or bike, you can taste the spirit of Niagara in every wine you sample in this region.

"Wine country" refers to the approximately 42 square miles (108 sq km) of fertile plain bounded by Route 405 to the south, the Niagara River to the east, Lake Ontario to the north, and the Welland Canal to the west.

Most people exploring wine country find accommodations in Niagara-on-the-Lake. A majority of people use their cars to explore, while others hop on a tour bus. It is impractical to walk to wineries because of the distances involved, but cycling through wine country is gaining in popularity.

WINERIES

Inniskillin Winery

All contemporary Canadian wineries have roots that reach back to the **Inniskillin Winery** (1499 Line 3 Rd., NOTL, 888/466-4754, www.inniskillin.com, 10am-6pm daily May-Oct., 10am-5pm daily Nov.-Apr., tasting fee $3 and up per sample). In the early 1970s, the founders of Inniskillin decided to create world-class wines and were granted the first winery license in Ontario since the Prohibition era.

Their work in cultivating wine grapes adapted to Ontario's unique climate launched an entire industry. Driving into the winery, you'll notice architecture with hints of Frank Lloyd Wright. The estate originally belonged to Darwin Martin, who employed Wright to build several structures in the Buffalo area.

Although many of the vintages have received medals at tasting competitions, Inniskillin is particularly known for its ice wines. Tours ($20) are available on the hour 10:30am-4:30pm, and the Market Grill (open daily during summer) offers food pairings to complement their wines.

Château de Charmes

Another pioneer in Ontario winemaking is the Bosc family, owners of the **Château de Charmes Winery** (1025 York Rd., St. Davids, 905/262-4219, www.chateaudecharmes.com, 10am-6pm daily, tasting fee $1 and up per serving). The Bosc family championed the exclusive cultivation of *Vitis vinifera*, the European grape varieties known to yield the finest wines. They were in the vanguard of agritourism and built the sprawling Château des Charmes Winery and Visitors Centre. Tours are held daily ($15) in English, French, and Japanese.

Peller Estates

On the outskirts of Niagara-on-the-Lake, just before you drive into the village, there's a stunning estate surrounded by vineyards. **Peller Estates** (290 John St. E., NOTL, 905/468-4678, www.peller.com, 10am-9pm Fri.-Sat., 10am-7pm Sun.-Thurs., tasting fee $15) is a gorgeous winery with a first-class restaurant that should not be missed.

As you enter the winery, a fireplace with comfortable couches greets you. The structure is spacious yet warm and inviting. To the left is the wine boutique, where tastings are available. To the right is the winery's restaurant, which has received Zagat's highest culinary rating (Extraordinary). Tours are offered daily ($35); the tour includes a visit to the igloo-themed 10 Below Icewine Lounge.

Stratus Vineyards

Stratus Vineyards (2059 Niagara Stone Rd., NOTL, 905/468-1806, www.stratuswines.com, 11am-5pm daily May-Dec., noon-5pm Wed.-Sun. Jan.-Apr., tour and tasting fee $15, specialty tours $25 and up) is a modern winery dedicated to making top-quality wine while

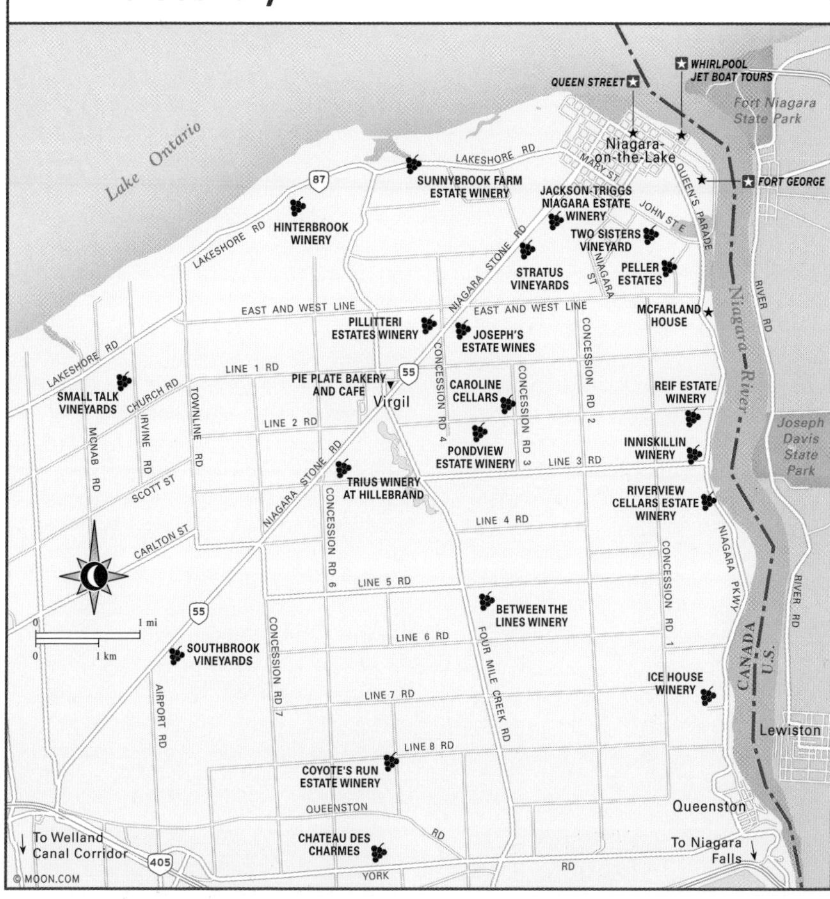

reducing the impact of that process on the environment. This is the only LEED (Leadership in Energy and Environmental Design) certified winery in Canada. The wines here are limited production, which means that many vintages are only available on-site rather than in stores. Stratus is renowned for its premium single-varietal reds and whites.

Jackson-Triggs Niagara Estate Winery

The architecture is as stunning as the wines at **Jackson-Triggs Niagara Estate Winery** (2145 Niagara Stone Rd., NOTL, 905/468-4637, www.jacksontriggswinery.com, 10am-6:30pm daily June-mid-Sept., 10am-5:30pm daily mid-Sept.-May, tasting fee $10). At the entrance is a magnificent, modern glass-and-metal barn. Its two huge sliding doors open in the summer, allowing visitors to pass through the building directly to the vineyards. The atmosphere is open, airy, and inviting. Tours (10:30am-5:30pm daily, $15) are offered every hour on the half hour.

Jackson-Triggs offers a full spectrum of wines. The Entourage Grand Reserve

Sparkling Brut 2009 is among its best. The winery also has a summer season of live concerts at its 500-seat outdoor amphitheater.

Reif Estate Winery

While many NOTL winery operations have an Italian or French heritage, **Reif Estate Winery** (15608 Niagara Pkwy., NOTL, 905/468-9463, www.reifwinery.com, 10am-6pm daily Apr.-Oct., 10am-5pm daily Nov.-Mar., tour and tasting fee $15) has its roots in Germany's Rhine Valley. The winery produces a complete range of good varietals. In 2017 Reif earned eight medals for various ice wines.

Caroline Cellars

Caroline Cellars (1028 Line 2 Rd., Virgil, 905/468-8814, www.carolinecellars.com, 10am-5pm daily Jan.-Mar., 10am-6pm daily Apr.-Dec., free tastings) is a family-owned and -operated winery that distinguishes itself by producing fruit wines in addition to traditional reds and whites. Both the plum wine and the cranberry winter harvest wine were medal winners.

Trius Winery

Trius Winery (1249 Niagara Stone Rd., NOTL, 905/468-7123, www.triuswines.com, 11am-6pm daily, tours noon-4pm daily, tasting fee $15, tour with tasting $39) was the first winery in Niagara-on-the-Lake to have a restaurant on-site. Today this spirit of innovation continues. Hillebrand focuses on the wine-tasting experience, with an emphasis on pairing wine with the proper food. Throughout the year, more than a dozen different tours and tastings are offered, each a unique experience. If you like red wine, try the Trius Red. A blend of cabernet franc, cabernet sauvignon, and merlot grapes, it was designated as the world's best red wine at the prestigious International Wine and Spirits Competition in London.

Between the Lines Winery

You'll taste local pride in every bottle of wine at the **Between the Lines Winery** (991 Four Mile Creek Rd., NOTL, 905/262-0289, www.betweenthelineswinery.com, 10am-6pm daily Apr.-Oct., 11am-5pm Tues.-Sun. Nov.-Mar., tasting fee $1 per sample). This small family winery is operated by the Wertsch brothers, who believe that vintners should trust the local grape varieties, rather than imitate those grown elsewhere. Their philosophy has resulted in wines that lack pretense, with the true taste of Niagara.

wines from Peller Estates

At this proud boutique winery, wines are small-batch and sold only on-site in the big red barn. For a unique wine, try the Lemberger, a red. Between the Lines is the only local winery to use lemberger grapes. Finding the winery is easy. It's on Four Mile Creek Road between Line 5 and Line 6 Roads (hence the name Between the Lines). Another recent innovation is Outset—sparkling wine in a can.

Sunnybrook Farm Estate Winery

The Niagara region is blessed with the ability to grow many fruits in addition to grapes. The **Sunnybrook Farm Estate Winery** (1425 Lakeshore Rd., NOTL, 905/468-1122, www.sunnybrookwine.com, 10am-6pm daily May-Oct., 11am-5pm Nov.-Apr., tasting fee $1 per sample) recognizes and celebrates this by making fruit wines. Apples, peaches, nectarines, cherries, and pears are among the fruits grown on the 10-acre estate and used in wine production.

Sunnybrook's unique boutique selection of fruit wines are not necessarily sweet—they are balanced with acidity to reflect the selected fruit's true flavor. An intriguing Chocolate Series of wines are featured, which blend dark chocolate with blueberry for an artisanal dessert treat. A new addition to the family is the winery's Ironwood Hard Cider complex featuring a tasty, tangy peach-ginger cider with 6.3 percent alcohol by volume.

Ice House Winery

Don't let the humble exterior of the **Ice House Winery** (14778 Niagara Pkwy., NOTL, 905/262-6161, www.theicehouse.ca, 10:30am-7pm daily July-early Nov., 11am-5:30pm daily early Nov.-June, tasting fee $20) fool you. Inside this rustic building (a barn once used for packing peaches) is an epicenter of ice wine delight. The Ice House is the only regional winery solely promoting ice wines, which is good news if you are an ice wine lover. The Ice Wine Tour aims to make you an "ice wine expert" by showing guests the vineyard where the process starts, with informative stops inside the production room for an explanation of the fermentation process. Your education is completed at the tasting bar with samples of ice wine, slushies, and cocktails.

Hinterbrook Winery

Find a cozy, smaller, rustic wine-tasting experience at **Hinterbrook Winery** (1181 Lakeshore Rd., NOTL, 905/646-5133, www.hinterbrook.com, 10am-6pm daily May-Oct., 11am-5pm daily Nov.-Apr., call for tasting reservations), located west of Niagara-on-the-Lake along the Lake Ontario shoreline. Although this region is not known for red wines, try the franc blanc, which is a white wine made from red cabernet franc grapes. Don't forget to ask about the NOMAD experience, which allows you to create your own wine labels.

Two Sisters Vineyard

The **Two Sisters Vineyard** (240 John St. E., NOTL, 905/468-0592, www.twosistersvineyards.com, 10:30am-8pm Tues.-Sat., 10:30am-6pm Sun.-Mon., estate tour and tasting experience $34) offers the best of both worlds. It is conveniently located within walking distance of the main village of Niagara-on-the-Lake but also provides a stunning vista of a sprawling vineyard landscape. As good as the wines are (the riesling ice wine offers hints of tangerine, lemons, and pears), the restaurant may be the star of the show. If you're planning a meal during your winery tour, make reservations at Kitchen 76 for an amazing experience.

Riverview Cellars Estate Winery

As you are driving north along the main parkway joining the falls with Niagara-on-the-Lake, consider a stop at **Riverview Cellars Estate Winery** (15376 Niagara Parkway, NOTL, 905/262-0636, www.riverviewcellars.com, 10am-6pm daily Apr.-Oct., 10am-5pm daily Nov.-Mar., tasting fee $5 and up). This family winery prides itself on small-batch

TOP EXPERIENCE

Bicycle Wine Tours

A fun and healthy way to tour wine country is by bike. Several reputable companies provide bike rentals and escorted tours.

- **Grape Escape Wine Tours** (215 King St., NOTL, 866/935-4445, www.tourniagarawineries.com, daily, $109) has a six-hour tour that includes bike rental, lunch, and several winery visits. Free pick-up and drop-off shuttle service is provided.
- **Zoom Leisure Bikes** (431 Mississauga St., NOTL, 905/468-2366, www.zoomleisure.com, June-Aug., $79) offers a four-hour tour to three wineries. Need to use a power assisted bike? Those are available for $20 extra.
- **Niagara Getaway Wine Tours** (92 Picton St., NOTL, 905/468-1300, www.niagaragetaways.com, hours vary by tour, $79-159) has the greatest variety of guided and self-guided bicycle winery tours in the area. The Gourmet Dinner and Wine Tour is one of the most ambitious tours at six hours, with four wineries, sixteen tastings and a three course dinner.
- **Premier Cycling Tours** (NOTL, 905/328-9323, www.premiercyclingtours.com, Sat.-Sun. May-Oct., $70-110) offers full and half day guided tours. Premiere's full day, six-hour tour includes four wineries and a dinner. The half day tour visits three wineries and includes a snack. Departing locations vary based on your tour selection.
- **Vino Velo Bike Wine Tours** (1511 Niagara Stone Rd., NOTL, 905/468-1280, www.vinovela.ca, daily May-Oct., $60-90) is great for a curated bike tour of Niagara-on-the-Lake. The guided tours include a tasting at four wineries plus a casual picnic. For adventurous cyclers on a budget, try their self-guided tour which includes your bike rental, helmet, map, and tastings at three wineries.

Not one for biking? Bus tours to the wineries are also available (page 158).

vintages grown on their 25-acre farm that straddles the beautiful lower Niagara River. Sometimes smaller wineries differentiate themselves with friendlier service—and that is the case here. Wines are reasonably priced, and there is a family atmosphere that contrasts pleasantly with some of the larger, more exclusive estates in the region. The family is branching out and producing some innovative sparkling wines in a can.

Pondview Estate Winery

Over the years, the family operating **Pondview Estate Winery** (925 Line 2 Rd., NOTL, 905/468-0777, www.pondviewwinery.com, 10am-6pm daily May-Oct., 10am-5pm daily Nov.-Apr., tour and tasting fee for 3 wines $16) has earned Ontario's prestigious Grape King designation, awarded annually to the best vineyard operator. The tradition continues today at Pondview, nestled in the heart of the NOTL wine region, south of the village and west of the river. This unpretentious winery offers a White Label Series of wines that deliver on a promise to be "perfect for backyard patio moments." If you are tasting on a warm summer day, try the wine slushie or an ice wine shooter for a refreshing treat.

Joseph's Estate Wines

The namesake of **Joseph's Estate Wines** (1811 Niagara Stone Rd., NOTL, 905/468-1259, www.josephsestatewines.com, 10am-6pm daily May-Oct., 10am-5pm daily Nov.-Apr., tasting tours by reservation only) pioneered ice wine creation in this region. Joseph's offers a full spectrum of wines crafted from grapes grown on their estate, with bottles ranging from $12 to over $300 for a rare 1998 ice wine. The beauty of this winery is that it is smaller and caters to small groups and couples (versus wineries that accommodate motor coach groups). The more intimate, less commercial experience is perfect for longer conversations about the wine you are tasting and how it is produced.

Pillitteri Estates Winery

If you are looking for an award-winning winery, **Pillitteri Estates Winery** (1696 Niagara Stone Rd., NOTL, 905/468-3147, www.pillitteri.com, 10am-8pm daily June-Sept., 10am-6pm daily Oct.-May, tastings $5 and up) has earned more than 450 medals in international and domestic wine-tasting competitions. It is also the world's largest estate producer of ice wine, so it's hard to beat the selection here; the Vidal Icewines are highly recommended and worth the cost.

Small Talk Vineyards

Find good wine and conversation at **Small Talk Vineyards** (1242 Irvine Rd., NOTL, 905/935-3535, www.smalltalkvineyards.com, 10am-6pm daily May-mid-Oct., 11am-5pm daily mid-Oct.-Apr.). Here the emphasis is on the experience. That's why you should take the vineyard tour (it employs an open-top wagon with pink seats and is pulled by a tractor), which is unlike any other tour in the region. The tour emphasizes the charming and natural aspects of winemaking rather than the technical minutiae common to such tours. While at the winery, keep your eyes open for creative signs, engaging bottle labels, and other entertaining marketing gimmicks.

Small Talk is bold and unique because it embraces nontraditional winery products such as cider. For something you've never tried before, sample the Shiny Cider—a blend of locally grown apples and sparkling wine. The winery also promotes creative uses for its products, including mixed drinks such as Apple Pie (cider, whiskey, and ice wine) and Hard Cider Lemonade (cider, lemonade, and ice wine).

FOOD

Not content with simply baking their own bread, staff members at ★ **Ravine Winery Restaurant** (1366 York Rd., St. Davids, 905/262-8463, www.ravinevineyard.com, 11am-9pm Wed.-Sun., $24) locally source all their ingredients. That means growing their own grapes and herbs and raising their own livestock. This über-organic philosophy results in well-paired food and wine, along with interesting conversations with employees who enjoy describing your dish's origin. The restaurant's exterior is that of a simple prairie home, while the interior has a simple but warm ambience with plenty of wood and rustic earth tones. For every entrée on the menu, there is a suggested wine pairing. The frittata main, for example, pairs nicely with the 2018 Small Batch Riesling.

Most restaurants could learn a thing or two from **Benchmark** (135 Taylor Rd., NOTL, 905/641-2252, www.ncbenchmark.ca, 11:30am-2pm Tues., 11:30am-2pm and 5pm-9pm Wed.-Sat., $25), a teaching restaurant on the campus of Niagara College, where students cook under the supervision of teachers and professional chefs. The emphasis here is on locally sourced ingredients and a dynamic menu with many vegan and vegetarian choices. The restaurant is modern, mixing wood and metal in its design, with glass windows overlooking the local vineyards and farms.

You can savor the art of wine and food pairing at the **Trius Winery Restaurant** (1249 Niagara Stone Rd., NOTL, 905/468-7123, www.triuswines.com, 11am-6pm daily, $45) on the grounds of the Trius Winery. Chef Frank Dodd says the menu is "locally inspired" and reflects various ingredients that are in season. The white fish fillets are caught in Lake Huron, and the lamb, duck, and beef are locally sourced whenever possible. The restaurant is in a stunning stone building with high ceilings, hardwood floors, and a contemporary feel. Large floor-to-ceiling windows add to the bright, natural ambience of the dining area. When the weather is nice, head to the outdoor patio. It has a beautiful view of the vineyards gently rolling out before the distant escarpment, and the sound of the large fountain drowns out background noise.

The ★ **Peller Estates Winery Restaurant** (290 John St. E., NOTL, 888/673-5537, www.peller.com, noon-2:30pm and 5:30pm-8:30pm Sun.-Fri., noon-2:30pm and 5pm-8:30pm Sat., $50) sets the standard for winery dining in Niagara-on-the-Lake. The winery is a massive French château surrounded by picturesque lawns and vineyards. At the entrance, you are greeted by a large fireplace and stairs that wrap around to the restaurant. The vaulted ceiling of the indoor dining area creates a spacious yet intimate setting. The outdoor patio is wonderful, affording great views of the vineyards while you eat. The menu philosophy here is different from that of other restaurants, with dishes served à la carte. However, many diners come here for Chef Jason Parsons' signature menu, a five-course meal ($106). If you choose this option, make a reservation at 6:30 pm to sit by a window or out on the patio to enjoy the beautiful sunset.

As you walk into the **Pie Plate Bakery and Cafe** (1516 Niagara Stone Rd., Virgil, 905/468-9743, www.thepieplate.com, 10am-6pm Tues.-Sun., $18), your nose immediately confirms that all the food here is homemade. This delightful restaurant is small, comfortable, and warm, with a country ambience. The Pie Plate shines if you're looking for a light lunch served quickly at the edge of the NOTL region. Try the pear-and-brie sandwich on a baguette. The thin-crust pizzas are superb, especially the My Kaptain spicy Italian sausage and caramelized onions. At 5pm, the menu changes to small plates, meaning light fare served in small portions. Check the blackboard when you walk in for the daily small-plate menu.

GETTING THERE AND AROUND

The most popular ways to tour wineries are by car, bus, or bike (page 156). If you're making a day of it and want to include lunch or dinner, planning ahead is essential. You can make your own map or use an online map generator (www.winecountryontario.ca).

Bus

Bus tours are popular in NOTL because they are safe, fun, and convenient. Many tour operators will pick you up and drop you off at your hotel. **Grape and Wine Tours** (855/682-4920, www.grapeandwinetours.com) provides pickup service from Niagara Falls or NOTL. Its three-hour, three-winery tour is $79. **Grape Escape Wine Tours** (866/935-4445, www.tourniagarawineries.com) offers pickups in NOTL (Niagara Falls pickup is extra) for its four-hour, four-winery tour ($84). **Niagara Wine Tours International** (800/680-7006, www.niagaraworldwinetours.com) makes pickups in NOTL, Niagara Falls, or St. Catharines. The four-hour, four-winery tour is $84.

Welland Canal Corridor

A 25-mile (40-km) line cuts through Ontario's Niagara Peninsula, joining Lake Ontario and Lake Erie: the Welland Canal. The canal has shaped the economic fortunes of this region, drawing people to small towns along it since the early 1800s. Towns such as St. Catharines, Welland, Thorold, and Port Colborne were founded and then thrived because of this waterway.

Today the towns along the canal look to the Welland Canal for transportation as well as recreation, tourism, and community identity.

1: Peller Estates Winery Restaurant **2:** St. Catharines Museum and Welland Canals Centre

1

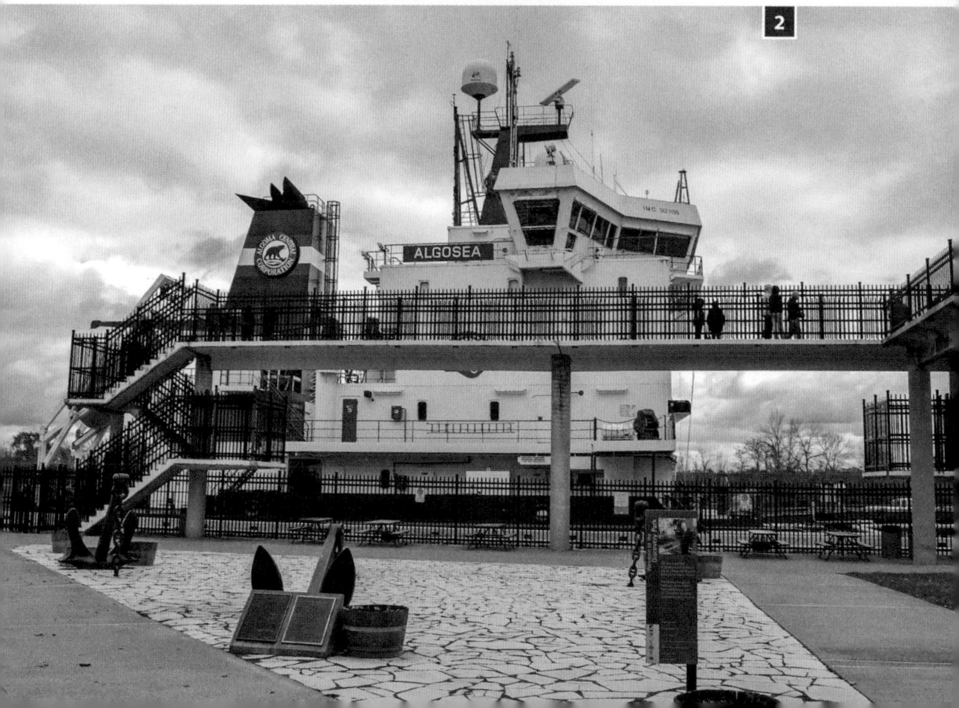

2

Together, they make up a vibrant corridor that redefines the role of the Welland Canal while embracing its industrial heritage. Tourists who view the magnificent lake freighters on the canal are discovering reasons to stay longer: engaging museums, heritage sites, and entertaining festivals.

Adjacent to the southern portion of the canal is Fort Erie. This fort is steeped in the history of the War of 1812, when it guarded the mouth of the Niagara River and witnessed one of Canada's bloodiest battles. Today the fort's guns are quiet; the former fortress is now a symbol of more than 200 years of peace between Canada and the United States.

SIGHTS

St. Catharines

Known as the "Garden City" because it contains more than 1,000 acres of parkland and trails, St. Catharines is the Niagara region's largest municipality. This region is where the Welland Canal was developed by William Hamilton Merritt, its tireless champion. Merritt had served for the crown during the War of 1812, when he devised the idea to create a canal to bypass Niagara Falls. St. Catharines grew in population, political importance, and wealth as the Welland Canal prospered.

During the mid-1800s, the city earned a reputation for supporting the abolitionist movement. Former and escaped enslaved people found a welcoming community in St. Catharines; by 1850, 800 of the town's 6,000 residents were Black. In fact Ontario's first all-Black hockey team—the St. Catharines Orioles—was founded here in 1932.

The city's population soared from 40,000 in 1950 to 130,000 by the 1980s due to the availability of manufacturing jobs at plants like General Motors of Canada. Since the turn of the 21st century, St. Catharines has seen manufacturing jobs being replaced by jobs in the service industry, especially in call centers.

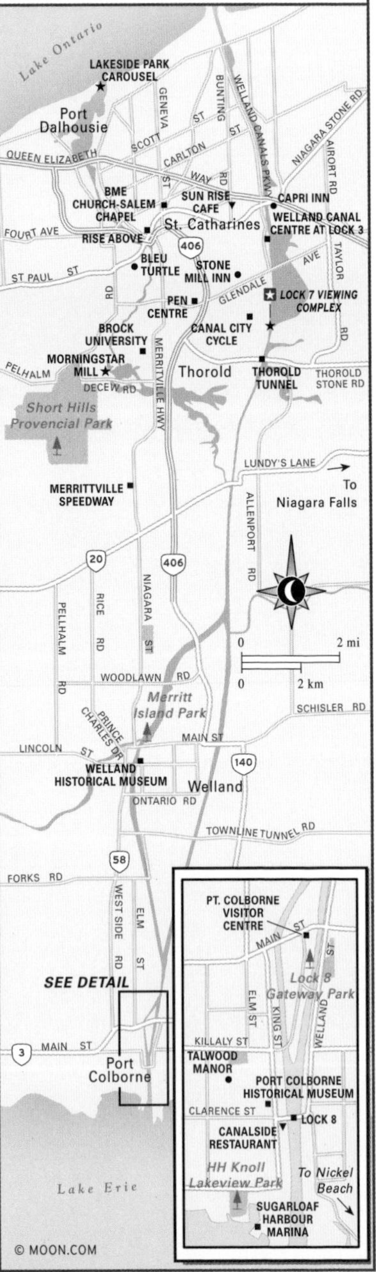

ST. CATHARINES MUSEUM AND WELLAND CANALS CENTRE

To get any closer to a lake freighter, you'd have to be a sailor! The **St. Catharines Museum and Welland Canals Centre** (1932 Welland Canals Pkwy., 905/984-8880, www.stcatharines.ca, 9am-5pm daily, $5 suggested donation) gives you a front-row seat as huge ships ascend and descend 45 feet (13 m) in this lock. You'll be amazed at how these behemoths ease through the lock with just a few feet to spare on either side. Wave to the sailors and try to guess what the ship is carrying (40 million metric tons of goods traverse the canal each year).

The museum is small but packed with information on the Welland Canal and local history. The staff is quite friendly and knowledgeable. Ships ply the Welland Canal April-December. Call on the morning of your visit to find out when ships are passing through Lock 3 or go online (www.greatlakes-seaway.com) for the schedule. The Lock 3 viewing platform is free and open to the public. Visitors usually spend about an hour here, watching the lock in action and investigating the museum.

THE SALEM CHAPEL, BRITISH METHODIST EPISCOPAL CHURCH

When slavery was legal in the United States, many escaped enslaved people found freedom and refuge in Canada. **The Salem Chapel, British Methodist Episcopal Church** (92 Geneva St., 905/682-0993, www.salemchapelbmechurch.ca, tours by appointment, $5) was among the most important stops on the Underground Railroad.

Originally built in the 1820s, the church was expanded in 1851 to meet the needs of the growing congregation. Abolitionist Harriet Tubman lived in St. Catharines from 1851 to1858 and was among the church's members. The church functioned as Tubman's home base as she rescued enslaved people from plantations in the southern United States. The building today is a simple chapel, having retained some of its original 1851 architecture, including benches hewn from walnut logs. The predominantly Black congregation is believed to be the oldest of its kind in Ontario. This church is one of many Underground Railroad heritage sites in southern Ontario.

PORT DALHOUSIE AND LAKESIDE PARK CAROUSEL

At one time, **Port Dalhousie** (www.portdalhousielife.com) was the terminus for the Welland Canal. Modern improvements have changed that, but Port Dalhousie still maintains its waterfront charm. This community in St. Catharines has waterfront access, beaches, historic lighthouses, and the original pier of the second Welland Canal. While most of St. Catharines is urban, Port Dalhousie is more like a beachside resort. On weekends, locals and visitors alike take the 15-minute drive from the city center to enjoy Port Dalhousie's lake views, beaches, and sunsets.

One of the major attractions in Port Dalhousie is the **Lakeside Park Carousel** (1 Lakeport Rd., 905/934-1221, www.stcatharines.ca, 10am-9pm daily June-Aug.) This stunning antique carousel was donated to the local government with one string attached—the fare for riding the carousel could never be more than a nickel. That promise has been kept, and for just five cents you can hop aboard and ride on any of 68 different animals.

The ride was originally built between 1898 and 1905 in Brooklyn. It has been lovingly restored and maintained. Depending on the weather, visitors can spend an hour or more exploring the lighthouses, shops, and sights in Port Dalhousie.

MORNINGSTAR MILL

Step back in time with a visit to the **Morningstar Mill** (2714 Decew Rd., 905/688-6050, www.morningstarmill.ca, 9am-1pm Tues. and Thurs., 10am-3pm Sat.-Sun. mid-May-Oct., free). After emigrating from Bavaria, Wilson Morningstar settled in the American colonies. Being a loyalist, he moved to Canada during the American Revolution. Eventually, he purchased this tract of land near the Decew Falls and harvested the moving water to power a gristmill.

Today the original Morningstar house and mill remain. Other structures here are faithful reproductions of 19th-century agricultural buildings. You can tour the buildings as volunteer docents recount the story of the Morningstar family and life during the early 1800s. The grounds are quite picturesque. Plan to spend an hour here. Call ahead to check if the mill is open for tours, since it is staffed by volunteers and hours of operation can vary day to day. Check out the site's Facebook page (www.facebook.com/morningstar.mill) to see if the mill is grinding grain on the day of your visit. Based upon supply, you can purchase whole grain and rye flour ground at the mill.

Thorold

Just five minutes south of St. Catharines is the historic canal city of Thorold (www.thoroldtourism.ca), with a population of 18,000. It is here that the Welland Canal climbs up the Niagara Escarpment.

★ LOCK 7 VIEWING COMPLEX

The **Lock 7 Viewing Complex** (50 Chapel St. S., 905/680-9477, www.thoroldtourism.ca, 9am-7:30pm daily July-Aug., 9am-4pm daily June and Sept., free), perched atop the Niagara Escarpment, allows you to view Locks 4-7. From this vantage point, you also can see Niagara Falls in the distance as freighters pass through the locks and climb the escarpment. It is truly amazing to see ships 740 feet (225 m) long by 77 feet (23 m) wide glide through the locks with just a few feet to spare on either side. When a vessel completes its journey through the Welland Canal, it has been raised or lowered more than 30 stories.

When the indoor viewing area is open, enjoy a complimentary maple syrup cookie and a copy of *Tommy Trent of the Welland Canal,* an informative guide to the basics of the Welland Canal. The staff at the complex will answer questions about the canal and the region's attractions. They may tell you about the legend of the Kissing Rock, which is along the canal near the viewing complex. Lore has it that a handsome sailor known as Charles Snelgrove would bring his women friends to the rock for one last kiss before he set sail. Other mariners heard of this ritual and soon began bringing their partners to the rock for a proper send-off. The Kissing Rock became a tradition, and it is said to bring good luck to those who use it wisely.

Plan on spending an hour at the viewing complex, depending on how many boats are in the locks and how long you'd like to embrace at the Kissing Rock.

Port Colborne

Port Colborne (www.portcolborne.ca) is the southernmost lock on the Welland Canal. It has the ambience of a small canal town. Emigration here started in 1790, with the population surging after completion of the first Welland Canal in 1833. As a gateway to Lake Erie, Port Colborne serves as a hub for many seasonal cottage residents, who flock to the quaint canal area for its shops and restaurants.

The **Port Colborne Historical and Marine Museum** (280 King St., 905/834-7604, www.portcolborne.ca, noon-5pm daily May-Dec., free) is a treasure for history lovers. The museum consists of a small campus of buildings restored to their 19th-century charm. The museum's main site is the 1869 Georgian revival-style home and carriage house of Arabella Williams. The campus also includes a log cabin schoolhouse, a marine blacksmith shop, and a reproduction of the parapet of Port Colborne's lighthouse. The museum has marine artifacts such as the wheelhouse from a tugboat and a lifeboat from the SS *Hochelaga*. Top off your visit to the museum with a light afternoon tea at Arabella's Tea Room, a fully restored 1915 Edwardian cottage that is small but elegant.

Port Colborne is a great spot for watching massive boats navigate through the locks.

Fossil Heaven

Can you keep a secret? One of the best places in Canada to find fossils is just outside of Port Colborne. Here you can see the remnants of million-year-old fossils. In a landscape littered in fossils, there are so many that you cannot walk two steps without seeing one.

During the Paleozoic era, this land was the bottom of a vast warm, shallow sea that teemed with aquatic life. Those creatures died and millions of them are fossilized in the rocks of a former quarry that is now a protected conservation area. The most common fossils found here are trilobites and brachiopods. Trilobites are those menacing-looking ancestors of the horseshoe crab. Brachiopods, like small clams and corals, take on various shapes with many looking like tubular branches.

This former quarry pit, now owned by the Niagara Peninsula Conservation Authority, is known as the **Wainfleet Wetlands** (10638 Quarry Rd., Wainfleet, 905/788-3135, www.npca.ca, 8am-8pm daily). The quarries on either side of the road have been filled with water, which is great for swimming, canoeing, or fishing (little anglers can catch sunfish all day long). But the stars are the fossils, some of which are more than 12 inches (30 cm) in length.

This is a protected area. Sadly, there is evidence that collectors have removed some fossils, which is prohibited. Find this hidden gem on Quarry Road, west of Port Colborne off Route 3. It is a truly beautiful and unique area that allows you to walk among a fossilized sea of creatures that lived and died 100 million years before dinosaurs made an appearance on this planet.

Port Colborne's Lock 8 is among the longest in the world, at 1,380 feet (420 m). Most visitors will only need to spend two hours in Port Colborne.

Fort Erie

Fort Erie (www.forteriecanada.com) is a vibrant border town, just across the Niagara River from Buffalo, and 18 miles (29 km) south of Niagara Falls. In the heart of vacation country, Fort Erie's population swells from 30,000 to 40,000 each summer as cottage dwellers flock to the area's beautiful beaches.

★ OLD FORT ERIE

An active fortification during the War of 1812, **Old Fort Erie** (350 Lakeshore Rd., 905/871-0540, www.niagaraparksheritage.com, 10am-5pm daily mid-May-Aug., 10am-4pm Mon.-Fri., 10am-5pm Sat.-Sun. Sept.-Oct., $13.27 adults, $8.41 children 6-12) dates back to the late 1700s. In 1764, after Britain won the French and Indian War, redcoats built a modest fort near the water's edge along the Lake Erie shoreline. After the American Revolutionary War, Britain built a much larger fort a little farther inland, which still guarded Lake Erie and the entrance to the Niagara River.

This national historic site comes alive each July when reenactors dramatize the 1814 siege of Fort Erie. More than 1,000 British troops lost their lives, were injured, or were captured. The reenactment is a dramatic retelling of the violent clash that occurred when British troops attempted to capture the fort, which was held by American forces. During the two-day reenactment, visitors can take guided tours of the fort as well as British and American troop encampments. The evening tour by lantern light is fun. Visitors will also witness various reenactments of skirmishes and assaults from the siege battle.

The fort offers visitors an authentic glimpse into the lives of the soldiers and families who occupied the fort in the 1800s. Restored buildings include the guardroom, soldiers' barracks, and the powder magazine. The officers' quarters have real artifacts from an officer who lived here, such as the "traveling bed" of Captain Kingsley of the 8th Regiment of Foot. The canopy bed and other portable furniture were constructed so officers could easily transport them.

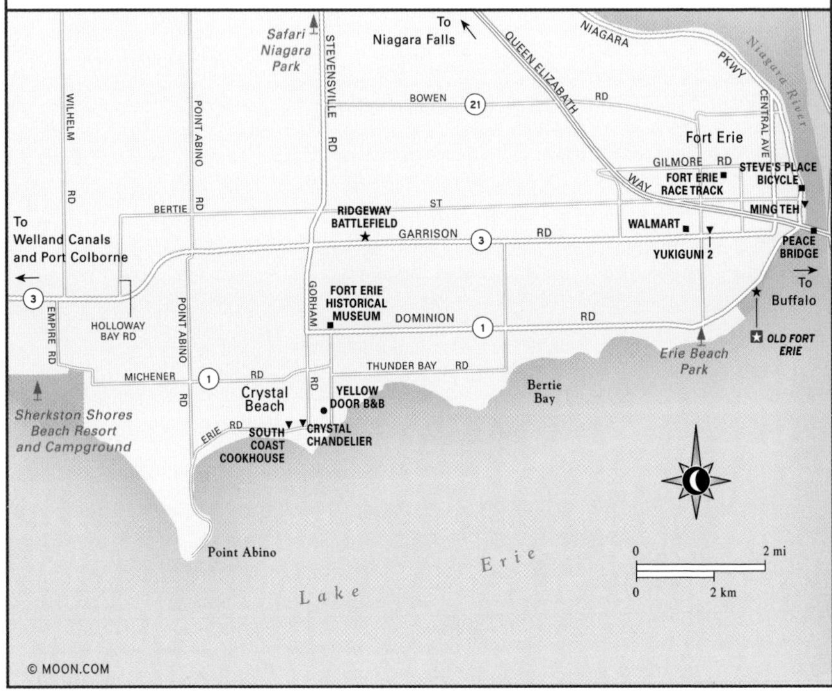

Fort Erie is great fun for families; a visit will take about two hours.

RECREATION

Bicycling

Biking is growing in popularity in this region, and many adventurous cyclists are discovering the **Greater Niagara Circle Route** (www.regional.niagara.on.ca), an 86-mile (138-km) loop of paved paths that joins Lakes Erie and Ontario. The path is an amalgam of five trails along the Niagara River to the shore of Lake Ontario. The route follows the Welland Canal and then connects Port Colborne with Fort Erie. An association of bed-and-breakfast operators in the Welland, Fort Erie, and Niagara region has a website (www.cycleandstayniagara.com) with excellent information on cycle routes and accommodations that are bike friendly.

There are 12 smaller bike loop routes within the region as well. Maps and descriptions are online at the **Cycle Niagara** website (www.cycleniagara.com), which has excellent information on accommodations and bike repair shops near the loop routes.

The wineries of Niagara-on-the-Lake are becoming a top destination for novice and veteran cyclists. Several tour operators offer escorted group tours through wine country. For those who want to go at their own pace and customize a route, there's a map and an app online (www.niagararegion.ca).

For bike rentals in Fort Erie, contact **Steve's Place Bicycle and Repair** (181 Niagara Blvd., Fort Erie, 905/871-7517, noon-6pm Tues.-Fri., 10am-3pm Sat., $25/day).

1: Port Colborne Historical and Marine Museum **2:** Old Fort Erie

YVON DUPRE JR.

Museum
port colborne
280 KING ST.

OPEN DAILY
MAY-DEC. 12-5
FREE ADMISSION

1

2

The Battle That Made Canada

Driving west along Route 3 outside of Fort Erie, you'll pass a small sign letting you know that you're passing the Ridgeway Battlefield. Today it is a pleasant, small, park-like pull-off from the main highway. But in 1866, a violent clash at this spot changed Canada forever.

Here, Fenian soldiers fought Canadian militia on June 2, 1866. The Fenians were a group of Irish Americans, many of whom had been recently discharged from fighting for the Union in the American Civil War. These battle-hardened soldiers and their leaders believed that attacking Canada would cause the British to leave Ireland.

About 1,000 Fenians gathered in Buffalo and covertly made their way across the Niagara River with the assistance of sympathetic Irish people who worked the grain mills on Buffalo's waterfront. The Fenian Raiders took control of Fort Erie and marched west, eventually meeting Canadian troops who had set up defensive positions along Limestone Ridge (known today as Ridgeway).

However, for unexplained reasons, Canadian troops broke ranks, which resulted in chaos. When the dust cleared, nine Canadian soldiers and six Fenians lay dead, and the Fenians emerged the victor. The Fenians retreated toward the U.S. border, where they discovered that a U.S. Navy gunboat was patrolling the Niagara River, effectively cutting off supplies and more troops. This resulted in most of the Fenians leaving Canada and surrendering to U.S. military forces in the region.

This invasion was supposed to be part of a larger coordinated military campaign by the Fenians. That effort never came to fruition. The goal of strong-arming Britain by invading Canada was a failure. However, the Battle of Ridgeway did have an unintended impact on the Canadians; concern about homeland defense galvanized a movement to unite the separate provinces of Canada into a confederation, which led to the formation of Canada as the nation we know today.

For bike rentals in Thorold, contact **Canal City Cycle** (23 Front St. S., Thorold, 905/964-8056, www.canalcitycycle.com, 8am-8pm daily, $35/day).

Horseback Riding

HorsePlay Niagara (11061 Ellsworth Rd. N., Port Colborne, 905/834-2380, www.horseplayniagara.com, daily by reservation only, $50/hr) puts you in the saddle for leisurely rides along nature trails near Port Colborne. More experienced riders can gallop on the sands of a Lake Erie beach with their instructor ($80). Couples can indulge in a 2.5-hour Romantic Picnic Ride ($165 pp).

Motorsports

If you have the need for speed, **Merrittville Speedway** (2371 Merrittville Hwy., Thorold, 905/892-8266, www.merrittvillespeedway.com, Apr.-Sept., time and admission vary by event) has fast-paced action. Saturday evening stock-car races are the most popular events at the 0.3-mile (0.5-km) banked clay speedway.

FESTIVALS AND EVENTS

For 16 days from mid-May through early June, St. Catharines hosts the **Niagara Folk Art Festival** (St. Catharines, www.folk-arts.ca). Canada's longest-running heritage festival celebrates diversity by highlighting the numerous cultures of the people who call Ontario home. You'll experience music, dancing, food, and arts from a spectrum of cultures, including artists from Africa, Europe, and Asia. Events are hosted throughout St. Catharines, including the opening ceremonies on the front steps of St. Catharines City Hall.

St. Catharines also hosts Canada's largest single-day music festival. Known as **S.C.E.N.E.** (St. Catharines, www.facebook.com/scenemusicfestival), it draws more than 140 bands and other musical acts to the city on the second Saturday in June. The Market Square (91 King St.) is the hub, with all music stages and venues within walking distance of each other. Music ranges from alternative to rock to folk, and the acts are mostly independent bands from Canada, although the festival now attracts international artists.

Have a blooming good time throughout June at the **Welland Rose Festival** (Welland, 905/732-7673, www.wellandrosefestival.com). At several venues throughout the city, various events highlight Welland's traditions and talented citizens. Festivities include a baby contest, grand parade with marching band complete with bagpipes, juried art show, and coronation ball.

In the first week of August, Port Colborne comes alive during its **Canal Days Festival** (Port Colborne, 888/767-8386, www.portcolborne.ca). For four days, tall sailing vessels arrive at Port Colborne and become the highlight of the festival. Visitors can board the ships, learn about maritime history, and go for a sail on Lake Erie. Each year, more than 300,000 visitors travel to Port Colborne to see the ships and other attractions, including a classic car show, a craft show, and nightly music entertainment.

SHOPPING

The Pen Centre

With more than 180 stores, **The Pen Centre** (221 Glendale Ave., St. Catharines, 905/687-6622, www.thepencentre.com, 10am-9pm Mon.-Fri., 9am-6pm Sat., 11am-6pm Sun.) is this area's largest mall. Among the most popular stores are Aéropostale, American Eagle, Sears, and The Bay. The Pen also features four restaurants and a 10-screen multiplex.

FOOD

Every region has its legendary breakfast joint, and in St. Catharines it's the **Sun Rise Cafe** (136 Bunting Rd., St. Catharines, 905/685-1100, 6am-2pm Mon.-Wed., 6am-3pm Thurs.-Sun., $10). The restaurant doesn't have a website and its Facebook page hasn't been updated since 2014, so maybe locals are trying to keep this place secret! The restaurant is clean and simple, with everything you'd want in a great breakfast place. The reasonable prices are why it gets crowded here. Service is fast, and the wait times are minimal. The banana-split breakfast parfait and the Greek omelet with feta cheese and spinach are crowd pleasers.

The best vegan restaurant in southern Ontario is in St. Catharines. **Rise Above** (120 St. Paul St., St. Catharines, 289/362-2636, www.riseaboverestaurant.com, 11am-10pm Tues.-Sat., 11am-3pm Sun., $15) has an ambitious but tasty menu. The mac and cheese is so good that you won't believe it doesn't contain cheese. The Italian meatball sub features chickpea "meatballs" smothered in a creamy cashew mozzarella and served on a fresh baguette. The most expensive entrée is $18. This place is also a vegan bakery. The desserts rock, and you can always order goodies to go.

In the shadow of Bridge 21 on the Welland Canal, you'll find the **Canalside Restaurant** (230 West St., Port Colborne, 905/834-6090, www.canalside.ca, 11:30am-11pm daily, $18). The view of passing freighters is wonderful, and so is the food. Sit indoors or on the patio—it's a perfect setup for travelers looking for reasonable food and local scenery. A surprisingly diverse menu features a spiced maple peameal wrap as well as a lobster and chorizo jambalaya entrée. You can browse the abundant and interesting nautical memorabilia while waiting for your meal.

Of the many good Asian restaurants in southern Ontario, **Ming Teh** (126 Niagara Blvd., Fort Erie, 905/871-7971, 5pm-10pm Mon., 11am-10pm Tues.-Sun., $12) is among the best. For years, Americans have crossed over the Peace Bridge to dine at this wonderful restaurant. Portions are large, and the food is always made to order and fresh. Ask to be seated along the rear of the restaurant to view the swift waters of the Niagara River on its 18-mile (29-km) journey toward the falls.

The best Japanese restaurant in Fort Erie is **Yukiguni 2** (660 Garrison Rd., Fort Erie, 905/994-8506, noon-9pm daily, $14). The exterior is a little drab, but the inside is warm and inviting, and the staff is very personable. Consistently fresh seafood is the key to this restaurant's success. The dinner menu is varied, and the Yukiguni Box, which features separate portions of chicken teriyaki, shrimp tempura, *gyoza*, and California rolls in a compartmentalized dish, is a local favorite. Try the two-appetizers-for-$10 deal; the portion sizes are enough to qualify as an entrée at most sushi places.

Just down the shore from Fort Erie is Crystal Beach and cottage country, lovingly referred to by locals as Canada's South Coast. The **South Coast Cookhouse** (423 Derby Rd., Crystal Beach, 905/894-7037, www.southcoastcookhouse.com 11:30am-11pm Sun.-Thurs., 11:30am-midnight Fri.-Sat., $18) is a casual, family-friendly restaurant close to the beach, with a kitchen open longer than most other eateries in the area. The Cookhouse has a lot of typical pub fare, but it's known for its large chicken wings. Unless you are a veteran wing consumer, stay away from the suicide-style wings (very, very hot) and instead try the chipotle-mango-sauce wings. On summer weekends, there is live music, a wonderful accompaniment to watching the sunset and enjoying a choice of 20-plus beers.

The small community of Crystal Beach doesn't have any fine-dining establishments, but it does have **The Crystal Chandelier** (3878 Erie Rd., Crystal Beach, 905/894-9996, www.thecrystalchandelier.com, 4pm-9pm Wed.-Thurs., 4pm-11:30pm Fri., 11:30am-11:30pm Sat.-Sun., $22), with a romantic ambience and good food. The menu is contemporary, with a few surprises such as the meat loaf Calabrese—a nice Italian twist on an old favorite. The patio is a wonderful place to dine during the summer, as the beachgoers pass by and the sun sets over the water. On summer evenings, the Chandelier hosts live music. If you want a quiet meal, make reservations by 6pm. The music, featuring local acts, is lively and begins at 9pm on Saturdays and Sundays.

Lucky travelers will go to Bridge 13 on the Welland Canal to find **Taris on the Water** (25 W. Main St., Welland, 905/788-0123, www.taris.ca, 11:30am-10pm Sun.-Fri., 4pm-10pm Sat., $25). The restaurant is the only dining establishment on the canal, and the owners have optimized the view to complement their menu. Pork schnitzel with cheese, cabbage, bacon, and apple salad is delightful. If you like vegan dishes that taste like meat, try the Vegan Spaghetti and Beyond Meatballs with pesto.

If you're looking for pub grub served in an English pub atmosphere, then pop into **Ye Olde Squire Restaurant** (800 Niagara St., Welland, 905/714-7821, www.yeoldesquirewelland.com, 10am-11pm Mon.-Thurs. and Sat., 10am-midnight Fri., 10am-10pm Sun., $17). If you love a lighthearted atmosphere and prompt service (especially at lunch), then you'll like the Squire. The head chef has an aversion to anything frozen, so all meals are prepared fresh. The diverse menu includes typical pub favorites such as fish-and-chips, Steak and Guinness Yorky Bowl, and traditional shepherd's pie. Reservations are a good idea on Friday and Saturday evenings when the restaurant becomes crowded after 6pm.

ACCOMMODATIONS

Stone Mill Inn (271 Merritt St., St. Catharines, 905/680-6455, www.stonemillinn.ca, $239) is a unique property blending modern decor and amenities with traditional charm and architecture. St. Catharine's only boutique hotel was once a cotton mill, originally built in 1865. Among the 35 spacious rooms are eight Jacuzzi suites and two-story loft suites with ample space for four and a jetted bathtub. Unmatched in St. Catharines, the property is 20 minutes away from Niagara-on-the-Lake or Welland.

Cyclists will feel right at home at the **Talwood Manor** (303 Fielden Ave., Port Colborne, 905/348-5411, www.talwoodmanorbb.com, $175). This B&B has four rooms and all the comforts you need. Cyclists will like the manor's proximity to trails and indoor overnight bike storage. The B&B's hostess makes you feel at home by providing wine before dinner, tea, cookies, and genuinely caring service.

Affordable, clean, and conveniently located, the **Capri Inn** (391 Ontario St., St. Catharines, 905/684-8515, www.capriinn.com, $119) in St. Catharines has everything a value-conscious traveler requires. There is no elevator in the two-story motel, so choose a room on the first floor to avoid carrying gear up the stairs. Try to reserve a room at the back of the property for good views of the canal and less traffic noise.

The **Yellow Door B&B** (308 Helen St., Crystal Beach, 289/876-8399, www.yellowdoorbandb.com, $125) is a homey B&B offering three rooms in the nestled in a residential street in the Crystal Beach area. Your host, Deidre, prides herself on accommodating guests needs and is known for her Irish breakfast scones. Rooms are comfortable but the bathroom is shared for all three rooms. Although open year round, this B&B shines in the summer due to its proximity to Bay Beach.

GETTING THERE AND AROUND

Most visitors drive as they explore this region. Fort Erie is 18 miles (29 km) away from Niagara Falls. Take the Niagara Parkway along the Niagara River for a scenic route. St. Catharines is about 12 miles (19 km) away from the falls, a 15-minute drive on the **Queen Elizabeth Way (QEW).**

Driving south from St. Catharines to Port Colborne (22 mi/35 km) should take less than 30 minutes. The major roads are Routes 406 and 140. You'll pass through Thorold and Welland on the way.

The QEW connects Fort Erie to St. Catharines. Route 406 joins the QEW in St. Catharines and then goes south, generally parallel to the QEW, passing through Thorold and Welland, and terminating in Port Colborne. Highway 3 connects Port Colborne to Fort Erie.

Niagara Regional Transit (www.niagararegion.ca) connects St. Catharines, Welland, Port Colborne, Thorold, Fort Erie, and Niagara Falls with buses that run Monday-Saturday. One-way fares ($6) cover transfers to each town's municipal transit service.

For-profit bus operators offer fewer options—**MegaBus** (www.ca.megabus.com) provides daily motor coach service between Fort Erie (Vince's Robo Mart, 21 Princess St.) and St. Catharines, at the St. Catharines bus terminal (70 Carlisle St.), but there are no other stops in the region. The journey from Fort Erie to St. Catharines costs less than $11.

Rail service is minimal in this area as well; trains stop at St. Catharines (5 Great Western St.) but no other communities in the area. **VIA Rail** (www.viarail.ca) has daily service between Niagara Falls, Ontario, and St. Catharines with a 21-minute trip ($23). **GO Transit** (www.gotransit.com) offers service connecting Niagara Falls and St. Catharines twice daily ($6.30).

Background and Essentials

The Landscape

Geography both divides and unites this region. The U.S. and Canadian sides of Niagara Falls are physically separated by the Niagara River, but they share these same geographical features that give the region its identity.

About 12,000 years ago, the entire area was covered by a glacier that was more than 1 mile (1.6 km) thick. As the earth's climate warmed, the glacier retreated. The glacier's movement created the basins of the Great Lakes, and the melting glacier filled the lakes with freshwater.

Today the Great Lakes contain 20 percent of all the liquid surface freshwater in the world.

The Great Lakes flow from Lakes Superior to Michigan to Huron to Erie, and then to Lake Ontario. Lake Erie is more than 320 feet (98 m) higher in elevation than Lake Ontario, which means the water flows downhill (via the Niagara River) between the two bodies of water. The river flows over an escarpment during its journey downstream, resulting in Niagara Falls. Just 12,000 years ago, Niagara Falls was 7 miles (11 km) downstream. The erosive power of the water cut a gorge from its original location, causing the waterfall to recede to where it is today.

The region's soil is fertile and allows for cultivation of diverse crops, including corn, tomatoes, strawberries, potatoes, beans, grapes, gourds, and lettuce. The region is known for the production of tree fruits such as apples, cherries, peaches, and pears. It also has abundant forests, woodlands, meadows, and small rolling hills. Gorges such as Niagara's can be formed because much of the area's rock is sedimentary and relatively soft, making it that much easier for erosion and changes in the landscape to occur. Fossils abound here, evidence from the warm and shallow sea, teeming with life, that existed many millions of years ago. Most of these fossils were formed 240-425 million years ago. The most often spotted fossils are Trilobita (seafloor crustaceans), Crinoidea (sea lilies), and Gastropoda (snail shells).

CLIMATE

Summer and autumn are the best times to visit the Niagara region. Winters are cold, snowy, and windy. Spring is unpredictable and can have snow, rain, and sunshine all in the same day.

The average July temperature is 81°F (27°C); the average January temperature is 32°F (0°C). Summers are moderate and comfortable, with temperatures rarely reaching 90°F (32°C). In the fall, highs average 60°F (16°C).

The annual precipitation is 40 inches (101 cm); to provide a comparison, New York City averages about 46 inches (116 cm). In winter, Niagara Falls can expect a total of 77 inches (196 cm) of snow. Portions of Buffalo receive 94 inches (238 cm) of snow.

FLORA AND FAUNA

Niagara has a healthy mix of urban, suburban, and rural spaces, from cities to sprawling farmlands to forests.

Animals

The largest animals here are whitetail deer, bobcats, coyotes, turkeys, and foxes. In the parks surrounding the falls, you will see squirrels (black and gray) but may also encounter chipmunks, rabbits, groundhogs, woodchucks, skunks, turtles, snakes, and raccoons in nearby hiking areas.

Bird-watchers trek to the Niagara area because it's along a major migratory path that annually attracts birds from as far north as Greenland and as far south as Florida. The Niagara River corridor has gained international recognition by conservation groups as a Globally Significant Important Bird Area—the first such designation in all of North America. The National Audubon Society designated the entire river as Globally Significant in 1996 to raise awareness of the river as a major food source for migrating birds.

Because Niagara's waters are generally free of ice, migrating birds can find fish, whereas many other sources of food on their path are frozen over. In November, the river is visited by more than 100,000 gulls of 19 different species, some of which have traveled from Siberia. Most of these birds are traveling south from arctic Canada and Greenland. Numerous species of swans, ducks, and geese live here year-round or migrate through the area. Many waterfowl gather near the base of Niagara

Previous: fireworks display over Niagara Falls in summer.

Falls, where there is a large supply of dead or stunned fish.

Other birds typically found in this area include robins, hummingbirds, blackbirds, cardinals, chickadees, cormorants, doves, finches, jays, and crows. Larger birds such as herons, cranes, owls, and hawks are seen regularly, with rare appearances by falcons and eagles.

Plants and Trees

Although nearly all the old-growth forest is gone, there is a remarkable diversity of trees in the woodlands of the Niagara region. Maple, elm, birch, beech, ash, dogwood, sycamore, oak, cherry, chestnut, and willow trees thrive. By 1833, nearly all the white oak trees on Grand Island were harvested and milled, eventually shaped into barrels for rum in the West Indies and planks for Yankee boats in Boston.

Some of the more common plants of the region include goldenrod, irises, geraniums, roses, milkweed, and various grasses. Poison ivy, poison sumac, and stinging nettles may be found near woodland paths in the area.

ENVIRONMENTAL ISSUES

Niagara Falls, New York, is still recovering from the legacy of generations of high-polluting industries that once operated here. In the early 1900s, manufacturers were drawn to Niagara Falls because of the inexpensive and reliable electric power. Many major names in industry, including Alcoa, Union Carbide, Olin, DuPont, Hooker, Carborundum, and Occidental, generated jobs, economic growth, and chemical by-products. The boom lasted through World War II and into the 1970s.

The Meaning of "Niagara"

The origins of the name "Niagara" are shrouded in mystery because the native people who lived here did not have a written language. Some scholars believe the word comes from a group of local people named the Niagagarega. Others say Niagara is derived from the Neutral Nation word, "Onguiaahra," meaning "the strait." Some local guides may tell you that the term means "neck" or "thunder water."

Although many of the industrial plants have closed, a toxic legacy remains. The first U.S. federal Superfund cleanup site was Love Canal, a school and community about 7 miles (11 km) from the falls (and within Niagara Falls city limits), built on a chemical landfill. In the late 1970s, the federal government purchased the homes of 950 families near the dump site, paid to relocate them, and then began remediating the area. According to government officials, there are pollution concerns for dozens of similar sites in the region.

Thanks to aggressive cleanup efforts, tougher environmental regulations, and a decline in heavy manufacturing, the region is much cleaner and safer. A more symbiotic relationship between industry and regulators has emerged as the community balances the need for both manufacturing jobs and a livable environment. Wise conservation measures have led to an abundance of fish and game for outdoor enthusiasts. Several species have enjoyed resurgence in the region, including wild turkeys, red-tailed hawks, eagles, and foxes.

History

EARLY PEOPLES

Long before Europeans visited the Niagara region, native peoples inhabited the land. Some groups were attracted to the area because outcroppings of flint yielded important tools, such as arrowheads and hide scrapers. Others came here for the abundance of nature—forests filled with wild game and waters packed with fish. Many who stayed cultivated the soil and harvested corn, squash, pumpkins, and beans.

Prior to the 1500s, the various tribes within the area sometimes fought against each other. Around 1570, the Cayuga, Onondaga, Mohawk, Seneca, and Oneida tribes banded together to form the Iroquois League, a confederacy with social laws and government institutions designed to promote peace among its members. In 1722, a sixth nation, the Tuscarora, joined the Iroquois League.

The Iroquois Confederation dominated the region and greatly influenced the fate of all native people in this area. The Iroquois went to war with two local tribes, the Eries and the Neutrals, resulting in the destruction of those tribes. The remaining Eries and Neutrals fled, were killed, or were assimilated into other tribes.

EUROPEAN SETTLEMENT

Europeans began exploring this region in the 1600s.The French and the British traded with the native peoples, swapping iron tools, firearms, blankets, and other wares for beaver pelts. During the French and Indian War, the alliance of the Iroquois with the British was instrumental in allowing England to gain control of the region in 1759.

For a few years, there was peace in the area. The region's sparse population began to grow as the American Revolutionary War started. Many American colonists who were loyal to Great Britain sought refuge across the border in Ontario. For the six tribes of the Iroquois Confederacy, the American Revolutionary War was the source of massive in-fighting. The Tuscarora and Oneida leaders sided with the Americans, while the Cayuga, Mohawk, Seneca, and Onondaga leaders allied with England. When England lost, American troops pushed the English-allied tribes from central and western New York in a sustained military campaign in 1779. Some of these Iroquois crossed the border and settled in Canadian territory.

WAR OF 1812

By the turn of the 19th century, the region saw modest population growth as farmers began clearing fields and planting crops. The War of 1812 erupted as the United States declared war on Great Britain over trade policies and English impressment of U.S. sailors, a practice in which English soldiers boarded U.S. vessels and seized any American sailors who had deserted from the British Navy. Many contemporary historians believe that the conflict was, in reality, a thinly veiled attempt by the United States to annex Canadian territory.

The bloodiest fighting of that war occurred in the Niagara theater. In October 1812, U.S. forces crossed the Niagara River and briefly took control of the cannon that was strategically placed atop Queenston Heights. The U.S. invaders were eventually repelled, but Canada lost its most able young general, Isaac Brock. In another dark chapter of the war, retreating U.S. forces burned down the village now known as Niagara-on-the-Lake. In retaliation, British forces crossed the border and burned Lewiston, Niagara Falls, and Buffalo. At the end of the conflict, neither side gained or lost territory. Eventually, peace negotiations yielded an agreed-upon, fixed boundary between Canada and the United States.

EVOLUTION OF CANADIAN GOVERNANCE

Following the war, Ontario struggled to define itself politically. Some residents favored an aristocratic form of government with access to positions of power limited to an elite group, many of whom were British-born transplants. This type of governance was opposed by others loyal to the Crown but resistant to the creation of a powerful class of unelected "nobles."

Building resentment led to unrest and a brief and unsuccessful armed rebellion in 1837 by William Lyon Mackenzie. The seeds of reform were sown, and Great Britain recognized that its colony in Canada was capable of limited autonomy. A governor would preside over a territory or colony, but that governor would implement the will of a democratically elected legislature. The first steps were taken toward Canada's complete autonomy and the creation of Ontario as a province.

ECONOMIC DEVELOPMENT

The opening of the Erie Canal in 1825 fundamentally changed the region's economic destiny. The canal placed Buffalo at the terminus of the nation's first superhighway, making it the crossroads for raw materials traveling east and immigrants heading west. Buffalo became the 6th busiest port in the world, and by 1900 it had more millionaires per capita than any other American city.

The Canadian side of the border prospered as well, although the growth was more measured. The Welland Canal was built as a competitor to the Erie Canal and was improved over the years. In Niagara Falls, Canadians considered tourism to be the main industry. Americans embraced Niagara for tourism but also fostered heavy industrialization of the area. Both regions experienced population and economic growth through the 1950s.

THE GRIP OF THE RUST BELT

The United States was rocked by two events that paralyzed the economic fortunes of Buffalo-Niagara. In 1959, the St. Lawrence Seaway opened, allowing large oceangoing ships to bypass the port of Buffalo. Buffalo's waterfront slowly atrophied, changing from a robust, vibrant center of trade and transport to a graveyard for massive grain silos that were no longer needed. The knockout punch came in the form of the general decline of manufacturing in the United States, which was particularly acute in the Northeast during the 1970s and 1980s. Buffalo and Niagara Falls joined cities such as Pittsburgh, Cleveland, Milwaukee, and Detroit in what became known as the Rust Belt.

The Rust Belt cities witnessed the closure of many manufacturing plants, the loss of jobs, and inner city decay. Both Niagara Falls, New York, and Buffalo saw their populations decrease by 50 percent, which led to a shrinking tax base and concentrations of poverty. Attempts to bring jobs back to the region were hampered by high tax rates, labor unions, and a bureaucracy that was unfriendly to business. The Canadian region near Niagara Falls suffered a similar fate, although not as severe as Buffalo.

BRIGHTER FUTURE

By the late 1980s, Canada recognized that Niagara Falls needed more attractions to become a multiday vacation destination. Federal, provincial, and local leaders collaborated on a plan to build up their side of the border with a casino, high-rise hotels, golf courses, and infrastructure that significantly enhanced the visitor experience. Public and private spending helped create a heritage-and-tourism corridor that now stretches from Fort Erie to Niagara-on-the-Lake. This effort is evident today as you stand at the falls and see that the Canadian side is much more commercially developed than the American side.

The Schoellkopf Power Plant Disaster

When people try to harness the power of nature, sometimes nature strikes back. A good example is the Schoellkopf Power Plant disaster. As you look along the U.S. side of the gorge just north of the Rainbow Bridge, you'll see that the wall of the gorge is interrupted by an artificial facade. It is here that the Schoellkopf Power Plant harnessed flowing water for electricity, starting in the late 1800s. However, in June 1956, the water turned the tables and caused catastrophic damage.

On the day of the power plant collapse, employees noticed water leaking into the plant along the wall adjacent to the gorge. Soon the trickle turned into a torrent, and within a few hours, a large portion of the plant was pushed from the gorge and slid to the water below. The explosive force of the event propelled debris across the river and onto the Canadian shore. Forty workers escaped the collapsing building, but 39-year-old Richard Draper, a maintenance foreman, was not as fortunate and was killed. The exact cause of the disaster is still debated, although most believe groundwater pressure or a small earthquake caused the collapse.

On the U.S. side, Buffalo and Niagara Falls are experiencing positive change. In 2018, New York State completed an upgrade to the Niagara Falls State Park facilities, spending more than $25 million. A movement to increase access to the gorge by changing roadways is gaining momentum, and a portion of the Robert Moses Parkway has been removed and replaced with green space. Tourism agencies are trying new ideas that give tourists a reason to stay here longer than one day. One such initiative is bringing more live entertainment, food vendors, and free, family-oriented activities to Old Falls Street in downtown Niagara Falls.

Buffalo's once-slumbering waterfront and the downtown area are enjoying a true renaissance, with private developers transforming historical buildings into loft apartments, boutique hotels, and entertainment venues. Grain silos on the inner harbor are being used for tours, rock climbing, music festivals, and art performances. Former high-polluting factories are now facilities for high-tech light manufacturing, requiring a skilled labor force. A city that was once known for its low self-esteem and lack of desirability has found growth and confidence by embracing its industrial, political, and economic heritage.

Government

New York's government is led by a governor who holds power over hundreds of appointments, and a legislature consisting of a 61-member Senate and 150-member Assembly. Members of both houses are elected for two-year terms, and each house has standing committees concerned with public policy issues. The governor also appoints non-legislative commissions to investigate such issues as education aid and welfare administration. The state's finances are overseen by an independently elected state comptroller.

New York is divided into 62 counties that are subdivided into towns and cities. The towns contain villages, most governed by an executive, usually a mayor. Despite its decreasing population, Buffalo is still the second-largest city in New York State. Niagara Falls' population of 48,000 ranks it as the 13th-largest city in the state. Both Buffalo and Niagara Falls are governed by mayors who work with elected councils. Buffalo is located in Erie County; Niagara Falls is in Niagara County. The combined population of the two counties is 1.1 million.

Canada is a democratic constitutional monarchy in which a sovereign acts as head of state, but the national Parliament makes decisions and holds power. The monarch of England functions as a symbolic and ceremonial representative.

Canadians elect a prime minister who heads the parliamentary government, which is composed of two chambers: the Senate and the House of Commons. Members of the House of Commons are elected by citizens, while Senate members are appointed by the governor-general with the prime minister's recommendation. Government responsibilities are shared among federal, provincial, and territorial governments.

Ontario is 1 of 10 provinces, analogous to a state in the United States. Citizens in the Province of Ontario elect representatives to a legislature known as the Assembly of Ontario. The party with the most elected members in the Assembly forms the government and chooses a premier for the province who acts as an executive.

Ontario is divided into 444 municipalities. These can be as large as Toronto or as tiny as a village of 100 people. There are several types of municipalities, and each has different governing responsibilities, such as raising taxes, maintaining highways, or administering emergency services. It is typical for a mayor and several councilors to make decisions at the municipal level.

Niagara Falls, with its population of 88,000, is the 23rd-largest city in Ontario. The City of Niagara Falls, Ontario, has a mayor and eight councilors who are elected to four-year terms. Toronto is one of the largest cities in North America.

Transportation

GETTING THERE

Air

As of October 2021, U.S. citizens over the age of 18 will need a **REAL ID,** state-issued **enhanced driver's license,** or a **passport** for all domestic air travel.

Many air travelers depart from New York City to arrive at the falls. The best way to do this is to land at the **Buffalo Niagara International Airport** (BUF, 4200 Genesee St., Buffalo, 716/630-6000, www.buffaloairport.com). Flights originating from LaGuardia, JFK, or Newark airports are frequent and last less than 90 minutes. With a little preplanning, you can snag a round-trip flight for less than $350. Once at the airport, it is easy to rent a car for the 25-minute drive to Niagara Falls. Taxis are clean and plentiful at the curb outside the baggage claim area on the ground floor. The fare from the airport to the U.S. side of the border is $65; $75 is the fare to the Canadian side of the river (border delays will add costs to your fare).

Fliers may opt to use the **Niagara Falls International Airport** (IAG, 2035 Niagara Falls Blvd., Niagara Falls, NY, 716/297-4494, www.niagarafallsairport.com) because it is conveniently located close to the falls. However, it is only serviced by two regional air carriers, **Allegiant Air** (www.allegiantair.com) and **Spirit Airlines** (www.spirit.com), so flight options are limited. Keep in mind that the rental car/taxi trip from this airport is 15 minutes, comparable to landing at the Buffalo airport.

International travelers may use Toronto's **Pearson International Airport** (YYZ, 6301 Silver Dart Dr., Mississauga, 416/247-7678, www.torontopearson.com). Pearson handles flights from 64 different airlines and is Canada's busiest airport. Sedan transportation from Pearson to Niagara Falls, Ontario, is over $200. If you don't mind ride sharing,

Niagara Airbus (905/374-8111, www.niagaraairbus.com) offers one-way service for individuals starting at $100.

Train

Amtrak (800/872-7245, www.amtrak.com) offers service between Buffalo and Niagara Falls with stops on both sides of the border. Amtrak's **Empire Route** joins New York City and Niagara Falls with three daily runs. The **Maple Leaf Route** runs once daily, connecting New York City with Toronto via the falls. One-way fare from New York City to Niagara Falls, New York, is $70; $88 to Niagara Falls, Ontario.

Bus

Bus travel from Toronto to Niagara Falls is cheap and easy aboard **MegaBus** (877/462-6342, www.megabus.com). Buses depart more than 10 times daily from Toronto. The two-hour one-way trip is just $19.

If you're traveling by bus from New York City, **Greyhound** (800/661-8747, www.greyhound.com) is your most reliable bet. Trips to Niagara Falls (New York or Ontario) cost $55-85 one-way and will last about nine hours. You may save some time by choosing a route that has no transfers.

Be careful if considering a low-cost transportation-plus-hotel package sold by bus companies that offer New York City to Niagara Falls service. Some of these trips do not include attractions or meals, and they may use substandard hotel accommodations. In the past, "guides" aboard these buses have used high-pressure sales tactics on their non-English-speaking guests to inflate the costs of food and attractions. Check the trip itinerary to see how long you are staying at the falls; then determine if that time is sufficient for you to appreciate this wonderful destination.

Car

Niagara Falls is referred to as a rubber-tire destination, meaning that most visitors drive here. If traveling from New York City, plan on a 400-mile (643-km) journey to Niagara Falls, New York. The best route takes you west and north through Pennsylvania on I-80 and I-81, eventually depositing you onto the New York State Thruway (I-90). These roads are dependable and well traveled, which is something to consider if you are traveling during the winter, when snowy conditions exist. Several towns and cities midway along the route (Binghamton and Cortland) are particularly scenic during the autumn months and are worthy of a rest stop.

Driving from Toronto is fast and easy, as long as you are able to escape the traffic of Toronto. Plan on a 90-minute drive (80 mi/130 km) using the Queen Elizabeth Way (QEW). Large electronic traffic signs will alert you to delays caused by volume or construction. Right-hand or middle lanes are safest; you can expect cars speeding in excess of 80 miles per hour (128 kph) to zoom by you in the passing lane. The QEW takes you along the western edge of Lake Erie to Route 420, the main artery into Niagara Falls, Ontario.

If you are crossing the border by car, there are two bridges you should consider using: the Lewiston-Queenston Bridge and the Rainbow Bridge. The Lewiston-Queenston Bridge is north of the falls and accepts tractor-trailers, buses, and autos. The Rainbow Bridge accepts cars and buses only. Use the Niagara Falls Bridge Commission website (www.niagarafallsbridges.com) on your smartphone to determine which crossing is best for you.

Organized Tours

Several tour companies provide transportation and guide service for those seeking to join a group tour of Niagara Falls. All tour companies listed here will provide customer pickups at the address you specify. Among the reputable providers are **Niagara Airbus** (800/268-8111, www.niagaraairbus.com), **Bedore Tours** (800/538-8433, www.bedoretours.com), and **Gray Line** (877/285-2113, http://graylineniagarafalls.com). Customized private tours that include transportation are available through **Niagara Falls Walking Tours** (716/997-2245, www.

niagarafallswalkingtours.com) and **See Sight Tours** (888/961-6584, www.seesight-tours.com).

For heritage tours of Buffalo, try **Buffalo Double Decker Bus** (716/246-9080, www.buffalodoubledeckerbus.com) or, for walking tours, the **Preservation Society** (716/852-3300, www.preservationbuffaloniagara.org).

GETTING AROUND

The vast majority of visitors to Niagara arrive by car. Outside of Niagara Falls, Ontario, public transportation is not robust and is designed to serve locals, not visitors.

In New York, I-90 is the main highway running east-west, from Albany to Buffalo. In Buffalo, big-city traffic is virtually nonexistent, although congestion can occur during weekday commute times. The statewide speed limit for open highway driving is 65 miles per hour (104 kph). Speed limits for cities, towns, villages, and smaller roads are considerably slower and are posted. If you're visiting in the winter months, snow may make for less-than-ideal driving conditions. Local radio stations and highway signs provide warnings and weather information.

The main thoroughfare on the Canadian side of the border is the QEW, which joins the Niagara region to Toronto. The QEW's top posted speed limit is 100 kilometers per hour (62 mph), although traffic moves faster the closer you get to Toronto. Except for construction areas, there is not much traffic in the Niagara region. Most of the traffic laws are the same for Canada as New York, except that radar detectors not legal in Ontario.

Major car-rental companies operating out of the Buffalo airport include **Alamo** (800/327-9633), **Avis** (800/831-2847), **Budget** (800/283-4387), **Enterprise** (800/736-8222), **Hertz** (800/654-3131), and **National** (800/227-7368). In Ontario, drivers 21 and over may rent a vehicle. The minimum age to rent a vehicle in New York State is 18. Be advised that in both Ontario and New York, rental agencies are likely to add a "youthful driver" surcharge to renters under the age of 24.

Travel Tips

CROSSING THE BORDER

U.S. citizens crossing the border into Canada must have a passport, passport card, Nexus card, or enhanced drivers license (issued by a select number of U.S. border states). Technically, U.S. citizens do not need a passport to enter Canada; however, U.S. regulations require that you have the proper documentation to re-enter the United States. The typical border inspection lasts less than three minutes, especially if you are prepared.

Have your documentation ready to present to the inspector. Remove your sunglasses, mute your radio, and pay attention (ask everyone in the car to put away electronic devices). Inspectors are concerned if there is inconsistent information among people within the vehicle. Make certain that everybody knows where you're going and how long you are staying. You may not bring mace, pepper spray, or stun guns across the border. If one parent is traveling with a child, it is recommended that the absent parent create and sign an informal letter of permission.

Travelers with criminal records are likely to receive extra scrutiny when crossing into Canada. Infractions including a DUI may prevent your entry into Canada. Border agents have some discretion in these matters, so it pays to be respectful, sincere, and honest. If someone in your vehicle has a criminal conviction, the entire group may be asked to remain in the car while that person is questioned further inside the immigration offices.

Which Is the Best Side?

During the 1800s and for much of the 1900s, Niagara Falls, New York, was considered *the* destination when visiting Niagara. Since the 1960s, that situation has changed, and Niagara Falls, Ontario, dominates in tourism (in its number of visitors, hotel rooms, etc.). A friendly rivalry exists across the border as each destination claims to be number one. But which side is the best?

The answer is they *both* are.

Each side has its own distinct advantages and challenges. The Ontario side of the border boasts the better view. Without a doubt, this is true—you can see all three of the waterfalls that make up Niagara Falls from the Canadian side. The vista here is clearly superior. However, the Ontario side is also more crowded and is ringed with high-rise hotels that some feel detract from the natural beauty of the falls.

The New York State Park at Niagara Falls has many more opportunities to experience the water up close. The park facilitates a relationship with nature that is much more visceral. By state law, the park is prohibited from becoming over-commercialized and overdeveloped. Fewer tourists make for shorter lines at attractions. But the U.S. side faces its own challenges—outside of the park, the downtown area is not nearly as vibrant as its Canadian counterpart. Top-quality hotels and restaurants are few in comparison to Niagara Falls, Ontario.

The best advice is to experience both sides of Niagara Falls. Think of Niagara as a region, not just a single attraction. If your situation permits, explore both sides of the border and you'll discover that each has its unique charm and character.

If you are not a U.S. citizen and you're entering Canada, find out if you need a visa or other documentation by using an interactive form on Canada's Immigration and Citizenship website (www.cic.gc.ca).

For the current wait times at border crossings, call (800/715-6722) or go online (www.niagarafallsbridges.com) for updates on which border crossing to use based on traffic volume.

MONEY

Banks on both sides of the border are usually open 9am-3pm Monday-Friday, with some branches open 9am-1pm Saturday. Many banks offer 24-hour ATMs. Check with your bank to see if your debit card will work at Canadian ATMs. Most larger banks participate in international networks that permit cash withdrawals in other countries. There may be fees associated with these transactions.

U.S. and Canadian currency fluctuate in relative value, which means that sometimes the U.S. and Canadian dollar are at par and sometimes not. Businesses set their own exchange rates and policies on accepting foreign currency. There are two ways to make certain that you know the exchange rate you're receiving. The first is to use your own credit card for all transactions; the other is to purchase Canadian currency at your local bank before you leave the United States.

CELL PHONES

It is important to know your cell phone carrier's policy on roaming charges if you intend to use your phone in Canada. Roaming charges, especially for data, can quickly add up. If your carrier charges roaming fees for service in Ontario, you may consider turning off phone functions that require data roaming and data sync. Switching your phone to airplane mode ensures that your phone will not roam, but you cannot make or receive calls in this mode. You can, however, use Wi-Fi in airplane mode. Another option is to contact your carrier and see if they have a service package for Canada, which would allow you full use of your phone's functions, while avoiding roaming fees.

RECREATION

Parks

The Niagara region abounds in lovely green spaces most of the year. New York has an excellent park system that includes Niagara Falls State Park and Fort Niagara State Park in Youngstown. Admission is free, although there may be a charge for parking. If you visit multiple parks during the same day, you only need to pay for parking one time—just show your receipt from the first park as you enter subsequent ones. Of the state's 178 parks, 17 are in the Niagara region. For the best information on park amenities and activities, call 518/474-0456 or go to the state's website (www.nysparks.com).

Also on the U.S. side of the border, **Erie County** (www2.erie.gov) and **Niagara County** (www.niagaracounty.com) operate regional parks. Look online (www.bfloparks.org) for information on Buffalo's historic Olmsted system of parks.

Not to be outdone, **Niagara Parks** (www.niagaraparks.com) provides many outdoor attractions, such as Queen Victoria Park, Fort Erie, Queenston Heights, Niagara Glen, and the Niagara Parks Botanical Gardens. Niagara Parks is governed by the Niagara Parks Commission, a special administrative body created by the province. Niagara Parks is financed by park revenue.

Camping

Camping is very popular in the Niagara region, with dozens of campgrounds with tent and RV spaces as well as cabins. Camping spots in New York State's campgrounds start at $15 a night; there are four in the region, and it is wise to reserve spaces online (www.newyorkstateparks.reserveamerica.com) well in advance of your trip. Across the border, Ontario Parks offers camp spots starting at $38.70 a night. For more information and reservations, call 888/668-7275 or visit the website (www.ontarioparks.com).

HEALTH AND SAFETY

Outdoor Safety

Before heading onto the hiking trails of Niagara, be sure you know where you're going and what you're doing. Check with park officials about trail conditions and weather. Be sure your equipment is functioning properly, and don't head out alone.

Lyme Disease

Anyone who spends much time outdoors in this region should be aware of the symptoms of Lyme disease. The bacterium that causes the disease is carried by the deer tick, which lives in brush, meadows, forests, and even lawns. In early stages, the disease is easily treatable with antibiotics, but if left unattended, it can lead to serious neurological, heart, and joint problems.

Many—*but not all*—of those infected develop a red circular rash around the bite location within three days to one month. The rash usually begins with a small red dot that expands to a diameter of 1-5 inches (2.5-12 cm). The expanded rash may feature a bright red border and a hard, pale center, often resembling a bull's-eye on a target.

The rash is usually accompanied by flu-like symptoms. These may include fatigue, nausea, vomiting, diarrhea, pain in the muscles and joints, stiff neck, swollen lymph glands, headaches, fevers, chills, sore throat, dry cough, dizziness, sensitivity to the sun, and chest, ear, and/or back pain.

Wear light-colored clothing to make it easier to spot ticks, and long pants and long-sleeved shirts to discourage them from coming in contact with your skin. Tuck pants' cuffs into socks and use an insect repellent with a 25-30 percent DEET content around clothing openings and on exposed skin.

Use gloves and tweezers to remove ticks; grasp the tick's head parts as close to your skin as possible and apply slow, steady traction. Wash both your hands and the bitten area afterward. Do not attempt to remove ticks by burning them or coating them with anything like nail polish remover or petroleum jelly. If you remove a tick before it has been attached for 24 hours, you greatly reduce the risk of infection.

Crime

In Niagara Falls, New York, the state park has its own police force that caters to the needs of visitors. The Parks Police Headquarters is located across from the Gorge Discovery Center, which keeps response times short and provides maximum visibility for visitors. The tourist area adjacent to the park is patrolled by the Niagara Falls city police. Some neighborhoods beyond this zone are economically depressed and have higher crime rates. Because of the importance of tourism to the local economy, police frequently patrol the tourist areas downtown.

In Niagara Falls, Ontario, Niagara Parks also has their own police force, with headquarters in Queen Victoria Park. Officers here are highly visible and patrol in cars, on bikes, and on foot.

No matter where you visit, always put valuables such as cameras and GPS units inside your car's trunk and lock your car doors. Using common sense and staying alert are the best ways to avoid crime while on vacation in Niagara. In general, tourists are extremely safe any time of day or night when traveling within the parks on either side of the border.

ACCESS FOR TRAVELERS WITH DISABILITIES

Travelers with disabilities will find many accessible attractions in the region. Nearly all the attractions on the U.S. side are ADA-compliant. Niagara Falls State Park features curb cuts and paved paths for people who use wheelchairs. All buildings in the park are accessible, including restrooms, visitors centers, restaurants, theaters, the Observation Tower, and the Maid of the Mist.

Ontario does not mandate sweeping accessibility regulations, although many businesses and government agencies are striving to increase access. Major attractions such as Table Rock Welcome Centre, the Skylon Tower, WEGO buses, Niagara Hornblower Cruises, and the Butterfly Conservatory are all accessible.

Help for travelers with disabilities is available through the **Society for Accessible Travel and Hospitality** (212/447-7284, www.sath.org), a nationwide, nonprofit membership organization that collects data on travel facilities around the country.

New York State residents with disabilities should apply for the **Access Pass,** which provides free entry to most state parks and recreation areas. For an application, contact **New York State Parks** (Empire State Plaza, Albany, NY 12238, 518/474-2324, www.nysparks.com).

SENIOR TRAVELERS

The **Golden Age Program** provides New York State residents age 62 or older with free entry to state parks and recreation areas any weekday, excluding holidays. Simply present your current driver's license or nondriver photo ID card at the entrance gate.

WORK STUDY

The **Council on International Educational Exchange** (CIEE, 7 Custom House St., 3rd floor, Portland, ME 04101, 207/553-7600 or 800/407-8839, www.ciee.org) provides information on low-cost travel and work-study programs in the United States, including New York State. The CIEE also sells the International Student Identity Card, good for travel and entertainment discounts.

Resources

Suggested Reading

HISTORY

Aherns, Edward W. *The Devil's Hole Massacre.* Sanborn, NY: Rissa Productions, 2004. Well-researched tale of a grim chapter in Native American and settler relations.

Berton, Pierre. *Niagara: A History of the Falls.* Albany, NY: State University Press, 1992. An accessible and thoughtful history of the falls from a prolific Canadian author.

Gromosiak, Paul. *Water Over the Falls: 101 Most Memorable Events at Niagara Falls.* Buffalo, NY: Western New York Wares Inc., 1996. Humorous vignettes of interesting people and events in Niagara.

Jackson, John N., John Burtniak, and Gregory P. Stein. *The Mighty Niagara: One River—Two Frontiers.* Amherst, NY: Prometheus Books, 2003. The most comprehensive study of the border that separates and unites the United States and Canada.

Kriner, T.W. *In the Mad Water: Two Centuries of Adventure and Lunacy at Niagara Falls.* Buffalo, NY: J and J Publishing, 1999. Captures the dark side of those who have made their final journey at Niagara.

Malcomson, Robert. *A Very Brilliant Affair: The Battle of Queenston Heights, 1812.* Toronto, ON: Robin Brass Studio, 2003. Well-written and balanced account of the Battle at Queenston Heights in the War of 1812.

NATURE AND RECREATION

Duling, Gretchen, Dennis Duling, Karen Noonan, Toby Jewett, and Linda Fritz. *From the Mouth of the Lower Niagara River: Stories of Four Historic Communities.* Buffalo, NY: Western New York Wares Inc., 2012. Fascinating study by local authors of communities along the Niagara River.

Freeman, Rich, and Sue Freeman. *Bruce Trail: An Adventure Along the Niagara Escarpment.* Fishers, NY: Footprint Press, 1998. An excellent hiking guide to the Bruce Trail.

Gromosiak, Paul. *Goat Island: Niagara's Secret Retreat.* Buffalo, NY: Western New York Wares Inc., 2003. A quick read on the beautiful details of Goat Island.

Schuman, Michael, and Deborah Williams. *Natural Wonders of New York: Exploring Wild and Scenic Places.* Toledo, OH: Country Roads Press, 1999. Describes many of the state and local parks in Western New York.

TRAVEL

Kowsky, Frank. *Buffalo Architecture: A Guide.* Cambridge, MA: MIT Press, 1981. Complete and scholarly guide to Buffalo's architecture.

Sheridan, Jan. *Buffalo Treasures: A Downtown Walking Guide and Driving Tour of Frank Lloyd Wright Homes.* Buffalo, NY: Western

New York Wares Inc., 2006. Quick guide to the architecture of Buffalo.

Wooster, Margaret. *Somewhere to Go on Sunday: A Guide to Natural Treasures in Western New York & Southern Ontario.* Buffalo, NY: Prometheus Books, 1991. Practical guide to many natural areas that are off the beaten path.

Internet Resources

HISTORY

The Erie Canal

www.eriecanal.org

Discover how this humble waterway shaped a nation and why it is still important today.

Niagara Falls Public Library

www.nflibrary.ca

The Niagara Falls Public Library in Ontario has many images and books available online. The historical images section is well worth a look.

Niagara Falls Thunder Alley

www.niagarafrontier.com

The grassroots website details the history of the falls, as well as information on current attractions; it emphasizes the natural beauty of the region.

RECREATION

Cycling the Erie Canal

www.ptny.org/canaltour

This website offers ways to enjoy the Erie Canal on a bike.

Cycling the Niagara Ontario and Welland Canal Region

www.cycleandstayniagara.com

It's an indispensable site for serious cyclists biking along the Welland Canal-Niagara trails.

Hiking Trails in Western New York

www.wnyhikes.com

This informative website lists the best hiking trails in Erie and Niagara Counties.

New York State Office of Parks, Recreation & Historic Preservation

www.nysparks.com

New York State's listing of all state-operated parks includes excellent information on amenities and fees.

Ontario Trails Council

www.ontariotrails.on.ca

This nonprofit organization promotes hiking in Ontario.

EVENTS

Canalside Buffalo

www.buffalowaterfront.com

Hundreds of events hosted on Buffalo's waterfront are listed here.

Gusto

www.buffalonews.com/gusto

Gusto is the entertainment guide for Buffalo's only daily newspaper, *The Buffalo News.*

Niagara This Week

www.niagarathisweek.com

Use this website to find out what's going on in southern Ontario during your stay.

Old Falls Street

www.fallsstreet.com

Old Falls Street is a vibrant area immediately adjacent to Niagara Falls State Park in New York. Check their schedule for daily activities in the summer.

Step Out Buffalo

www.stepoutbuffalo.com

This online publication is dedicated to highlighting entertainment in Western New York.

Winter Festival of Lights

www.wfol.com

This is the best website for information on the Festival of Lights in Niagara Falls, Ontario.

TOURIST INFORMATION

Clifton Hill

www.cliftonhill.com

The website is a guide to the über-touristy area of Niagara Falls, Ontario, known as Clifton Hill.

Niagara Falls Bridges Commission

www.niagarafallsbridges.com

Crossing the border? Check here for the best bridge to cross the Niagara River. This livestreaming website can save you hours of traffic time.

Niagara Falls State Park

www.niagarafallsstatepark.com

This is the official site of Niagara Falls State Park in New York.

Niagara Falls Tourism

www.niagarafallstourism.com

The commercial site features attractions, restaurants, and accommodations on the Canadian side of the falls.

Niagara Parks

www.niagaraparks.com

The official site of Ontario's Niagara Parks is very reputable and informative.

Niagara USA

www.niagara-usa.com

On this comprehensive website are attractions and events in Niagara Falls, New York, and Niagara County.

Tourism Niagara

www.tourismniagara.com

The website promotes attractions in southern Ontario. Look here for convenient packaged regional itineraries.

Visit Buffalo Niagara

www.visitbuffaloniagara.com

Check here for information on Erie-Niagara County attractions, plus excellent suggestions for adventures.

Index

H

I

JK

L

M

N

O

P

QR

S

TU

VWXYZ

List of Maps

Photo Credits

Title page photo: Philcold, Dreamstime.com;

page 2 © Niagara Parks; page 3 © Joel Dombrowski; page 6 © (top left) Niagara Parks; (top right) Niagara Parks; (bottom) Niagara Parks Commission; page 7 © (top) Ontario Tourism Marketing Partnership Corporation; (bottom left) Niagara Parks; (bottom right) Niagara Parks; page 8 © Niagara Parks; page 10 © (top) Drew Brown; (middle) Destination Niagara USA; (bottom) Destination Niagara USA; page 11 © (top) Destination Ontario; (middle) Drew Brown; (bottom) Drew Brown; page 12 © (bottom) Niagara Parks Commission; page 15 © (bottom) Niagara Parks Commission; page 16 © (top) Niagara Parks Commission; page 18 © (bottom) Ontario Tourism Marketing Partnership Corporation; page 19 © (top) Elovkoff, Dreamstime.com; page 21 © Niagara Parks Commission; Niagara Parks; page 22 © (top) Niagara Tourism and Convention Corporation; page 23 © Niagara Parks Commission; page 24 © (top left) Destination Ontario; (top right) Leonid Andronov, Dreamstime.com; page 31 © (top) Niagara Parks; (bottom) Niagara Parks Commission; page 34 © (top) Destination Ontario; (left middle)Niagara Parks; (right middle)Niagara Parks; (bottom) Niagara Parks; page 36 © courtesy of Library of Congress; page 39 © (top) Destination Ontario; (left middle)Niagara Parks Commission; (right middle)Niagara Parks; (bottom) Destination Ontario; page 44 © (top) Niagara Parks; (bottom) Niagara Parks Commission; page 48 © (top) Joel A. Dombrowski; (bottom) Destination Ontario; page 52 © (top) Niagara Parks; (bottom) Niagara Parks; page 54 © Niagara Parks; page 62 © Erix2005, Dreamstime.com; page 63 © (top left) Ian Whitworth, Dreamstime.com; (top right) Destination Niagara USA; page 71 © (top left) Demerzel21, Dreamstime.com; (top right) Destination Niagara USA; (bottom) Patricia Hofmeester, Dreamstime.com; page 74 © (top) Destination Niagara USA; (bottom) Destination Niagara USA; page 76 © (top) Destination Niagara USA; (bottom) Kim Smith; page 79 © (top) Destination Niagara USA; (bottom) Destination Niagara USA; page 83 © (top) Destination Niagara USA; (bottom) Destination Niagara USA; page 90 © (top) Destination Niagara USA; (left middle)Destination Niagara USA; (right middle)Nickjene, Dreamstime.com; (bottom) Destination Niagara USA; page 97 © Paul Brady, Dreamstime.com; page 98 © (top left) Drew Brown; (top right) Destination Niagara USA; page 105 © (top) Demerzel21, Dreamstime.com; (bottom) Paul Brady, Dreamstime.com; page 110 © (top) Drew Brown; (left middle)Carol Bell, Dreamstime.com; (right middle) Elovkoff, Dreamstime.com; (bottom) Joel Dombrowski; page 112 © Destination Niagara USA; page 122 © (top) Markjonathank, Dreamstime.com; (bottom) Sandra Foyt, Dreamstime.com; page 130 © (top left) Destination Niagara USA; (top right) Destination Niagara USA; (bottom) Destination Niagara USA; page 133 © Destination Niagara USA; page 136 © Joel A. Dombrowski; page 137 © (top left) Destination Ontario; (top right) Niagara Parks; page 142 © (top) Joel A. Dombrowski; (bottom) Destination Ontario; page 144 © (top) Niagara Parks Commission; (bottom) Niagara Parks Commission; page 147 © (top left) Joel A. Dombrowski; (top right) Joel A. Dombrowski; (bottom) Joel A. Dombrowski; page 150 © Joel A. Dombrowski; page 154 © Joel A. Dombrowski; page 159 © (top) Destination Ontario; (bottom) Joel A. Dombrowski; page 165 © (top) Joel A. Dombrowski; (bottom) Niagara Parks Commission; page 170 © Destination Niagara USA

Acknowledgments

This third edition of the guide benefitted from the infusion of new ideas, experiences, and passion from Brian Hayden. Brian is the Communications Manager for Visit Buffalo Niagara, the agency tasked with promoting the Buffalo-Niagara region. Brian is a proud Buffalo native, who moved back home after spending eight years away at college and as a newspaper reporter and social media manager. Brian's contributions are reflected in the Buffalo, Lockport, and Niagara Falls, New York sections of this book.

Both Brian and I are graduates of Syracuse University's S.I. Newhouse School of Public Communications. Twenty-three years separate our graduation dates!

Special thanks to my wife, Jenn, who tolerates my deadline stress each time the book is revised. The stunning beauty of Niagara cannot hold a candle to her.

ROAD TRIPS AND DRIVE & HIKE GUIDES

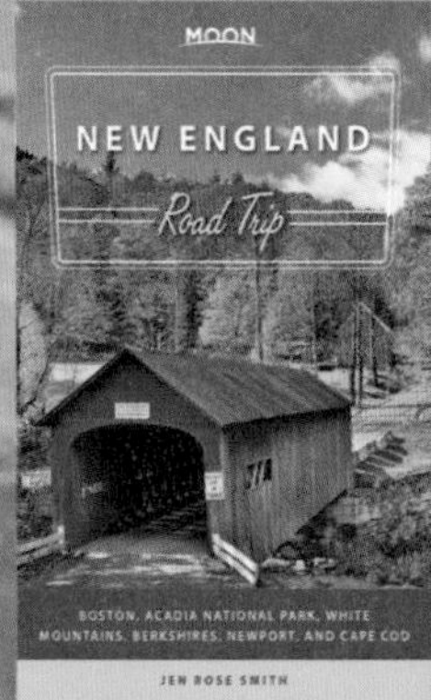

MOON.COM | ROADTRIPUSA.COM